FLIRTING WITH FAME

FLIRTING WITH FAME:

A Hollywood Publicist Recalls 50 Years of Celebrity Close Encounters

DAN HARARY

BearManor Media
2022

FLIRTING WITH FAME:
A Hollywood Publicist Recalls 50 Years of Celebrity Close Encounters

© 2022 DAN HARARY

All rights reserved.

No portion of this publication may be reproduced, stored, and/or copied electronically (except for academic use as a source), nor transmitted in any form or by any means without the prior written permission of the publisher and/or author.

Published in the United States of America by:

BearManor Media

4700 Millenia Blvd.
Suite 175 PMB 90497
Orlando, FL 32839

bearmanormedia.com

Printed in the United States.

Typesetting and layout by BearManor Media

ISBN—978-1-62933-924-5

ADVANCE PRAISE FOR *FLIRTING WITH FAME*

I first met Dan on the set of my TV show *New Lassie* back in 1989, and he and I became friends very quickly. He was a terrific publicist and generated a great deal of media coverage for our series. I enjoyed his book, *Flirting with Fame,* because he is so open and honest about his encounters and adventures with celebrities–some very funny, some odd, and some even hard to believe–but all told from an "everyman's" point of view. Dan quite often found himself in rather bizarre circumstances while interacting with famous people–like having a staring contest with Barbra Streisand, twice; smoking a joint in silence with Jill Clayburgh in Central Park; talking with Billy Crystal about Chinese food at Sid Caesar's funeral or introducing his mother to Mel Brooks and finding out they both went to the same high school. In this book, Dan successfully encapsulates his 50 years of "celebrity close encounters," all while serving the reader as a skillful narrator. I wish him only the best of luck with his new career as an author!

– *Dee Wallace, Actress, Teacher, Healer, Star of E.T.: The Extra-Terrestrial* (1982)

I don't think too many Hollywood professionals other than Dan Harary would be so painfully open and brutally honest about some of his strange misadventures during a long showbiz career–like the perils of pissing off Arnold Schwarzenegger, Sally Field, Jerry Seinfeld, and Kirsten Dunst's mother; insulting Meryl Streep, Harvey Keitel and Julia-Louis Dreyfus; accidentally catching actress Karen Black naked in the shower; hitting on Rene Russo while on a date with another woman; or meeting his hero, Sylvester Stallone, while urinating! Are all of his stories one-hundred percent true? Well, he is a publicist after all! To anyone looking to connect with his inner Zelig, and to any fan of the entertainment industry during the past half-century, I'd say that Dan's book, *Flirting with Fame*, can guarantee the reader a truly unique–and fabulous–ride.

– *Marc Summers, TV Host, Producer,*
Star of Double Dare (1986)

Dan Harary was an excellent publicist when we worked together on the *New Gidget* TV series in the mid '80s. I always enjoyed his company and when he told me he was now an author, I was delighted to see that he'd branched out beyond his PR duties. His book, *Flirting with Fame*, was very entertaining and I laughed out loud several times while reading it. Who else but Dan would forget Meryl Streep's name while talking face-to-face WITH MERYL STREEP HERSELF? He shares countless tales, all written in an engaging way, of how his life often accidentally crossed paths with celebrities from every area of show business. His stories convey to the reader a sense of his almost disbelief that he was even interacting with them in the first place! Dan's stories are charming and humorous. He is the ultimate Hollywood fan and I am proud of his new accomplishments as an author.

– *Caryn Richman, Actress, Teacher,*
Spokeswoman/Star of The New Gidget (1986)

Dan Harary is the Leonard Zelig of Hollywood, the Forrest Gump of show business. Wherever there is a celebrity, he'll inevitably be close by. Whether this is due to his persistent stalking or simple coincidence is a legitimate question. What's undeniable is Dan's colorful ability to spin a great story. His book is a treasure trove of golden star anecdotes from 50 years of his truly unique life.

– *Ray Richmond, Longtime Hollywood Journalist and Author of*
Betty White: 100 Remarkable Moments in an Extraordinary Life (2021)

Like Dan himself, *Flirting with Fame* is funny, captivating, surprising, enlightening, eloquent, touching, brutally honest and eminently enjoyable. Chronicling a career that has seen this talented author regularly interact with an unbelievably diverse range of film, television, music and theatrical luminaries, this book is a must-read for anyone who loves the entertainment industry or just wants to spend some quality time with their favorite celebrities. I read it straight through in a few hours and you probably will, too. Let's just hope Dan is already working on a sequel!

– Peter Berk, Author/PR Executive

Folks from out of town tend to assume that greater Los Angeles is simply teeming with famous people everywhere you look. Not true, unless you're Dan Harary. While many of his title flirtations were professional in nature, even while off-duty Dan seems to attract celebrities like a metal detector finds buried treasure–encounters he relates with great brio and a delightfully self-effacing sense of humor. Some anecdotes are uproarious, some are surprisingly touching. For anyone looking to connect with his inner Zelig, it's a fabulous ride.

– Ron Mulligan, Writer/Editor and Former CBS TV Executive

ACKNOWLEDGEMENTS

First off, I'd like to thank all the countless celebrities from film, TV, theater and music I've met, worked with or interacted with since 1972. I've enjoyed meeting you all and it was these magical moments that inspired the theme of this book.

Thanks to my mother, Joan, for her encouragement over the years with my creative writing. For my college graduation from Boston University, she bought me a ring with a quill pen embossed on it. I've been trying to live up to her dreams for me ever since.

Thanks to Ben Ohmart at Bear Manor Media for offering me a book contract within an hour of my pitching *Flirting With Fame* to him! Ben, you rock! My longtime friend, Ray Richmond – thanks, man, for suggesting Bear Manor and for your book review quote! To my agent, Francesca Romero–I so appreciate all your hard work with editing this book.

Thanks to Ron Mulligan, Peter Berk, Marc Summers, Dee Wallace, and Caryn Richman for their wonderful book review quotes; and to Steve Walter, Brad Shron, Tobin Tellers, Shauna Krikorian, Mike Garfinkel, Heather Burgett, Mitch Zamarin, Ava Cadell, Jamie Hoffer, Todd Masters and Ron Mendelsohn for the decades of shared laughter, martinis and friendship.

A special shout-out thank you to Mark & Tina Echeverria and Andrea Scuto from the Musso & Frank Grill. I'm thrilled that we all found each other.

Last, but certainly not least, thank you to my wonderful, talented and beautiful Anjuli for being such a caring and encouraging daughter. She is my pride and joy–the greatest gift I've ever received. To paraphrase Singer Debby Boone, "She Lights Up My Life!"

DJH/Spring 2022
Beverly Hills, CA

CONTENTS

Introduction   1

Chapter One: 1956-1974 – Little Drummer Boy/The Monkees/Rock 'N Roll at The Sunshine Inn   3

Chapter Two: 1972-1974 – Springsteen   10

Chapter Three: 1974-1980 – College Daze/Joan Rivers Gives Advice/McCartney Winks/Close Call with Woody Allen/Brooke Shields is Magnetic   18

Chapter Four: 1980-1985 – Poverty in Venice/Jerry Seinfeld's First Fan/Peeing with Robert Wise/Mike, My First Monkee/Hanging with Hugh Hefner   30

Chapter Five: 1985-1987 – Lunch with a Monkee/ Gilligan in Hawaii/Madonna Blows a Kiss/Harassing Sally Field/Barbra Streisand Stares Again   56

Chapter Six: 1987-1989 – Sid Caesar's Dogs/Jay Leno's Underwear/Uncle Miltie is Old/Karen Black is Naked/ Dying a Divine Death   63

Chapter Seven: 1989-1996 – Scrapping Lassie's Star/ Seinfeld Remembers/Sting Goes the Wrong Way/Crosby, Slick, Nash & Dan/Two Moon Men/Jerry Lewis Winks/ Insulting Meryl Street/Blinded by Michael Jackson/ Marky Mark's Pecs/Julia's Dress Has a Tag/The Who's Private Concert/Mary Tyler Moore in Vegas/Sam Kinison's Ladies/Jean Smart Gives a Hug   79

Chapter Eight: 1996-2009 – Asbury Launches/Arnold Snarls/Biggie Smalls Gets Killed/Jack Black Is Stoned/Jenna Jameson Gets Naked/Jimmy Kimmel is My Neighbor/A Go-Go Writes Lovelace/Rene Russo Wants My Bone   117

PHOTOS   153

Chapter Nine: 2009 – Help! I'm In Love With A Supermodel!   177

Chapter Ten: 2010 – Hollywood & Vine/Meeting Spielberg/George Lopez in Wax/Skinny Barry Manilow/Jonah Hill Gets Stunned/Billy Bob is Rude   193

Chapter Eleven: 2011-2017 – Asbury Agency Arrives/Wrangling KISS/The Cowsills' 50th Anniversary/Billy Crystal Likes Chinese/Annoying Nancy Sinatra/Spiritual Carlos Santana/Kim Kardashian Has Big Boobs/Directing Yoko Ono/Sexy Times with Dr. Ruth   207

Chapter Twelve: 2017-2019 – Musso & Frank Turns 100/Danny Trejo Wants My Daughter/Lucy Liu Sends a Wink/Ann-Margret is My Dream Girl   237

Chapter Thirteen: 2019-2022 – Barney's Turns 100/Hello Covid My Old Friend/Charlie Sheen's Ex-Wife Calls/Drew Carey Loves to Bowl/Alan Arkin Send a Note/Billy Joel's Drummer Stands Corrected/Goodbye Mike Nesmith/Star Trek: 25/A Musso Dinner with a Legendary Beach Boy/The Vanity Fair "Young Hollywood" Oscars Party   242

Afterword   254

Photo Credits   257

Celebrity Encounters Index   259

For Anjuli

FLIRTING WITH FAME:
A Hollywood Publicist Recalls
50 Years of Celebrity Close Encounters

PREFACE

In the summer of 1964 when I was eight years old, my father met Ed Sullivan at Newark Airport and got his autograph. When he came home, my dad handed me the small piece of paper, which read:

*To Dan, Bob and Mike,
Best Regards, Ed Sullivan*

The time frame stands out because my brother Michael had JUST been born.

Unfortunately, that slip of paper is now long gone, along with my hair.

I clearly remember being dumbfounded that my father had shaken hands with a man who had shaken hands with The Beatles!

That small event made me realize that famous people who appeared on TV, in movies, on the radio, on stage, and on records, actually DID EXIST in real life. It was my very first glimpse into the exciting "other side" of my quite ordinary universe.

Little did I know on that summer day back in '64, that I would personally experience countless "close encounters" with celebrities of all shapes and sizes on both coasts, during the course of the next six decades.

INTRODUCTION

I'm just an ordinary Joe from New Jersey who made his way to Hollywood, became established as a Publicist, and eventually owned and operated his own entertainment industry PR Agency for 25 years. Becoming a "Publicist" (which sounds like "Pub-la-CYST"– a dangerous growth that should be removed immediately) was never something I'd anticipated, planned on, thought about or pursued.

It quite simply "just happened" along the way.

Let's start at the beginning. My first "close encounter" with a celebrity was in early 1972–singer/guitarist Richie Havens. I was 15 at the time. It was a thrill that I still remember quite vividly.

Since then, I've met, worked with, interacted with, "almost met," or been waved at, nodded at, or winked at, by many dozens of famous people–some living legends–in the fields of TV, film, music, the stage and politics.

Among these celebs were a Vice President, a few of the world's biggest porn stars, and two men who walked on the Moon!

Given the small potatoes neighborhood I came from, I think it's interesting that for some God-only-knows reason, I was predestined to be a fame-adjacent "Zelig" for most of my adult life. Of course, if YOU worked within the entertainment industry as a producer, director, writer, studio executive, cameraman, celebrity publicist, hair or makeup artist, etc., the stories you are about to read won't be very impressive. People with those occupations work with major stars like these all the time.

Perhaps also intriguing is the fact that the only other person I know of who came from my hometown, and also wound up "fame adjacent," is my childhood best friend, Steve Walter.

Steve is the owner and general manager of Manhattan's legendary Cutting Room nightclub. During the past 50 years he, too, has met, worked with, or interacted with countless celebrities from across all genres.

In fact, Lady Gaga was discovered at Steve's club in 2006, when she began performing there as Stefani Germanotta!

If one were to combine the list of famous celebs I've encountered with those who have circled Steve's orbit, you'd have a nearly complete tally of the entertainment industry's most famous people.

How two nice, conservative Jewish boys from a suburban '60s neighborhood along the Jersey Shore ended up rubbing shoulders with America's biggest stars is anybody's guess.

For background intel, please read this book. I hope you enjoy!

Chapter One

1956-1974

LITTLE DRUMMER BOY/THE MONKEES/ROCK 'N ROLL AT THE SUNSHINE INN

I was born in Neptune, New Jersey, during the summer of 1956; the product of a very musical family. My father, who was an electronics engineer for the U.S. Department of the Army for almost 50 years, had a beloved hobby–playing the trombone in big bands and dance bands, large and small. My mother, professionally both a teacher and later a probation officer, was also a noted singer, accordionist, actress, pianist, playwright, poet, artist and stage producer. Each of my parents performed musically for many decades in front of live audiences throughout Monmouth County, New Jersey. They most often performed in separate bands and shows, but for several years in the SAME combo - Harry Hurley's Big Band – broadcasting live on WJLK Radio.

My brothers and I grew up in West Deal, just adjacent to the legendary Asbury Park. In 1973, Asbury would become quite famous after Bruce Springsteen entitled his first album *Greetings from Asbury Park*. (More about Bruce to come.)

When I was seven, my parents insisted I take piano lessons. I studied classical music until the age of 10 and was quite accomplished, even performing at various local area piano recitals. Although I was very good, I never enjoyed the piano. My teacher, Professor Galliani, was a tyrant.

When I turned 10, my life took a dramatic turn. In the fall of 1966, NBC TV presented The Monkees (1966) and their music. As manufactured and "fake" as they may have been at the time, they rocked my world to its core. While I loved The Beatles' music, I was quite young when the Fab Four first conquered America in 1964. I had only one of their albums, had seen them perform once on *The Ed Sullivan Show* (1948) when I was 7, and watched their film *HELP!* (1965) at an Asbury Park movie theater.

The Monkees were something else entirely. Here was a rock band comprised of four funny guys with long hair, who cranked out hit song after hit song on a WEEKLY TV SHOW! They were instantly accessible to me, in spite of the fact that we only had a black and white television set back then. I bought all of their records, playing them until the grooves were scratched beyond repair.

My brother Bob and I would even dance to Monkees' records together in our den.

The arrival of The Monkees on TV had a second impact on me. I became obsessed with Micky Dolenz, their drummer (whom I would befriend 20 years later). Watching him (pretend to) play the drums made me realize I no longer wanted to study classical piano. I HAD to play the drums, too. I hounded my parents incessantly to buy me a drum set. Eventually the agreement became that I could start taking drum lessons along with my continued piano lessons, and IF I stuck with BOTH, I would get drums as a Bar Mitzvah present when I turned 13.

I initially took drum lessons for two years, learning all the rudiments on a little rubber drum pad and later on a red sparkle-colored snare drum, all under the tutelage of local area professional drummer Bill Weir, who always smelled of bourbon. Finally bailing out on the piano, my parents realized that playing drums was my passion. One of the greatest moments of my life was the day my father took me into Brooklyn to a Sam Ash music store to order a sky-blue pearl Ludwig drum set. When he wrote out that check for $350.00, I was stunned to my core. That was a fortune as far as I was concerned! I honestly didn't know he had access to that kind of cash.

At the age of 12, two years into my love affair with drums, a friend of mine gave me an extra ticket to attend a concert at Asbury Park's Convention Hall featuring the band Iron Butterfly. At the time, not only was their "In-A-Gadda-Da-Vida" the biggest "acid rock" song of 1968, but it also featured the first recorded rock and roll drum solo. While watching Iron Butterfly, I stood during the course of that drum solo, trying to glean just how drummer Ron Bushy was able to accomplish such a remarkable feat. From then on, I became obsessed with attending live rock concerts at Convention Hall, and during the next six years, would see dozens of shows there by such iconic bands as Mountain, YES, Chicago, Ten Years After, Black Sabbath, Humble Pie, The Eagles and Grand Funk Railroad. During a show by Emerson, Lake & Palmer, I leaned against the front of the stage, just feet in front of–and underneath–Greg Lake. A mesmerizing moment!

My beautiful Ludwig drum set was shipped to my house in the fall of 1968, just 10 months shy of my Jewish birthday milestone. As one of the very few kids my age with a professional-quality drum set, I was quickly sought out by the various guitar players from my neighborhood. I jammed, briefly, with a few local garage bands, before meeting Steve Walter in Hebrew School. Steve was to become a lifelong friend, noted guitarist, and later in life the owner of the world-famous Cutting Room nightclub in Manhattan.

Starting in 6th grade, Steve and I put rock bands together with other fellow student guitarists, bassists, and keyboard players. Our bands had such names (taken from a dictionary) as Radiation, Grain, Eclipse, and later Mr. Spud, which our bass player Scott thought was the real name of the "Mr. Potato Head" toy. Our bands performed contemporary songs by iconic '60s and early '70s bands such as The Rolling Stones, The Young Rascals, Creedence Clearwater Revival, The Who, Led Zeppelin, The Allman Brothers Band, Mountain, Cream, Grand Funk Railroad, Jefferson Airplane, and dozens more.

Steve and I were so in love with playing rock music and with our bands that we wanted to embellish our performances with a "light show." We melded our allowances and along with the generosity of Steve's father, designed and built a fully functioning stage lighting rig that included both multicolored floodlights that appeared on the stage floor in front of us musician/performers, as well as a "wet" light show that projected-onto a huge white bedsheet suspended behind our band–oozing, swirling blobs of colors, shapes and kaleidoscopic imagery.

We were the only band in town that had its own light show.

One day when we were high school sophomores, Steve got a call from a senior he knew named Lucas. Lucas, who ran a "wet" light show but didn't have front stage lighting, was asking Steve if he and his friends could use our flood lighting rig for a concert by singer/guitarist Richie Havens. At the time, Lucas was the Stage Manager and Lighting Director for a small rock concert venue in Asbury Park–one block west of the Atlantic Ocean–called The Sunshine Inn. The hall, originally known as the Hullabaloo Club, had been converted from a Hertz rental car garage into a theater, and was fast becoming a rock music mecca, presenting bands from across the U.S. and Western Europe, several of which would later become quite famous.

Steve then called me, and I rushed over to his house on my bike. Lucas and his friends arrived, and together we carried our lighting gear up from Steve's basement into Lucas' car. He drove us to the Sunshine Inn, where we hurriedly had to set up our floodlights. We arrived around 7:30 pm. Richie Havens was slated to begin his show promptly at 8:00.

Huffing and puffing, sweating and shaking, Steve and I quickly got our lights up and running. We then hopped into a small "lighting pit" area, which was in reality a hole in the very front right of the stage floor. We tested the lights once to ensure all was a go, and when he felt comfortable, Lucas told the Sunshine Inn owner that we were ready to begin the show.

There I was, standing up in a "hole" in a stage, watching Richie Havens take his stool and strap on his guitar. I was enthralled by his performance; here was one of the iconic stars of the 1969 Woodstock Festival and its subsequent 1970 movie, performing just a few feet from me! When he performed the song "Freedom," it blew our minds. I clearly remember the sweat flying off his face and hands.

After Havens' show, Steve and I went backstage to meet Richie. We shook his hand and he signed, for each of us, a Sunshine Inn promotional poster for his concert, writing: "A Friend Forever and Ever. Health. Peace. Love. Richie Havens."

The date of that show was March 24, 1972. It was my very first "close encounter" with a celebrity. I still have that poster; it proudly hangs in my living room in Beverly Hills.

After our success handling the lighting for that Richie Havens concert, Lucas asked Steve and I if we would like to take over his role as Stage Manager and Lighting Director for the Sunshine Inn in a few months, as he was preparing to leave the Asbury Park area to go off to college. Of course, we said a huge "YES!"

Having watched so many rock bands perform while stationed in a seat in the audience during the previous four years, suddenly I was "upgraded" to sitting INSIDE THE STAGE itself! During the course of the next 2-1/2 years, Steve and I would spend countless hours at the Sunshine Inn–that is, when we weren't in school, Shull, doing homework, or performing with our various bands at someone's birthday party, high school dance, or political fundraising event.

Among the dozens of bands Steve and I worked with at the Sunshine Inn were such now long-lost rock acts as Uriah Heep, Deep Purple, Mott The Hoople, the Edgar Winter Group, Renaissance,

Focus, Slade, Procol Harum, Quicksilver Messenger Service, the J. Geils Band, Seals and Crofts, Black Oak Arkansas, King Crimson, Billy Cobham, Rory Gallagher, Roy Buchanan, The Climax Blues Band, and so many others. (I'm sure Steve would remember all of them. He has an elephant's memory.)

Before and after these shows, Steve and I would set up (and later tear down) each band's equipment, schlepping amplifiers, drum cases, and especially heavy Hammond organs and other keyboards from the band's truck parked just outside, through the rear stage door, and onto the stage itself. We met and interacted with all of the road managers and roadies for these bands and, on occasion, were gently mocked by them as we, at ages 15, 16 and 17, weren't nearly as strong as they were. A few stories stand out:

- When the J. Geils Band began to play, our light show blew a fuse and they had to perform their first song in utter darkness. Their stage manager jumped into the lighting pit next to me and Steve, screaming at us. He LITERALLY pulled a huge chunk of hair out of his head, like Moe Howard used to do to Larry Fine in *The Three Stooges* (1922-1970) movies.
- After performances by Uriah Heep and Deep Purple, Steve and I lost much of our hearing for several weeks. I can still remember the high pitched "Hmmmmmm" noise that rang in my ears incessantly–it's miraculous we both didn't get tinnitus.
- While setting up the equipment for the Dutch band, Focus (whose sole hit song was called "Hocus Pocus"), their stage manager came up to Steve and I and shouted, "Tension Rods! Must have Tension Rods!" We had no idea what he meant. We finally figured out the poor man was begging us for "extension cords!"
- After I struggled for quite some time to lift my half of a Mellotron (keyboard) onto the stage, the lead roadie for

King Crimson jokingly said to me, "Danny, keep eating your porridge, and stay away from the young ladies!"

In addition to the bands listed above, three others stand out for obvious reasons:

- Fleetwood Mac: Steve and I worked with Fleetwood Mac before Stevie Nicks and Lindsey Buckingham joined the group. This was during their Bob Welch era. Before the show, I handed Mick Fleetwood and Christine McVie sodas, amazed at how tall Fleetwood was. Perhaps the most memorable moment of that show was a couple standing off to the right side of the stage, just in front of the lighting pit, during Mac's performance. This guy was humping the rear end of the girl standing just in front of him and when he finished, a clearly visible wet stain was prominent on his jeans!
- KISS: KISS' roadies set up their own lighting rig, so Steve and I only helped out with stage crew work for them. Their show at the Sunshine Inn was their very first ever concert not held in New York. After their performance, I went backstage and Gene Simmons, in full KISS kabuki makeup, asked me if I could get him and his bandmates some cold sodas. I had to quickly run several blocks down the street to purchase a case of Cokes, then ran back to him. When I handed him the soft drinks, he smiled up at me to say, "Thanks." The memorable part of this moment was that he had a ton of sweat slowly seeping through the cracks of his thick white makeup. His forehead, cheeks, chin and nose appeared to be "crying." It was so very creepy–and scary!
- The Bruce Springsteen Band: Ahh, good ole Bruce, so many stories. Where to begin?

Chapter Two

1972-1974

SPRINGSTEEN

Steve and I first saw Bruce Springsteen appear live on stage in early 1972 at the local area JCC (Jewish Community Center) in Deal, New Jersey, located just a few blocks from Steve's house. After seeing an orange-colored flyer there promoting an upcoming show by "Bruce Spring-STEIN" for $1.50, Steve and I purchased our tickets out of curiosity–we had never heard of him before. Plus, we assumed since his last name was Jewish, it would be kind of cool to see a fellow "Heeb" play rock and roll.

I'm sure today that misspelled flyer would be a collector's item.

Steve and I sat in the first row of the JCC's auditorium in folding metal chairs. Bruce and his group (not yet called the E Street Band) played INCREDIBLY LOUD music. According to Steve's memory, they played Bruce's early, original material, but not yet songs from "Greetings from Asbury Park." The band screeched so loudly I couldn't stand it. I left after maybe four songs. I clearly remember walking home from that show, thinking how much that music sucked.

Exactly one year later, Bruce and his band were booked to perform at the Sunshine Inn. While Steve and I spent many hundreds of hours working at The Inn, both with stage crew and stage lighting I, independently of Steve, also worked occasionally in the front office, answering phones and selling tickets to rock music fans.

I happened to be at The Inn alone when Bruce showed up to rehearse.

I was on the phone with someone asking about ticket prices for Bruce's two upcoming shows on February 10, 1973 ($3.50 for the 7:30 pm show, and $4.50 for the 10:30 pm show), when I heard a knock on the front office door. Finishing my call, I opened the door to see a scraggly-haired, very skinny guy holding a guitar case in one hand and the hand of a pretty brunette wearing purple stockings in the other. Not recognizing the man I'd seen perform on stage exactly one year earlier, I asked, "Are YOU Bruce Springsteen?"

He replied, "Yeah, man, that's me."

We shook hands, but I was more impressed with the purple-colored legs of his girlfriend than with him. I led the duo through the front office and up the short staircase leading to the stage inside the hall.

Next, Steve and the rest of Bruce's band members arrived. Together we all unloaded their truck and carried their amplifiers, drums and keyboards onto the stage. The band at that time was comprised of Danny Federici on organ, Garry W. Tallent on bass, Vinnie Lopez on drums, and Clarence Clemons–who had JUST JOINED–on saxophone.

Clarence showed up late: "Sorry guys, I just got outta jail. I was late on child support."

Once everything was set up, Steve and I stood on the stage about three feet from Bruce, while he and the band performed their first song during rehearsal: "Six-Eight-Four-Five-Seven-Eight-Nine"–a tune about a phone number. Later, Bruce was experimenting with the volume control knob on his guitar, making his instrument sound like a violin. Steve and I had never seen anyone do that before, and as a guitarist himself, Steve was impressed.

In rehearsal, Bruce and his band performed several other tunes (lost to my memory) before saying, "Okay, sounds pretty good. That's a wrap." Bruce and the band split, and Steve and I rode our bicycles back home.

The next day–concert day–the owner of the Sunshine Inn, Bob Fischer–a short, stout, obnoxious, Jewish man with a bad temper renowned for not paying his bills–showed up in a Cadillac, having driven to Asbury Park from his home in Queens. When Fischer realized that only 200 TOTAL tickets had been sold for BOTH of Bruce's two separate shows, Bob decided that Bruce would only do one show at 10:30 pm for ALL the ticket buyers. No one complained that I recall.

Note: At capacity, the Sunshine Inn held about 2,000 people. The 200 people who appeared for Bruce's show that night made the hall look virtually empty.

At this time, Steve had a girlfriend (Laura), so he decided to run the lighting board inside the stage pit with her. I volunteered to run the trouper/spotlight that was located midway through the venue, atop the left side bleachers.

Bruce and his band performed his entire first album, "Greetings from Asbury Park," that night. Having never before in my life hearing music like this ("Madman Drummers, Bummers, and Indians in the Summer, with a Teenage Diplomat" from "Blinded By The Light"), I had NO IDEA what he was talking about. His music sounded completely Martian to me. I had no connection to any of his material and could barely understand his words.

Steve and Laura apparently enjoyed the show far more than I did. Perhaps since they were inside the stage, they were better able to understand the lyrics?

After a 90-minute concert, Bruce, *et al.* went backstage for cold drinks. Then Bruce, with his purple-legged gal pal in tow, walked through the backstage hallway and past the front office to exit the building. Steve and I were in the office at the time and as he passed, Steve yelled out, "Hey Bruce, what'd you think of the light show?"

Springsteen stopped walking for a second, took a good look at Steve, then a good look at me. Smiling, he replied, "You cats were incredible!"

And just like that, he vanished. Like a "Spirit in the Night."

Just a few days later, Steve somehow heard through the grapevine that Bruce and his band would be rehearsing for an upcoming concert at Monmouth College, only a few miles from Steve's house. Steve and I rode our bikes over to the school's auditorium, then entered and walked up some bleachers to watch the rehearsal. While I, again, was no fan of Bruce or his music, Steve had gotten "bitten by The Boss," and was excited to watch him play once more. I was bored to tears during this rehearsal, but Steve seemed to be having a good time.

During a band break, Bruce's sax player, Clarence Clemons (may he rest in peace), walked up the bleachers to where Steve and I were sitting. He stood directly in front of us.

"Hey, would you guys be interested in working as our road crew? We're going down to Washington, D.C., next week, and we could use some help," he asked.

Steve and I looked at each other in amazement. I then turned to face the soon-to-become globally iconic sax man and said, "Clarence, we're only 16; we don't even DRIVE yet. Besides that, I'm pretty sure our fathers want us to go to college!"

Clarence paused. He took a long stare into Steve's face and then into mine and said, "Okay, that's cool. I understand." He turned and walked back down the bleachers to rejoin the band on the small auditorium's stage.

Was that THE LUCKY BREAK IN LIFE that Steve and I turned down? Of course, with Bruce becoming a living legend just two years later with the release of "Born to Run," Steve and I, had we accepted Clarence's offer–and killed our fathers by NOT going to college–could have seen the world, had sex with countless groupies, and become part of rock and roll history.

We'd also have become deaf and hunchbacked, having had to schlep heavy equipment around the world for the next fifty years.

During Bruce's show at the Sunshine Inn, Steve and I met Carl "Tinker" West, who was Bruce's first manager. Tinker hired Steve and I to run the spotlights at a concert he was producing at the Long Branch, New Jersey Armory–about 15 minutes north of Asbury Park–a few weeks later. The night we worked that show, Bruce showed up-along with drummer Vinnie Lopez and a girl in a remarkably short mini-skirt-and hung out at the front of the auditorium with Tinker. Bruce waved to Steve and I while we were precariously positioned high up on a raised – and rather shaky - lighting scaffold.

Several months after his show at the Sunshine Inn, Bruce was performing solo–just him and his guitar on a stool–inside the Student Prince bar, directly across the street from The Inn. Admission was $1.00. Steve and I were at The Inn that night, cleaning up and hanging out with owner Bob Fischer, when someone came in and told Bob that Bruce was at The Prince.

Bob invited Steve and I to cross the street with him to see the show. What's interesting to note here is that this was a BAR, and Steve and I were only 16 years old.

Bob had a beer, Steve and I had Cokes, and we watched Bruce's acoustic show. We sat about five feet in front of him. There were maybe 20 people in the room. Probably less.

When he took a break, Bruce hopped off the tiny stage, and walked up to Bob to say hello.

"Bruuucie, baby," Fischer said in his most obnoxious, guttural, salesman pitch. "Lemme be your manager, kid. I wanna represent you."

Bruce looked at Steve and I, kind of smiled (a wink maybe?) and said to Bob, "Thanks for the offer, man, but I'm okay. I'm with Tinker, but thanks anyway."

<u>Summer of 1973</u>: My mother dropped me off at West End Beach (Long Branch, New Jersey) for the day to sunbathe and swim. I sat on a towel, alone. Once I'd set myself up to relax, I glanced up the sand about 20 feet behind me to see Springsteen sitting, alone, on his towel. He seemed to be staring into space (and was probably orchestrating "Jungleland").

For the next two hours, Bruce Springsteen and I, and ALMOST NO ONE ELSE FOR MILES, sat on that beach, separate and alone. I was no fan of his music. Even though I'd already met him and had been within his orbit for months earlier that year, I simply had NO INTEREST in him. (Hard to believe now, I know, but sadly true.)

He saw me. I saw him. A quick nod, maybe? I will add that in those days I was VERY SHY and since he was seven years older than me, I wouldn't have felt comfortable walking up to him to talk, even if I had enjoyed his music. I will say that had Steve been there with me that day, it's likely the three of us would have spent the afternoon together.

When my mother returned to pick me up and take me home–again I didn't yet drive–we drove about a quarter-mile from the beach when I saw Bruce hitchhiking on the side of the road. He was holding a guitar with one hand, and the other featured a prominent hitchhiker's thumb.

"Hey Mom," I said to my mother as we passed Bruce, "see that guy over there? His name is Bruce Springsteen. He thinks he's a rock star!"

My mother and I chuckled as we simply drove on by.

Do I regret not talking to Bruce that day on the beach and not asking my mom to give him a lift? OF COURSE! Clearly, I'm a PUTZ! After all the various encounters I'd already had with him, I should have asked my mother to give him a ride simply out of basic human courtesy and kindness.

Because I was the big shot "know-it-all" who simply had no interest in his music or lyrics and had no idea what the hell his songs were about, I dismissed the very existence of the man who would soon become one of the most prominent, important, and successful musicians in the history of the world.

Bruce, I'm sorry we didn't give you a ride that day. I suck.

CODA #1: One day during my senior year of high school (early 1974), a friend of mine, Eric, already a huge Springsteen fan who'd had "The Boss" to his parents' home for dinner several times, told me he'd heard that Springsteen was "auditioning drummers" and maybe I should try out? Eric and I were playing handball in gym at the time. I told him I "didn't care for Bruce's music," but thanks for letting me know anyway."

Congrats, Max Weinberg. You avoided competing against the "stiff competition" of Daniel J. Harary! Such a PUTZ!

CODA #2: Jumping ahead five years, I was on a date in Red Bank, New Jersey, during the summer of 1979, when I saw Clarence Clemons and an attractive woman sitting at the next table in a small restaurant. I told my date, "I know him!", got up and sat, uninvited, at Clarence's table. He looked at me like I was an imbecile.

"Hey Clarence, do you remember me? I'm Dan, from the Sunshine Inn, back in '73."

He looked into my face, clearly annoyed, shook my hand and said, "Yeah, kind of, I guess." Clarence appeared to be physically exhausted and devoid of any human emotion.

I said, "Are your enjoying all the success? Is it fun?"

He replied in a dead-toned voice, "Man, it's a LOT of HARD WORK!"

Realizing he wanted nothing to do with me, I got up, left his table, and returned to my date.

Since she had no idea who Clarence Clemons was, not only was my date utterly unimpressed, she got pissed off at me for abandoning her for all of three minutes.

I never saw that woman again.

Chapter Three

1974-1980

COLLEGE DAZE / JOAN RIVERS GIVES ADVICE / MCCARTNEY WINKS / CLOSE CALL WITH WOODY ALLEN / BROOKE SHIELDS IS MAGNETIC

My father attended–and graduated from–Rutgers University in New Brunswick, New Jersey, so of course it was predestined that I, his first-born son, would also attend his *Alma Mater*.

Rutgers was about a 45-minute drive from our house. When I arrived there for my freshman year of college, I was just 18, had long dark brown hair halfway down my back, zits on my face that resembled slices of pepperoni on a pizza, had not yet smoked pot, and was a virgin. I had never in my life spent a night away from my parents. I was there solely because my dad wanted me to become a dentist.

My freshman year of college was a horror. While I got straight A's in my courses, I was hit by the severe genetic depression that runs rampant throughout my mother's family. I finally gave in to peer pressure and began smoking pot, which I greatly enjoyed, but that was small consolation to my self-loathing, doubt and complete lack of self-confidence.

During my freshman year, I did continue to attend as many rock concerts as possible. I schlepped out to Long Island to see Eric Clapton, then missed my train home and had to sleep on a bench at New

York's Penn Station for a night. I caught Renaissance at Rutgers and after the show went backstage. I'd met Singer Annie Haslam and Bassist Jon Camp the year before at the Sunshine Inn and wanted to say hello once again.

Most of the shows I saw were at Madison Square Garden in Manhattan by such top acts as The Rolling Stones, The Who, Led Zeppelin, David Bowie, John McLaughlin, Jeff Beck, George Harrison, Genesis, and Alice Cooper.

Funny story: A girl I knew from high school, Lori, also attended Rutgers. In what would have taken all of my courage to ask for a date at that time, I approached her one day on campus and asked if she'd like to attend a concert by Alice Cooper with me.

"Alice Cooper? Who's SHE?" Lori replied. (I'd meet Alice 12 years later.)

After my freshman year-during which I'd contemplated suicide on a daily basis, my parents were kind enough to realize that I was miserable at Rutgers and generously pooled their money so I could transfer colleges. During my freshman year, I'd taken my very first air-flight to visit Steve, who was attending the Berklee College of Music in Boston. We went to a George Harrison concert together at the Boston Garden. I was so enthralled with Boston that I begged, pleaded and cajoled my parents to send me there, as well. After a great deal of negotiations, my parents gave in and I transferred to Boston University for the rest of my college era.

At BU, I was enrolled in the School of Public Communications. I studied TV production, advertising, marketing, journalism, and multi-media production, but, notably, NOT public relations! It was the right place for me at the right time.

I was at BU from 1975-1978. Radio Shock Jock Howard Stern attended BU then, as well. I clearly remember him walking the hallways of the school. He was SO TALL, he stood out a mile. My friends were always asking me, "Did you listen to that crazy guy Howard Stern on the radio this morning?"

Howard had a BU radio show at the time. Since I was never an early riser–Howard's show was on very early in the mornings–I'm sorry to say I never did hear that show while he and I were both there. (I'd meet Howard 10 years later in Hollywood.)

During my sophomore year at BU (1976), Joan Rivers came to our campus to present a film she produced, *Rabbit Test* (1978), starring Billy Crystal. The film was about a man who becomes pregnant. While I thought the movie sucked, I always thought Joan was funny. After the film ended, a few students approached the comedienne to meet her. I had in my hand a copy of the BU student newspaper advertising her talk. I asked her to sign it for me; she did, and I still have that.

I said to her, "Hey Joan, I want to be a comedy writer for television. Do you have any advice?"

Her response, winking at me: "Move to Los Angeles as soon as you possibly can!"

Less than five years later, I would take her advice. Sort of.

In the early months of 1976, I joined a Beatles fan club at BU. I was the only male member of the club, which was comprised of about a dozen pretty girls.

I befriended the founder of the club, a girl whose name I do not remember. She told me that Paul McCartney and Wings would be appearing that summer at the Boston Garden. She told me if I gave her the money, she'd ensure that I, along with several other members of the club, got good seats.

Paul McCartney and Wings performed at the Boston Garden on May 22, 1976. The girls from my club and I sat in the VERY FRONT ROW, directly under Sir Paul. Since the girls I was sitting with were all clearly attractive, Paul was constantly winking and smiling at them throughout his performance.

At one point, I think during the song "Maybe I'm Amazed," I looked up at Paul and gave him a thumbs up sign. He looked directly at me, winked, and returned the gesture.

Other than once directing Yoko Ono to a restaurant bathroom decades later, that was the closest I ever came to "meeting" one of The Beatles.

In the spring of 1977, I took a home movie camera and recorded a short film capturing that year's Boston Marathon race. By that time, Steve's brother, Dean, had entered into BU, and the two of us spent the day together, drinking beer and shooting film.

Movie legend Jack Lemmon stood at the finish line at that year's Marathon, appearing as a special guest star.

With my Super 8mm camera in hand, I slowly walked toward Lemmon, clearly waving at him. Responding, he waved back at me and smiled for the camera. Nice guy!

My senior year of college, I was fortunate enough to score an internship with WNAC TV, Boston's ABC affiliate television station. My "job" there–not for pay but, instead, school credit–was to write news stories from AP and UPI wire copy for the 11:00 pm live newscast each weeknight. I also had to run the teleprompter, from which the newscasters read the news aloud to viewers. I worked there from 7:00-11:30 pm, five nights a week, for five months.

John Henning was the lead anchorman in those days. He was an iconic Boston legend at the time, the local "Walter Cronkite." He was a nice guy to me, except for the fact that nearly every night around 9:00, he would task me with getting him a strawberry milkshake from the Faneuil Hall Marketplace, several blocks away.

Running in freezing cold Boston nights during January and February 1978, to buy a rich man a milkshake always really pissed me off. I froze my balls off each and every time I had to scurry to fulfill this errand.

At least I got an "A" for that internship.

Steve and I both graduated from our respective colleges in May 1978, and together we returned to the New Jersey Shore. We rented a house one block west of Belmar Beach, and tried to put a post-college band together. After just one gig in which we sucked beyond repair, things fell apart pretty quickly. I decided then that I was not meant to become a professional drummer.

Steve's cousin, Paul, was the advertising salesman for a small monthly print magazine called *The New Jersey Boater*. The publication offered news and ads for owners and lovers of all things nautical along the Jersey Shore. From summer '78 to March '80, I was the Art Director for that magazine–my first "professional" job, post-Bachelor of Science Degree in Communications.

I was earning a whopping $140.00 a week.

Once a month, after we created the layout and design of the latest issue of the magazine, the staff of *The Boater* had to spend a full day placing mailing labels onto the magazines for subscribers, and then stuffing mailbags full of those publications so that the post office could disseminate them. This task always took a full eight hours.

During summer of '79, Woody Allen was shooting his film *Stardust Memories* (1980) along the beachfront in Ocean Grove, New Jersey–just a few blocks south of Asbury Park and about a 20-minute drive from Long Branch, where *The New Jersey Boater* office was located.

On the day that we had to perform our monthly "labeling and stuffing" ritual, I asked for an hour off for lunch, so I could drive down to Ocean Grove in an attempt to meet Woody Allen. Reluctantly, my boss said, "Okay, but be sure to get back in time to help."

After parking my car adjacent to the famous Ocean Grove Auditorium, I ran a few blocks toward the beach, hoping for a simple "Woody sighting." I looked down at the beach from the boardwalk above and saw Tony Roberts and a few actresses on the sand alongside a movie camera and a few large lights on massive stands.

As I was checking out the view below me, I heard footsteps to my left. I turned and suddenly realized that Woody Allen was briskly walking my way; in fact, he was walking DIRECTLY towards me! I was truly surprised to see him in person–he had been my comedy "hero" for many years, and I had long imagined that one day I would become a comedy writer–the "new Woody Allen."

My heart began beating a mile a minute and my palms got sweaty. "This is it," I said to myself, "here's your chance to meet your idol." When Woody was a mere few inches from me, I TRIED to say "Hi, Woody, I'm Dan. Nice to meet you," and I TRIED to move my right hand forward to shake his.

I couldn't do a thing. Frozen. Completely paralyzed. I made a funny noise from the back of my throat that sounded like a bird catching its tail in a windowsill. Woody turned toward me, gave me a puzzled look as though I were a space alien, then turned his head back facing forward, very quickly descending the stairs down to the beach, where his set and cast were awaiting him.

I came THISCLOSE to meeting Woody Allen, but I simply couldn't do it.

When I returned to my office, I was about 40 minutes late. My boss screamed at me, furious. When he finished, he asked, "Well, did you meet Woody Allen, at least?" to which I had to offer my pathetic, truthful denial.

I DID, however, write an article about my "close encounter" with Mr. Allen. It ran, along with my photo standing in front of the

Ocean Grove Auditorium, in an issue of *The Asbury Park Press*, my hometown daily newspaper, a few days later.

I'll wonder for the rest of my life if Woody ever read that story.

One night during the summer of 1979, I went to a nightclub in Asbury Park called the Warehouse to watch a performance by the singing duo, Flo and Eddie. The team was comprised of Howard Kaylan and Mark Volman from The Turtles. I enjoyed their show greatly and was truly impressed by their remarkable vocal harmonies.

For their last song that night, Howard said, "To close our show, we're gonna do a song that we JUST RECORDED WITH BRUCE SPRINGSTEEN! We hope you like it." They then performed "Hungry Heart," which was to become one of Bruce's biggest hit singles.

After the show ended, I was making my way toward the front exit of the building, when who should I see standing directly in front of me? Yep, Bruce. He was there with his best friend and fellow guitarist, Steve Van Zandt.

Completely taken by surprise to see Bruce again, I tapped him on the shoulder. He turned around.

I said, "Bruce, do you remember me from the Sunshine Inn days?" I should note that when Bruce used to see me around back in '73, I had VERY long hair and had not yet started to wear glasses. Here we were now, together again, SIX YEARS later; I had much shorter hair, a moustache and glasses. There is no way on Planet Earth that anyone short of my own mother would have recognized me after such a dramatic physical change in appearance.

I put out my hand to Bruce.

He glanced up at my face, curious, and then after about 10 seconds, a twinkle appeared in his eye and his face softened. He shook my hand, heartily with one hand, then grabbed my elbow with his other, and said, "Yeah, man, actually I DO remember you!"

I was amazed. "I just wanted to congratulate you on all your success, Bruce. Everyone's so incredibly proud of you."

"Cool, thanks man," Bruce responded, smiling broadly. Steve Van Zandt was waiting for Bruce a bit further below on the exit's staircase. I waved at him as well, but as he and I had never met previously, he simply had no idea who I was and I got no response.

After two years with *The New Jersey Boater*, I was bored to tears with my "career." My mother suggested I try to find a creative writing job in Manhattan. I had a week's vacation coming my way, so I hustled myself into the Big City; an uncle of mine was kind enough to let me use his office space there as a resume "pitching center."

During that week, I had a variety of interviews at various entertainment industry companies, but all the jobs I was interviewing for were secretarial. People asked me "do you take shorthand?" which, of course, I did not. I did have one friend from Boston University named Stu, whom I remembered had gotten a job right after college graduation at Columbia Pictures on Fifth Avenue.

I called Stu at work during my vacation week and asked him if he wanted to have lunch with me. He said he couldn't; he was too busy since he'd JUST gotten promoted to publicist and was entering the next phase of his career.

Then, out from the clear blue sky, I asked him, "If YOU just got promoted, who got your OLD JOB?"

He replied, "No one, yet. It's not even posted. Why don't you get your ass over here right now and I'll try to help YOU get it?"

I scurried over to 711 Fifth Avenue and within a few minutes met with Stu, up in the Publicity/Promotion/Advertising Department. Truthfully, I had NO IDEA what Stu's old job was, nor did I really know ANYTHING at all about the movie industry.

Regardless, Stu introduced me to an ancient, old-time movie marketer named Abe, who handled all of the East Coast promotions for films released by Columbia Pictures. (Abe was so old, he had been friends with the actual Warner Brothers!)

Stu introduced us, and I shook Abe's hand. He asked, "Are you as good as Stuart?"

I replied, "I have no idea, but if you give me a chance, I'm sure I can learn quickly." Abe studied my face for 10 seconds, then said, "Stu, bring him to HR. Sign him up."

"What just happened?" I asked Stu as we left Abe's office.

"Congratulations, Dan," Stu replied, "you now work for Columbia Pictures."

Between April and July, 1980, I was a Promotions Assistant in Manhattan for a major movie studio. Since I lived on the Jersey Shore, I also had to commute every weekday during those months, two hours EACH WAY on a bus, FOUR HOURS a day in transit! Breathing all of that carbon monoxide started to kill me–commuting for those four months was the hardest thing I ever had to do.

For the job itself, I was to serve as Abe's right-hand man. Among the highlights of that "glamorous" job (he said sarcastically), I had to:

** Hire gorgeous models to wear white hot pants with rear-ends embossed on their backsides while escorting them around Manhattan, handing out promotional fliers to the upcoming Columbia film, *The Hollywood Knights* (1980). It was so embarrassing! I also led actress Fran Drescher and comedian Robert Wuhl up to the private Columbia movie screening room, so they could watch themselves in that same heinous film.

** Wrap in gift paper, flower boxes and red ribbons, HEAVY, OIL DRENCHED, DISGUSTING used car parts (dipsticks, distributor caps, spark plugs, etc.) to mail to movie critics in promotional efforts to bring their attention to the upcoming Columbia film, *Used Cars* (1980).

** Serve as an errand boy for each of the publicists in our department. Among these tasks were: handing Director John Cassavetes a cup of coffee; asking Movie Producer Stanley Jaffe to approve an advertisement congratulating *Kramer vs. Kramer* (1979) on winning several Oscars; and chatting with renowned publicist Marvin Levy about Steven Spielberg's recent SPECIAL EDITION of *Close Encounters of the Third Kind* (1979). (Note: Marvin and I would remain friends for the next 40 years. He would introduce me to Spielberg in 2010. That story comes later.)

During my lunch hours while working in New York for Columbia, I would usually grab a quick sandwich someplace and walk a few blocks north to Central Park, where I would sit on the same rock every single day. Once during that walk, I watched Director Peter Bogdanovich direct Actor John Ritter and Playboy Model Dorothy Stratten during the making of the film, *They All Laughed* (1981). Ritter waved at me as I passed him.

One day while sitting on my Central Park rock, I glanced to my right to see Movie Actress Jill Clayburgh smoking a joint. It was so cool sitting next to a two-time Oscar nominated performer. We exchanged glances and she extended her hand to me, offering me a hit. I took it, inhaled, and handed the jay back to her. We never said a word to each other; instead, we just smiled during the very brief experience of sharing a high together.

During that summer of '80, I was miserable with my job, not to mention the fact that my romantic life was nil. While sitting on that rock in Central Park, I would daydream about writing Hugh Hefner a letter, asking him for his advice on how to meet attractive women in Manhattan. I actually ALMOST DID write that letter! I include this anecdote because exactly four years later, not only would I meet

Hef, but I would spend many hours of my life at the infamous Playboy Mansion West.

My best Columbia Pictures era stories concern Brooke Shields. Brooke, who had just turned 15, recently finished shooting what would become her first hit film, *The Blue Lagoon* (1980). She and her mother, Teri (known throughout the PR department as "Terrible Teri Shields"), would often come up to our floor to hang out with the people who would be promoting that important summer, 1980, Columbia release. (Teri called her daughter, "Brookie.")

NO ONE in the PR department at the time enjoyed dealing with Teri Shields. When a first cut of *The Blue Lagoon* movie was available, Abe asked me to escort Teri and Brooke to the private screening room upstairs. He told me to stay with them and ensure that they were "taken care of."

That is how it came to be that Brooke Shields, her mother, and I were among the first people on the planet to watch Brooke's breakout movie role. I sat next to Brooke–we three were the only people in the theater. Afterward, she looked sad. I asked her what she thought.

"I don't know," she replied. "I wasn't very good."

I responded, "Please don't say that. I thought you were terrific! This movie's going to be a big hit!"

Teri then said, "Thanks Dan. That's very kind of you to say. You're a good guy."

During the remainder of my time at Columbia, Teri and Brooke would always go out of their way to be extra sweet and kind to me. The other publicists were shocked–Teri Shields LIKED Dan Harary? How on earth did HE DO THAT?

My last thought about Brooke is this: One day she came up to the PR Department by herself. I was hunched over with my back turned to where she was standing, as I was filing some paperwork at the time. She didn't make one sound, yet I KNEW someone was standing in front of my desk. My body was LITERALLY PULLED around by some powerful force so I could face her. That's the only time in my life I've ever experienced that phenomenon.

Is there such a thing as a "magnetic personality?" Yes! Brooke Shields proved that to me right then and there, on a summer's day back in 1980, at Columbia Pictures on Fifth Avenue in New York City.

Chapter Four:

1980-1985

POVERTY IN VENICE / JERRY SEINFELD'S FIRST FAN / PEEING WITH ROBERT WISE / MIKE, MY FIRST MONKEE / HANGING WITH HUGH HEFNER

I'd made a huge fuck-up at Columbia Pictures one day and my boss, Abe, was so pissed he stopped talking to me. That, coupled with my daily four-hours on a bus, was more than I could handle, so I asked the head of the PR Department if she would be kind enough to "lay me off" so I could collect unemployment. She did and that was that.

During August and September, 1980, I was able to catch up on my sleep. I did some freelance graphics work for *The New Jersey Boater* and that income, plus my unemployment, kept me in food. My parents had gotten divorced back in '77, so I moved in with my mother and little brother Michael after my Manhattan nightmare ended. This allowed me to save a bit by not having to pay rent.

During the months I'd been commuting on the bus to and from New York City and the Jersey Shore, I'd often see on that bus a very attractive woman who never sat near me. I never was able to meet her; our paths never crossed, plus my shyness then was quite remarkable.

One day while staring at her from afar, I heard a voice in my right ear say, "Write a book about women–call it *Carrots*." I instantly realized that *Carrots* was meant as the metaphor of "a carrot on a stick." The beautiful woman on the bus was just beyond my grasp.

During my mini-vacation from working that late summer, I wrote a screenplay on my mother's dining room table called, "*Carrots*." I didn't really know what I was doing, but I thought the story might hold some potential as a writer's "calling card" in the future.

In mid-September, 1980, Steve and I got two phone calls that would change my life forever. Both were from friends of ours who were from Jersey–each was now living in Los Angeles. The two friends, who didn't know each other, had each invited Steve and I to "come visit" Los Angeles. The fact that they both called within a day or two of each other was purely kismet.

I asked my dad if I should go "visit" LA.

His reply? "SCHMUCK! Why don't you just MOVE THERE? That's where the entertainment industry is. Don't visit. Move!"

Thus, the remainder of my life was decided at that moment. "Oh, okay, Dad. I will."

I literally did not know where Los Angeles was on a map at that time. I'd never heard of the Hollywood Sign, the stars on the "Walk of Fame," or any other iconic L.A./Hollywood landmark. I'd never even owned a Beach Boys album. I knew that Columbia Pictures had a studio out there, and that Johnny Carson and *Laugh-In* were filmed in "beautiful downtown Burbank," but that was the extent of my knowledge.

In a few quick weeks, I sold off all of my New Jersey possessions, excluding my drum set; a coin collection from my grandfather; my used piece-of-shit car; my record albums, stereo, and other small items I owned at the time. The grand total of my stash was $2,000.00. This was more cash than I'd ever seen before in my life.

While my mind was set on flying out to L.A. to stay, Steve came along with me simply to visit. On our flight from Newark to LAX, there was an all-you-can-eat buffet lunch! Steve and I were shocked– that buffet offered more food to passengers than my parents served my entire family at my Bar Mitzvah!

Arriving in Southern California, Steve and I were greeted by our mutual friend Ronnie, a kid I used to play baseball with in West Deal during the mid '60s. Ronnie was kind enough to put us up on the couches in his living room. He was living with an attractive red-head at the time named Adrienne.

That first day, Ronnie drove Steve and I all around L.A. It wasn't long before we saw Kenny Rogers in a huge white Rolls Royce careening down a steep road up in the Hollywood Hills, almost hitting us. That night, we ate dinner at Canter's Deli, sitting next to Beach Boy Carl Wilson and Actress Carol Kane.

"Welcome to L.A.," Ronnie said.

Steve was a man on a mission during the next three weeks, ensuring that he and I absorbed as much of California as possible, albeit without a car. Ronnie had to work, so Steve and I took buses everywhere. We walked everywhere else. I got blood blisters on my feet that took forever to heal.

Steve and I also took side trips up to San Francisco (we could have seen The Go-Go's perform at a bar there for a $2 cover charge, but I was too tired) and down to San Diego, where we stayed with our friend Eric from our Hebrew school/high school days. In a short, three week-span, we ran through a "greatest hits" tour of California's three most famous cities.

After we stayed at Ronnie's place for just one week, our other L.A.-friend, Joanne, and her fiancé, John, invited Steve and I to stay on their couches for the rest of our time in town. They lived in a crappy apartment building in Venice Beach. Actually, the building was ON Venice Beach.

After our three weeks together ended, Steve and I took a cab to LAX. We hugged and wished each other well. I watched as Steve flew back by himself to New Jersey, realizing that for the first time in my entire life, I was virtually alone. My parents, my brothers, Steve, my friends back along the Jersey Shore, even my childhood Rabbi, were all now in my rearview mirror.

The time had come for me to make something of myself. I was 24 years old, healthy and strong. I had an original screenplay and was living rent free on Venice Beach with two incredibly kind and charitable friends.

Oh yeah, by the time Steve flew back home, I was down to $6.00 total. In life.

With Steve gone and my friends Joanne and John having to work full-time, I was left alone, daily, in the small Venice apartment. I had one simple goal: to somehow get a job in "Hollywood." I had no money, no car, and very few clothes, but I did have my slate grey business suit–the one I'd worn back at Columbia Pictures in New York.

Having learned how to get around L.A. pretty well via buses, cabs or on foot, I would make my way to the gates of each of the major movie studios, and simply try to just walk right through. This move, while clearly naïve, did actually work just once, at MGM Studios! I walked through those famous Culver City gates wearing my grey suit and carrying a briefcase, waving to the security guards, who waved at me in return! They must have assumed I was a big-shot New York executive of some kind. Little did they know I was penniless and completely clueless.

As I walked through the MGM Studio lot, I was on cloud nine. It was the coolest place I'd ever seen. "People actually get paid to work here?" I thought to myself.

The best moment came upon me quite quickly. As I began walking, I glanced to my right to see Bo Derek and her husband, John, walking a few yards ahead of me. Bo was, at that time, the biggest sex symbol on Earth, with her hit movie, *Ten* (1979), having come out exactly one year before. Bo was so remarkably attractive I actually gasped out loud. (This would happen to me three times more in the future with three other equally gorgeous actresses.)

As I saw Bo and John Derek moving further away from me, I looked to my left and who should be standing there but actor Larry Hagman, star of TV's *Dallas* (1978). In fact, by remarkable coincidence, the world-famous "Who Shot JR?" episode of *Dallas* would air LATER THAT SAME WEEK (November 21, 1980) as my little MGM trek!

Hagman, standing next to his silver sports car, stood mesmerized, clearly staring at Bo Derek's supernatural ass as it shimmied away from the both of us. He then turned his head toward me–I stared at him–and together, without one word uttered, we both shook our heads back and forth as if to say, "Oh my God, can you believe that? Was that not the most REMARKABLE ASS in the history of female-kind?"

Larry then hopped into his little sports car and drove off and away, into television history.

The next week, I had to go to the Unemployment Office in Culver City to try to get my money from the East Coast transferred to me in California. While walking through Culver City that day just blocks from the Unemployment Office, I noticed several large production trucks parked in front of the city's Civic Center Auditorium Building. I also saw numerous heavy black cables running power from the trucks to inside the building.

Curious, I walked into the civic center and quickly realized that a scene from *Dallas* was being filmed. In the scene, Patrick Duffy, who played "Bobby Ewing" on that series, was standing on a stage, asking the members of the audience to vote for him in an upcoming election. There were about three dozen extras filling up the room, wearing "Bobby Ewing for Congress" hats, blowing noisemakers and throwing confetti, while red, white and blue balloons were dropping from the ceiling. A semi-fan of *Dallas* at the time, I was intrigued, and silently glided along the far-right wall of the building, standing behind a bank of bright lights.

While leaning against the wall I heard, "Hi, there!" coming from behind me. I turned to my right to see the gorgeous Actress Victoria Principal ("Pam Ewing") also leaning against the wall just inches from me. Her smile was wide. I actually turned around to see if she was talking/smiling at someone else. Nope, it was ME!

I said, "Hi Victoria, so cool to meet you. This looks like a lot of fun."

She replied, "It's great when everyone knows what they're doing. Somedays this takes forever."

I couldn't believe that one of TV's most beautiful and famous women was having a conversation with ME–a penniless schlub who was walking to the Unemployment Office around the corner in a desperate attempt to embellish his last six bucks!

A small voice inside me said, "Ask for her phone number." Based on the way she was flirting with me, I think that bravado MIGHT have worked out in my favor. However, given my poverty, no car, on-going depression and complete and utter lack of any kind of self-confidence or self-worth, I instantly ran out of things to say to her.

When the scene was completed, the director called, "That's a wrap!" The crowd dispersed and I turned to leave.

"Bye-bye," Victoria called to me, waving.

I later learned that she was dating Director Steven Spielberg at the time.

I lived on a couch in Venice Beach for exactly one year, during which time I sent out resumes, made phone calls, and schlepped to virtually every corner of Los Angeles County taking interviews, again, mostly for secretaries in the entertainment industry who knew shorthand. I also continued to work on and edit my screenplay, *Carrots*.

Once my unemployment money from New Jersey finally found its way to L.A., I had a regular steady income, and no longer had to eat saltine crackers and peanut butter for dinner. (My dad flew out to L.A. once to feed me, fearing my starvation.)

Living right on Venice Beach was a blast then for a hetero young man, although there were a few glitches. I would often hear gunshot blasts going off just outside my window at all hours of the night. For two weeks after John Lennon was assassinated (12/8/80), I was incredibly paranoid that someone was going to sneak up behind me and blow my head off with a gun every time I had to walk through Venice alone at night.

Living adjacent to the concrete Venice "Boardwalk" was truly an eye-opening experience. There were incredibly hot girls in string bikinis roller skating everywhere; men working out with weights on Muscle Beach; and Hari Parry, the iconic "Man from Mars," playing his guitar while roller blading. All were met by me with shock and awe.

It was during this time frame that I met Bill Murray (roller blading); Jacqueline Bisset (who asked if I had any change for a parking meter); Dick Van Dyke (who wanted to know what flavors of ice cream were being offered at a small refreshment stand while we were both standing in the same line and waiting); and Dudley Moore (who reached for the same last can of tuna fish on a supermarket shelf that I'd reached for).

"Go for it, Dudley," I said, jokingly. "It's on me."

His reply: "Thank you, kind sir."

I also met the legendary sci-fi writer, Ray Bradbury, one night nearby during a book signing and laughed out loud when Sidney Poitier waved to me as if to say hello, while parking his black Cadillac near my apartment building one sunny afternoon.

Finally, I decided I really HAD to start working. I looked through the Yellow Pages (there was no Internet then), and found a company called the "Good People Employment Agency." I called and they had me come in for a quick meeting. I told them I was available at any time to "do anything." They were kind enough to find me a series of temporary and sometimes "odd" jobs around town.

The first job assignments I ever had in L.A. were: selling women's clothing along Venice Beach; helping to pack into cartons the contents of an advertising agency that was in the midst of moving; typing legal documents for a Korean law firm; and serving as the receptionist for a soft-porn film distribution company.

The first real entertainment industry gig I got in Southern California (although only as a "temp") was working as a script typist for Bob Banner Productions. At the time, the company was producing the hit weekly music show, *Solid Gold* (1980). As I am an especially strong typist, I was well-liked there, and was given free tickets to attend *Solid Gold* tapings.

Finally, in early 1981, Good People scored me a job as a "gofer" for a new technology company called VHD. This company, a massive joint venture between the UK's Thorn-EMI, Capital Records, JVC, and Matsushita, was formed to produce "video-discs"–the predecessors to what would years later become DVDs. Unfortunately, this company was many years ahead of its time.

The best part of this job was that I was allowed to drive the company car–a brand new Toyota Corolla–to and from wherever my assignments would take me. I eventually was able to even drive the car home at night, so I wouldn't have to take three buses from Venice Beach into West Hollywood every day.

One day after I'd parked the company car across the street from our office building on Sunset Boulevard, I quickly started to run across Sunset without first carefully looking both ways. A huge white Bentley came to a screeching halt, just feet from me. While I was clearly in the wrong, the driver of that car, Comedian Paul Lynde from *Hollywood Squares* (1966), turned pale and slammed on his brakes, just avoiding turning me into a paraplegic.

"You okay?" he shouted out the window.

"Yeah. Sorry, Mr. Lynde," I replied, "I'm a moron."

Grateful that I wasn't dead, he patiently waited until I'd fully crossed Sunset before he sped off and away.

During Spring '81, the VHD company was going to be making a presentation at the Consumer Electronics Show in Chicago. I was tasked with helping the company's Vice President of Marketing schlep promotional materials to that event, while also helping to co-manage a press conference at the Drake Hotel.

Back then, there was a huge "adult" section within the Consumer Electronics Show, cleverly separated and hidden from view from the rest of the enormous convention hall. One day during that CES while I had some free time, I snuck back into the adult section to check it out. I quickly came upon a booth being run by iconic '70s Porn Star, Marilyn Chambers. Before I knew what was what, Marilyn came up from behind me, squeezed my ass, and whispered in my ear, "You want an autograph, baby?"

I turned and there she was, the woman who'd made *Behind the Green Door* (1972) infamous. "Sure," I replied.

Marilyn took out a poster for her new film, *Insatiable* (1980), signed it, rolled it up and handed it to me. "Check out my new movie, handsome," she purred. "I think you'll enjoy getting off to it."

I walked away, stunned. Was one of the biggest, hottest porn stars in the world flirting with me?

One morning, the head of VHD's Program Acquisition Department asked me to accompany her to a focus group event at a private home in Beverly Hills. We went into a very nice house and I saw, framed along the walls, awards presented to "Abby Singer" with "MTM Studios." Having watched *The Mary Tyler Moore Show* (1970) in high school, I recognized the name Abby Singer instantly as being the "Executive in Charge of Production," not that I knew what that term even meant at the time.

I asked a woman who obviously lived in the house, "Is Abby Singer home? I'd love to meet HER."

She replied, "Abby's my husband! He's a man."

Oops! I felt like a putz, but she laughed.

"Not the first time that's happened," she said.

After our focus group event had ended, Abby Singer came home. I introduced myself, shook his hand, and told him that I'd just come out to California from back east. It was a few days before Passover.

Abby asked, "Are you Jewish?"

I replied, "Yes.

He then said, "Got plans for the Seder?"

I answered, "No."

He said, "You do now."

Abby and his family had me over to their home for a beautiful Seder meal (April '81), the first Seder I'd attended in countless years. Abby felt that since I was new in town and didn't know many people, he'd be the guy to reach out and rectify that situation.

I was so very grateful I was almost moved to tears by the Singer family's kindness. At the end of the night, I wished them well, then drove the Corolla home.

The next week, I did one of the schmuckiest things I've ever done, professionally. I wrote a letter to a top Executive Producer at MTM Studios and said in the letter, "My good friend Abby Singer thought I should be working at MTM."

The truth was that Abby and I NEVER talked about me working for MTM, nor did I even have the balls to mention that notion to him during the entire Seder dinner.

Needless to say, I never heard from Abby or the Executive Producer at MTM I had written to, ever again. It was presumptuous and simply stupid. I wish I could take that one back.

One of the most demeaning aspects of my "gofer" job with VHD was getting the cars of the company's various executives washed, once a week. I felt that I was far above sinking to this level, but I do have to admit now that it was fun driving Mercedes, BMWs, Audis, and Jaguars up and down Sunset Boulevard.

Located on Sunset, just east of Laurel Canyon Boulevard, was a prominent site called Sunset Car Wash. I'd driven the BMW of one of my bosses there to be washed, and while watching the car get soapy-foamed-up through the window, who should be standing right next to me? Jerry Seinfeld! I'd seen Jerry perform exactly one year earlier in Manhattan, when Steve and I, on double dates, attended one of his shows at The Comic Strip nightclub. During that show, Steve and I cried from laughing so hard, our cocktail napkins became soaking wet with joyful tears.

"Jerry Seinfeld?" I asked.

"Yes?" he replied, stunned that I knew who he was. I stuck out my hand and we shook.

"My name is Dan. I'm your biggest fan."

He responded, "Really? Gee I didn't know I HAD ANY fans!" (True story.)

I continued, "I just moved out here from Jersey and I saw you last year in New York. You are the funniest comedian I've ever seen."

"Thank you very much," he said. "That's very nice to hear."

We then chit-chatted a bit while watching our cars go through the wash machine. "What brings you here today?" I asked.

"Well," Jerry said, "In a few hours, I'll be on *The Tonight Show* (1954) for the first time, so I thought my car should be clean."

"I'll be sure to watch," I said.

The date: June 5, 1981.

When our cars were done, I actually said, "You know, Jerry, we're both from the East Coast, and we're both about the same age. I'd really like to be friends with you. Can I get your phone number?"

A bit taken aback, he hesitated, then said, "Well, I don't give out my number, but if you ever want to reach me, you can call my manager, Jim." He gave me Jim's card–we shook once again and went our separate ways.

That evening, Jerry killed it on *The Tonight Show*, and Johnny Carson asked him to sit down on the couch–the first sign of Seinfeld's upcoming status within the entertainment industry. He would become a comedy legend about one decade later.

My friends and I would go on to see Jerry perform dozens of times in the coming months at The Improv in West Hollywood, and at The Ice House in Pasadena. We howled with laughter so loudly, he would regularly reply to us with, "Hey, what drugs are <u>you guys</u> on?"

Separately, I did actually reach out to Jerry's manager, Jim. He had me come to his office, and I handed him my screenplay *Carrots*. I asked him if he would "represent me."

He said, "Sure…let me see what I can do."

While it would take me another 41 years until *Carrots* would be published, I can honestly say that for a very short, glimmering moment in time, Jerry Seinfeld and I shared the same manager!

Jim died a few years after this took place.

MORE on JERRY SEINFELD to COME!!

I worked for VHD for most of 1981, but toward the end of the year I asked my boss for a raise and he told me, "Since you don't use your brains for this job, only your brawn, I can't give you more money."

It was a remarkable insult and I quit on the spot.

Perusing the *L.A. Times* Classified Section that December, I saw a small ad that read: "Administrative Assistant Wanted for the American Film Institute." I'd never heard of AFI before, but it had the word "film" in there, so I figured it wouldn't hurt to apply. I mailed in my resume and waited.

The following week, I was asked to come up to the AFI Campus. AFI had just relocated onto the site of the former Immaculate Heart High School in Los Feliz. There, I'd meet with Jean Firstenberg, the Head of AFI, for about 30 minutes. She told me that since she had also attended Boston University, she was going to hire me on the spot.

"Us BU graduates need to stick together," she said.

My new job, begun during the very start of January, 1982, was to serve as an administrative assistant to the guy who served as the General Manager of the AFI Campus. AFI was a prominent film/TV production college on beautiful, green grass-covered acreage in the Hollywood Hills. My job was primarily two-fold: to answer his phones and to type up his memos. This was still during the IBM Selectric typewriter days. Since the campus had very recently relocated to its new site, the building I worked in had no heat during winter and no A/C during summer.

Working there was a colossal chore.

I had to take two long bus rides (shades of Manhattan!) to get to AFI from my new apartment in the Mid-Wilshire district, and after leaving the second bus, had to walk up a very steep hill from Sunset Boulevard due north on Western Ave. It was a tough climb and not very enjoyable.

One morning while I was making my trek up Western, I saw a small film crew shooting a movie at a drive-through bank. I walked up to observe and saw a beautiful brunette sitting inside of the exterior bank teller's window. She looked quite bored, as the filmmakers were clearly adjusting their lights, cameras and microphones.

When this woman saw me, she smiled broadly and winked. I waved to her and she waved back. I had no idea who she was, but thought it was pretty cool that such an attractive woman would seemingly be flirting with me.

Many years later, I realized that that brunette was Debra Winger. She was shooting a scene from her upcoming film, *Mike's Murder* (1984).

I worked at AFI for a year and a half. During that time, I had a few other "close encounters of the celebrity kind."

Oscar winning Director Robert Wise, of *West Side Story* (1961) and *The Sound of Music* (1965) fame, was teaching a filmmaking course at AFI while I was there. For some weird reason, every time I needed to pee, HE ALSO needed to pee. We urinated together, side by side, dozens of times, and each time either he or I would say to the other, "We simply have to stop meeting this way!" This made us laugh out loud every single time!

AFI's acting class often had special guest stars come to campus to lecture the students. I sat in on the session when Dustin Hoffman appeared. He spoke at length about the art, craft and love he had for acting, often standing up and shouting, punctuating his talk with fists held high. It was an incredibly rousing talk, and even though I had no interest of any kind in acting, found myself remarkably inspired.

After the talk, Dustin made his way up the aisle to shake hands and chat with several students. I was seated next to the exit door and when he came my way, I reached out. We shook hands and I said, "And here's to YOU, Mr. Robinson."

He chuckled, grabbed my shoulder and replied, "Jesus loves YOU more than you will know!"

Okay, okay, that didn't really happen. He only bumped into me and said, "Sorry, kid." But I think my "version" above is funnier.

Another AFI session presented The Monkees' guitarist Mike Nesmith who, at that time, was spearheading the burgeoning art form of music videos and had just recently produced his own project called, "Elephant Parts" (1981).

I went up to the auditorium early to get a good seat and since no one was yet inside, took a chair in the lobby near the front doors. I looked across from me and there was Mike, sitting alone directly opposite me.

"Hi there," he said, "how are you?"

Since I had mentioned earlier that The Monkees were Gods on Earth to me during childhood, I became a bit tongue-tied.

I said, "Uh, I'm good, thanks. You're Mike Nesmith!"

He chuckled. "Well, yeah…that's what they tell me," he answered.

I'm sure he could tell I was flustered and I couldn't manage to say much more to him. I was too busy flashing back to 1966, dancing to The Monkees' songs with my brother Bob in our den.

Just then, a crowd of AFI students entered the lobby. Mike got up and we all entered the auditorium. He talked about the future of music video production. Mike was actually one of the pioneers of MTV, and he presented his "Elephant Parts" video to us.

For weeks afterward I was in a daze. I'd (sorta) met one of my childhood heroes!

The only perk I was able to manage from my boring AFI job was stealing the movie passes from my boss when I retrieved his mail. In those days, the Motion Picture Academy of Arts & Sciences–the organization that hands out the Oscars–sent my boss free passes to attend private industry screenings of all the new major studio movie releases.

Also, I should note: I met a girl on New Year's Eve 1982 named Kim at Chippendales nightclub in Culver City. I met her just one week before I began my job at AFI. Kim and I fell in love very quickly and would remain together for the next 11 years.

I'd stolen a movie pass for the film *Gandhi* (1982) from my boss and invited my girlfriend Kim to meet me at the Academy's screening room in Beverly Hills. I should mention this is the best screening room in Los Angeles. I arrived early, got my seat and was saving a second one for Kim, who would soon be arriving separately, after her work shift as a junior nurse at a Santa Monica hospital had ended.

Every few minutes from my seat, I would turn my head around and look up the aisle to see if Kim had yet arrived. During one of those "head turning" moments, I suddenly realized that two women, who were sitting directly behind me, were STARING at me intensely. When I noticed them, I stared back. Each woman appeared shocked and dumbfounded. They were witnessing a ghost, and the ghost was me!

The women? Angie Dickinson and Dinah Shore!

I clipped another movie pass from my boss to see *Return of the Jedi* (1983) at the USC screening room. I took my visiting mother with me. It was a very small screening room. My mother and I sat next to Harrison Ford. My mother, who knew nothing about the "Star Wars" universe, kept talking out loud during the show. I tried to shush her, but that didn't help much. During one scene in which Harrison Ford was the primary actor, my mother said, "He's not bad looking," to which the REAL Harrison Ford, sitting right next to her, said, "Thanks lady."

I wanted to disappear into the floor.

I stole a movie pass for the premiere of a Sean Connery film, *Wrong is Right* (1982), which was held at the Mann's Chinese Theater on Hollywood Boulevard. After the film ended, I was standing right behind James Bond himself. As we started to walk outside, a strong gust of wind blew through the lobby of the theater. Mr. Connery's toupee started flopping around the top of his head a bit. He instantly put his hand upon his head to keep the rug in place, then looked behind him to see if anyone else had noticed. Since I was DIRECTLY behind him, he knew he was busted.

"Don't tell anyone, okay, Sonny?" he whispered to me.

"Of course not, Mr. Connery," I replied. "Didn't see a thing!"

Katherine Helmond, the star of ABC's *Soap* (1977) TV series, was attending AFI as a directing student. She would often come in to meet with my boss to discuss her curriculum. We always said hello to each other, and she once asked me if I was also a student.

I told her, "No, just a secretary, but I'd rather be a comedy writer."

"Don't give up," she told me. "It isn't easy but if you persist, I'm sure you'll get there eventually."

A few non-AFI celeb moments took place during this time frame: one afternoon, Kim and I went out for ice cream at a Carnation ice cream store in the mid-Wilshire area of L.A. As we licked our cones, we saw Muhammed Ali and one of his daughters eating their ice cream at another table. No one else was in the store.

Kim said, "Let's go meet him!"

I replied, "Are you serious? That's Muhammed Ali! I can't meet him!"

She said, "Come on," so we walked over.

"Hey, Mr. Ali," Kim said, "Can we get your autograph?"

Ali smiled up at her, took out his pen and signed a small napkin that was laying on his table.

"Thanks, Champ," I said, stunned to my socks by who I was talking to.

Ali nodded his head, then continued eating his hot fudge sundae. He never spoke a word.

Kim and I were on a double date with our friends Ron and Melanie, both of whom worked with me up at AFI. We were in a restaurant off Sunset Boulevard, a block from the former Columbia Pictures Studios (now Sunset/Gower Studios) movie lot. While eating dinner, we noticed two very attractive brunettes at a nearby table.

The occasion for this double date was Ron's birthday.

When our waitress brought out a cake with candles aflame, we began singing "Happy Birthday." The two women nearby–Kate Jackson (*Charlie's Angels*, 1976) and JoBeth Williams (*Poltergeist*, 1982) – rushed up to our table, joined in with the singing, and asked if they could sit with us and share the dessert.

That was fun. They were super cool. A real "Hollywood" moment.

One sunny Saturday afternoon in summer, 1983, Kim and I were riding bikes through Santa Monica. At one point, we arrived at a red traffic light, so we pulled our bikes off to the side of the road, waiting for the light to change. I looked to my right and saw a woman, wearing a very large straw hat, leaving a women's clothing store and carrying several bags. Just off to her right was a long black limo and a chauffeur clearly waiting for her to hop in.

As I was observing this woman, she glanced over in my direction for one second, saw me, then turned, rushing toward her car. A few seconds <u>later</u>, she stopped cold in her tracks, turned her head to look at me AGAIN, and STARED at me for about 20 seconds without making a sound. I stared back at her while wondering, "Do I look like your long-lost child? Why are you looking at me that way?"

After our staring contest finally ended, the woman jumped into her car and the limo took off.

A minute or two after Kim and I began riding our bikes again, it dawned on me. The woman who couldn't stop staring at me? Barbra Streisand!

My AFI post bored me to tears, so one day I was reading the Hollywood trade papers (*Variety* and *The Hollywood Reporter*) looking for jobs and saw an ad for "Production Assistant" at the Playboy Channel. I'd never heard of the Playboy Channel at that point, but figured it might be cool to work while surrounded by naked girls.

I interviewed for the Production Assistant job, which was for a new cable TV series called *Sexcetera–The News According to Playboy* (1983). I met with one of the show's executive producers, Pam, and we had a fun conversation about life. We met (in the now former) Playboy Building on Sunset Boulevard near La Cienega. (A large bunny head logo adorned the exterior of the building at that time.) I don't think we even discussed the job itself at all. The pay for this PA job was $100.00 more a week than what I was making at AFI, and I was in real need of the money. At the end of the interview, I told Pam, "Look, I'd really like this job and oh, by the way, today is my birthday."

The date: June 17, 1983.

Pam called me at home that night. "Happy birthday, Dan, you're hired."

So that's how I joined Playboy Enterprises, a company I'd work at for the next two and a half years.

During my first six months at Playboy, I was indeed a P.A., which was a lowly job comprised of typing scripts, running errands, and managing the teleprompter for the once monthly tapings we had in which our two co-anchors, Dan Cain (a Boston area TV reporter) and Crystal Smith (a former Playboy centerfold model), would read "sex news" aloud to viewers. The job was exactly the one I'd performed during my senior year college internship in Boston at WNAC TV–only with stories about penises and vaginas instead of stories about blizzards.

I worked for *Sexcetera* for six months and, once again, was bored to tears. The job was no challenge. One day during a lunch break, I saw a notice in the cafeteria. It was a posting from HR for a "Publicist" wanted for The Playboy Channel. I ripped the paper off the bulletin board and marched upstairs to the Executive's Office from which the notice had been issued.

Without an appointment, I managed to wrangle a spontaneous meeting with the Head of the Playboy Channel and the Head of Playboy Home Video. The two men (only one of whom already knew me) interviewed me for the position, with one of them asking if I was "tenacious." For some reason, I was chewing gum during the interview and replied, "Sorry, I don't know what that word means."

They asked if I was determined not to give up if things became challenging. "Absolutely," I replied, still smacking my gum. "Tenacious is my middle name."

The two men laughed and suddenly I'd become the first ever publicist for The Playboy Channel. It was the very start of January, 1984.

Within a very short period of time, I found myself covering various Playboy events being held at the Playboy Mansion, where Hugh Hefner lived. I met Hef several times and he couldn't have been nicer to me. During the filming of a "Playmate Olympics," during which two teams of bikini-clad Playmates were competing in sports activities against each other in Hef's backyard, he stood next to me and we watched together as one of the bikini tops flew off of one of the girls.

"Never gets old," he said to me, winking. He patted me on the shoulder and walked off, wearing pajamas, smoking a pipe, and sipping his Diet Pepsi.

The man was my God.

One day we were holding a press conference at the Playboy Mansion to present the first series of Playboy Home Video (VHS) videotapes being released. I was assigned to check in members of the media who would be attending and I was stationed in front of the main gates that led onto the Playboy Mansion grounds.

There was a large, fake rock just in front of the gates, with a two-way speaker system installed inside the rock. Each time a member of the press arrived, I had to check his or her name off a list, and "tell the rock" it was okay to open the gates so this person could drive his or her car up the steep incline and onto the property.

The last person to arrive that day was Christie Hefner, Hef's daughter, who was also at that time an executive with Playboy Enterprises. I knew who she was the second she pulled up to me but, in a poor attempt at humor asked, "Name please?"

She looked at me like I was purple and sarcastically replied, "I'm Christie Hefner!" She was clearly annoyed.

I said, "Christie, I was just kidding! I know who you are!"

I wasn't sure if she became any less pissed off at me, but I "told the rock" Christie was here. The gates swung open and she started pulling up the drive.

"Can I get a lift?" I asked.

Hesitating for a second, she finally said, "Sure, okay, hop in."

That's how Christie Hefner and I spent a private minute alone together, up the long steep driveway that fed into the front of her dad's famous Playboy Mansion.

Part of my job as Publicist for The Playboy Channel was to write up the TV Guide-style summary listings for the various programs the channel presented each month to its viewers. The main series on the channel was called *The Playboy Magazine Show*, and each episode featured a sit-down interview with a major Hollywood star. The interviewer for each of these sessions was noted author Larry Grobel. I would sit a few feet behind Larry while he interviewed such notables as John Lithgow, Billy Dee Williams, Joan Collins, Neil Simon, Producer Allan Carr, Elliott Gould, and Sid Caesar.

I met all of those people, briefly. Much more on Sid Caesar to come later.

The one funny story I have during those celebrity interviews was when Larry and I were at Zsa Zsa Gabor's house. I had just entered, met Zsa Zsa, and as she welcomed me inside said, "Make yourself at home."

I turned and saw a very odd-looking, quite small wooden chair in her living room. While I was IN THE PROCESS OF SITTING DOWN ON IT, she screamed at me from across the room, "NO, NO, NO, DAHLINK! NOT THAT CHAIR! IT'S A VERY VALUABLE ANTIQUE!"

Fortunately, my ass never made it to the seat of that chair. As quickly as I'd begun to sit, I bolted upright and stood straight as an arrow. I think I spent the rest of that afternoon sitting on her carpet.

I was invited to attend a few evening parties at the Playboy Mansion while I worked there, but the most fun were the Halloween galas. At the event in '84, I met Garry Shandling. I was dressed up like a peacenik/guru with a long hair wig and a large peace symbol around my neck, while also wearing my Bar Mitzvah tallit around my shoulders.

"Who are you supposed to be?" Garry asked, while sporting a Superman T-shirt.

"I'm a Jew-Roo, Garry," I answered, "a spiritual advisor with Jewish tendencies. Instead of a Guru, I'm a Jew-Roo."

"Oh, cool, tell me more!" Shandling replied, sounding truly interested. Alas, our conversation was short-lived when a beautiful, 19-year-old, nearly-naked blonde called out, "Garry, come play with me!"

Shandling said, "Sorry man, gotta go," shook my hand, then skipped off to Hefner's grotto to join his little playmate.

I met Bill Maher there once too-only very briefly, as he seemed to have just had a verbal argument with his attractive black girlfriend.

Another Halloween party guest I'd meet was actor Robert Vaughn, the famous *Man from U.N.C.L.E.* (1964), whom I told how much my dad used to love that TV series. I also met Weird Al Yankovic, with whom I discussed at length how he'd gotten permission from famous songwriters to create his music video parodies. Al was dressed up like a giant "Joker" playing card. He and his wife couldn't have been nicer.

During my time as Playboy's first publicist, I was invited to attend a Publicists' Guild luncheon in Beverly Hills. When I entered the huge ballroom, I was simply stunned – I couldn't believe that thousands of other people in Hollywood were publicists, too! I didn't realize that the dopey profession I'd stumbled into was so prominent. I sat at a table with a wonderful man named Henri, now deceased, who introduced me around and suggested I join the Publicists Guild if and when possible. (I would, just about 18 months later.)

That afternoon, I met: Michael Caine, telling him that his movie *Shock to the System* (1990) was one of my favorites, to which he replied, "Oh, really? I rather enjoyed that one myself." I met Heather Locklear, who at the time was riding high with her success on TV's *Dynasty* (1981). I told her my mother and I both watched *Dynasty* religiously, and then called each other to compare notes. Her reply: "Your MOTHER, huh? Okay, not weird." She then turned and fled, probably thinking I was quite gay. I also met Danny DeVito, to whom I said, "Danny, you used to cut my best friend's grandmother's hair while standing on an apple crate back in Asbury Park!"

Panic-stricken, he responded, "Shooosh! Don't tell anybody I used to cut hair!"

I clearly touched a nerve there and he quickly scampered away, utterly humiliated.

One day while I was in my office on the top floor of the Playboy Building (my view on the right was of the gorgeous mansions in the Hollywood Hills; my view on the left was of the gorgeous models that came through the doors of the Playboy Modeling Agency on a daily basis), Shannon Tweed suddenly flew into my office and asked me where she could find a certain executive who worked in the building. Her appearance happened so quickly, and she was so EXTRAORDINARILY HOT that I actually gasped, losing my breath for the second time in my life–the first time being when I spotted Bo Derek at MGM. She stood there, staring at me like I was the village idiot, until I could regain my composure. At the time she was dating Hugh Hefner.

"Oh, hi Shannon!" I finally said. "Let me look that up for you."

I glanced at my company employee roster and told her the office number of the guy she was seeking. With that, she turned and disappeared as quickly as she'd entered, neither thanking me nor seeking any further communication.

The most fun I had during my years at The Playboy Channel was working and flirting with a number of the drop-dead-gorgeous *Playboy* Centerfold Playmates. I met virtually every one of the Playmates from '82-'85 and hired several of them to do photo shoots for me. Part of my job was to create interesting promotional photos to "illustrate" the TV shows, movies and specials airing on the network. For example, the first promotional image I had to create was for a show called *Sex on Earth* (1984). For that one, I hired a very pretty blonde (Laurie something) who posed in a light pink teddy. My photographer then superimposed her image against a nighttime star-filled sky, making it appear as though she was sitting atop Planet Earth.

For a TV show called *Inside Playboy* (1985), I hired March '84 Playmate Dona Speir to pose as a gypsy fortune teller. My photographer and I had her peering into a crystal ball in which he superimposed a Playboy Bunny head logo. After the photo shoot, I drove Dona to lunch at Carney's–an iconic hot dog/burger joint inside a train car on Sunset Boulevard. I had a very old, piece-of-shit Honda Civic at the time which would have impressed no one. After lunch, when we got back into my car, I said, "Dona, you are without question the prettiest girl I've ever met in real life. If I wasn't already engaged, I would so ask you out!"

Thinking I'd flattered her, I was expecting at the very least a "thank you" or a "that's sweet." I got, "Really? Uh, I don't think so. Sorry."

I later learned she was dating Bill Cosby at the time!

For a TV show called, *The Art of Playboy* (1984), I hired July '82 Playmate Lynda Weismeier. During that photo shoot, I had Lynda pose topless, covering her exposed boobs with one arm, while wearing an artist's beret and painting a large red Playboy Bunny head logo on a canvas. During that session, Lynda was not only <u>not</u> uncomfortable showing off her magnificent breasts, she even asked me and my photographer if we wanted to squeeze them! We didn't.

I walked her to her car afterward. She stared at me, virtually thrusting her low-cut cleavage in my face and said, "You married?"

I replied, "Uh, not yet, no. I'm engaged. But I am getting married next month."

She said, "Why?" Her simple question caught me off guard, and I doubted my own answer.

"Because I love my girlfriend?" I hesitantly responded.

Her reply, "Oh, that's too bad. We could've had some fun."

We drove off in separate directions, and it took a while for my blood pressure to return to normal.

For a TV show called *Hefner's Halloween Bash* (1985), I hired May '82 Playmate Kym Malin for a photo session. For that shoot, Kym wore a tight red bikini, sported Devil's horns, and was holding a red pitchfork. Her body was supernaturally perfect. There were times during the session I found it hard to breathe. I later learned she'd been voted "Most Perfect Body in Texas" a few years earlier.

While walking Kym back to her car after the shoot, she asked me if I could take her to a party being thrown by one of her friends in the music industry. She added that her boyfriend was out of town, and she didn't want to go alone. I'd been married for just one year at this time, and by pure happenstance my wife, Kim, was also out of town in Dallas, taking a computer training course for her new job as a travel agent.

I told Kym I would take her. The next night, I picked her up in my wife's brand-new Volvo, at her apartment near Venice Beach. She'd spent the day on the beach and her skin was so beautifully tanned she was literally "glowing." She hopped into the car and inserted an audio cassette tape of Sade singing "Smooth Operator." She opened the sunroof of the car and started dancing in her seat, her long blonde hair flying out through the ceiling. I was mesmerized by her beauty and kept reminding myself, "You're married, putz! You're married!"

We went to the party, had a few drinks, and danced to a few songs. Maybe two hours in, she told me she was "on fire." I touched her skin and it was so hot from her having laid out in the sun that day, I was scared for her. She asked me to take her home, and I did. I walked her up to the front stairs of her building and stopped. We then stared at each other for what seemed like an eternity. I had a little angel sitting on my right shoulder screaming, "DO NOT KISS HER! YOU ARE MARRIED! GOD WILL SMITE YOU DOWN!" while a little devil sitting on my left shoulder screamed, "KISS HER, YOU PATHETIC MORON! SHE'S A PLAYBOY PLAYMATE! YOU CAN TELL ALL YOUR FRIENDS!"

I'd never been more morally conflicted in my life. Finally, the pressure to "do the right thing" was overwhelming, and I decided to leave ASAP. I gave her a quick peck on the cheek and ran back to my wife's car. Once inside, I felt a weird sensation in the middle of my forehead. I looked in the rearview mirror and realized I had a HUGE, PUS-FILLED ZIT sitting right there, screaming to the world, "Hey, look at me!"

<u>The zit had not been there a few minutes earlier</u>! I swear this is true.

God clearly "marked" me with that zit to repulse Kym Malin and to ensure that there would be "no kisses" that evening for this just recently-married, and quite supernaturally schmucky, publicist.

Chapter Five

1985-1987

LUNCH WITH A MONKEE / GILLIGAN IN HAWAII / MADONNA BLOWS A KISS / HARASSING SALLY FIELD / BARBRA STREISAND STARES AGAIN

I was only making $450.00 a week at The Playboy Channel at the end of 1985, so I asked the CFO if he could raise me up to $500.00.

"Sorry, we don't have the budget, Dan," he told me. "You do good work and everyone around here likes you, but I can't give you a raise."

As Kim and I were discussing trying to start a family, I couldn't continue living on such a pittance. One day at Playboy, I confided in a female executive in the Promotions Department about my "non-raise." She told me she was dating the Senior Vice President of Advertising, Publicity and Promotion at Columbia Pictures Television in Burbank, and she knew he was looking for a new Senior Publicist to work there.

"Should I put in a word for you?" she asked me.

"Yes, of course!" I said, adding, "You might mention to him that I worked for Columbia Pictures in Manhattan in 1980."

A few days later, I got the call from this executive, Steve, and met with him. We had a great interview and he told me, "I'm the only guy around here, Dan. I'm surrounded by women. We need more testosterone in this office. You're hired!"

My weekly income, just like that, rose from $450.00 to $1,000.00! I was most grateful and felt I'd finally scored a real job in Hollywood. I started there in December 1985.

Columbia Pictures and Columbia Television were located at the far Northeast end of what was called the Burbank Studios at that time–the joint location of both Warner Bros. and Columbia. I had an office just across the lot with access to a golf cart-type vehicle which I could use to zoom around the studios during lunchtime.

During some of those lunches, I waved to Richard Dreyfus, Clint Eastwood, Michelle Pfeiffer, John Fogarty, and Jim Henson, shortly before his death.

I worked within the Syndicated TV Department of Columbia Pictures Television and was responsible for the publicity of three of their shows, *What's Happening Now!!* (1985), *The Real Ghostbusters* (1986), and *The New Gidget* (1986).

What's Happening Now!! was an updated version of the earlier *What's Happening!!* (1976), a series starring an all-black cast. For the new edition of the program, I worked closely with cast members Ernie Thomas, Heywood Nelson, Shirley Hemphill, Anne-Marie Johnson, and Reina King, sister of the now quite famous Actress/Director Regina King. Actor Fred Berry, who portrayed the character "Rerun" in the original series, quit the new show after just a few episodes.

For *What's Happening Now!!*, I attended every taping of the show and set up specific PR photos from the episodes for my purposes of promotion. One episode featured guest star Tempest Bledsoe, an actress from *The Cosby Show* (1984). I generated a good deal of PR from her participation on *What's Happening Now!!* within several black media publications.

During dinner breaks at *What's Happening Now!!* rehearsals, I became friends with the warm-up comic/MC Marc Summers. In fact, I'd originally met Marc on my third day ever in L.A., back in October, 1980, when he was the warm-up comic for a show called

Hour Magazine (1980-1989), starring Gary Collins. Marc would later become iconic to children during his time hosting *Double Dare* (1986) on Nickelodeon, the show that introduced green slime to the world. (More on Marc, now one of my best friends, to come.)

On May 25, 1986, I had the *What's Happening Now!!* cast, along with myself and my wife, Kim, participate in the national "Hands Across America" event–we were stationed in Century City. I remember that Ernie Thomas, the star of *What's Happening Now!!*, seemed to have a crush on my wife. We also met L.A. Mayor Tom Bradley that afternoon.

The second show I handled PR for was an animated series called *The Real Ghostbusters*, based on the original *Ghostbusters* (1984) movie written by Dan Aykroyd and Harold Ramis. I attended several voice-recording sessions for this show. I met Arsenio Hall, who voiced the character of "Winston Zeddemore," originally portrayed by Actor Ernie Hudson in the movie.

By pure coincidence, during this time frame Kim and I, during a trip to Manhattan, happened to meet Ernie Hudson inside our hotel lobby. I told him I was the publicist for the cartoon series.

He said, "I have no idea why they didn't ask ME to do that voice! I created that character!"

I also happened to separately bump into Harold Ramis one afternoon, when I was in Westwood purchasing movie tickets for Kim and me. As I stood in front of the ticket window at the theater, I turned to my left and saw him standing next to me. We shook hands and I told him I was the publicist for the new animated series.

"You know," he said, "Belushi was supposed to be in that movie."

"Really?" I said. "Instead of Bill Murray?"

"Yep," Harold answered. We made chitchat for a few minutes until his wife, and then Kim, arrived.

As a marketing idea for *The Real Ghostbusters*, I set up a promotion with a children's charity event held at a hotel in Beverly Hills. I hired my brother, Mike, to dress up like one of the "Ghostbusters," securing the costume from Columbia's Wardrobe Department. I also arranged for the original GhostMobile ambulance to park outside the hotel and placed a huge green "Slimer" ghost balloon in the lobby. The Slimer and my "Ghostbuster" brother were stationed there to pose for photos with the event's participants and their children. That's how I met Jaclyn Smith of *Charlie's Angels* (1976), Jane Seymour of *War and Remembrance* (1988) and Charlene Tilton of *Dallas* (1978).

My third TV show was *The New Gidget*, which starred Caryn Richman, and Dean Butler of *Little House on the Prairie* (1974). This show was shot on film, so not on videotape and not in front of a live studio audience. Most episodes were filmed on a beach in Malibu, so my job was literally to hang out in the sun on a beautiful SoCal beach for months at a time. I once appeared on camera on TV's *Entertainment Tonight* (1981) when they covered our show filming, but most of my time was spent flirting with Caryn Richman (we remain friends to this day), and some of the other cute bikini girls in lessor roles.

To promote *The New Gidget* in a few local markets, I accompanied Caryn and Dean to press/media events in Denver, San Francisco and Las Vegas. These trips marked the only time in my life I've ever flown First Class, to this day.

One day while filming interiors on a soundstage on the Burbank Studios' lot, Caryn told me she'd heard that Sally Field was shooting a movie on the next soundstage.

"Why don't you go see if you can get her to come over here and take a PR photo with me?" Caryn suggested. Field was filming a movie called *Surrender* (1987) at the time.

Realizing a great promotional idea when I heard one, I dashed off to the adjacent stage and as I arrived Sally Field was, in fact, just leaving her stage to return to her dressing room. She was wearing a bathrobe with curlers in her hair, as a few female assistants escorted her.

"Miss Field?" I asked.

She said, "Yes?"

I countered, "My name is Dan. I'm the publicist for *The New Gidget* TV show; we're filming right next door. Would you consider coming with me to take a PR photo of yourself with Caryn Richman, the new Gidget?"

Horrified, Sally replied, "Are you kidding me? Of course not! I wouldn't dream of it!" She then fled for her life.

The most fun I ever had handling PR for *The New Gidget* was during May, 1987, when the cast, crew and I flew to Oahu, Hawaii, to film several episodes on Waikiki Beach. Having never been to the Aloha State before, when I opened my hotel room drapes to see the view, a magnificent rainbow appeared just over Diamond Head. The scene was so remarkably beautiful, I had a few tears in my eyes.

The crew also shot one episode at Turtle Bay. Lo and behold, who should the special guest stars there be, but Bob Denver ("Gilligan") and Alan Hale, Jr. ("The Skipper,") the iconic stars of the syndicated series *Gilligan's Island* (1964). Both guys couldn't have been nicer, and I got my photo taken with each of them.

One late afternoon while strolling around the Burbank Studios' backlot, I saw a production taking place and a striking blonde girl dancing, alone, in the middle of a street. I stood off to the side to watch, and it took me a few moments to realize the dancing girl was Madonna. She was filming her "Who's That Girl?" music video (1987), while lip synching to the music that was being played by overhead speakers. During a break in filming, she glanced over in my direction, realized I was staring at her, and blew me a kiss. While I was never a big Madonna fan, I do have to say that was a pretty cool moment.

During another lunchtime walk around the studio lot, I strolled past a soundstage just as its side door was opening. Barbra Streisand, dressed in a hospital gown, had been filming *Nuts* (1987) at the time and had gone out into the alley for some fresh air. When I realized it was her, I stopped in my tracks. She turned, saw me, and STARED AT ME as though I was her long-lost brother from a past life. This staring contest went on for such a long time, I actually started to laugh out loud. I'd love to say I had the balls to introduce myself to her, but I didn't. We simply bore holes through each other with our eyes, until a production assistant came out from the soundstage door and called for her to return for her next scene.

As this was the second time in my life that Streisand and I experienced this staring contest, I came to the conclusion that perhaps it was the Brooklyn in my blood that she could smell from a distance, like a Vampire. (Both she-and my parents-were Brooklynites!)

My favorite story during my years at Columbia is this one. I have a first cousin named Franz Harary, a world-class illusionist/magician. Believe it or not, Michael Jackson "discovered" Franz while Franz was still in high school! In addition to his live appearances around the globe, Franz is also a designer of illusions for rock bands and other music artists. At the time I was working at Columbia, he was creating several on-stage illusions for Alice Cooper. As I was a big Alice fan, I got myself invited to attend a rehearsal at one of the soundstages in Burbank and even brought along my own photographer, in hopes of getting a photo of Alice and me together.

I was standing on the floor of the building, watching Alice Cooper and his band go through several numbers on the stage. As I observed, I glanced to my right and saw Micky Dolenz, the drummer from The Monkees and my boyhood hero, standing right next to me! Instantly, I introduced myself.

"Micky, my name is Dan. I played the drums for 20 years because of you!"

He replied, "That's great. I hear that a lot."

We watched the rest of the rehearsal and once it got quiet, he told me he was currently working with Columbia Television as a Director on *The New Mike Hammer* (1984) series.

"Come by and visit sometime," he said, before leaving.

After rehearsal ended, Franz introduced me to Alice Cooper, and I got my photo. I told Alice how much I'd loved him in high school, and he seemed most appreciative. I also told him about the time I asked a girl named Lori for a date to go see him in concert at Madison Square Garden, and she'd said, "Alice Cooper? Who's she?"

Alice replied, "Before I had a hit with 'School's Out,' that used to happen all the time."

Over the course of the next several months, I spent some free time with Micky Dolenz on the Columbia lot. One day we had lunch together in the studio commissary, and he asked me if I knew of anyone selling any mansions in Bel-Air.

"Uh no, sorry," I replied, as if I would know about MANSIONS FOR SALE IN BEL-AIR??!!

I also hung out with Micky a few times while he was directing episodes of *The New Mike Hammer Show*. During one such session, I asked him if he was aware that Columbia Television was currently planning an upcoming syndicated TV series called, *The New Monkees* (1987).

He replied, "Yeah, I heard about that. How incredibly fucking stupid! You can't replicate The Monkees anymore than you could replicate The Beatles. That show won't fly–it's the dumbest thing I ever heard in my life."

Micky was quite right. *The New Monkees* aired only 13 episodes during fall 1987, before dying a very swift and undistinguished death.

Chapter Six

1987-1989

SID CAESARS' DOGS / JAY LENO'S UNDERWEAR / UNCLE MILTIE IS OLD / KAREN BLACK IS NAKED / DYING A DIVINE DEATH

During summer, 1987, Coca-Cola, which owned Columbia Pictures at the time, eliminated Columbia's Syndicated TV PR Department, and my position vanished. This was rather scary for me because my wife, Kim, had just gotten pregnant with our first child. I was suddenly devoid of an income.

I scrambled and phoned virtually every person I'd dealt with during my past five years, working my Rolodex with a fine-toothed comb. Eliot, a publicist I'd worked with during my Playboy years on a show called *The Girls of the Comedy Store* (1986), told me that his PR agency was looking for a new Senior Publicist; was I interested? I hopped over to his company, Solters/Roskin/Friedman, and interviewed with him and his boss, Monroe Friedman.

Zip, zap, I was hired, and found myself with a slightly higher salary than I'd been making at Columbia. Instead of serving as an in-house publicist, I was now an "out-of-house" one, working for the most prominent celebrity PR firm in Hollywood.

When I was hired for Solters/Roskin/Friedman, the agency was representing Michael Jackson, Frank Sinatra, Barbra Streisand, Whitney Houston, Dolly Parton, Donna Summer, Van Halen, The

Monkees, and other huge stars I can no longer recall. On my first day on the job, I met the agency's founder, Lee Solters, a legendary old-school publicist who'd been Streisand's PR guy since her Broadway debut decades earlier.

Lee quickly assigned me to represent Comedy Icon Sid Caesar; up-and-coming Comedian Jay Leno; *National Lampoon* magazine founder Matty Simmons; a TV series called *Buck James* (1987) starring Dennis Weaver; a new cable TV network called *Shop TV* (1987); and Actor Robert Englund, best known as "Freddy Krueger" from the *Nightmare on Elm Street* (1984) films, who was now transitioning into becoming a film director.

My plate was FULL! These were A LOT of clients and I found myself busting my ass, working to secure as much media coverage for all of these people and companies as possible.

From '87 to '89, Sid Caesar was semi-retired and living in a modest mansion in Beverly Hills. He was still doing the occasional guest-starring role in a TV show or movie, but nothing compared to his legendary days with *Your Show of Shows* (1950). Sid was still a comedy giant and we once drove together to conduct an in-studio interview on Larry King's national radio show. Larry's producer, Pat Piper, shot a photo of Sid and I together after the interview was over.

I'd meet with Sid at his home, and we'd sit in his den, talking. The walls and shelves were covered with every imaginable award, trophy and honor, along with *TV Guide* cover stories and other magazine and newspaper articles about him. Sid wasn't the most pleasant man in the world, and he'd suddenly scream out for this wife, Florence, to "Bring me my lunch, NOW!"

I always felt sorry for the woman, who seemed beaten down by life and never said two words in my presence.

One day, a writer with *USA TODAY* came to Sid's house to work up a story about his releasing the old, classic *Your Show of Shows* episodes onto home video for the first time. The three of us (Sid, the writer, and myself) sat outside by Sid's pool and while the two men talked, Sid's two rather large, fairly aggressive dogs, suddenly found my pants quite fascinating. They took turns licking and chewing my pants, leaving putrid little tidbits of lunch in their wake. I had to gently, but firmly, "shoo" the dogs away, praying they wouldn't eat my crotch, all while trying to not interfere with the tape-recorded interview. Wasn't easy!

My favorite Sid Caesar story is this: Sid's manager, Larry, put Sid, Milton Berle and Danny Thomas together on a tour called, "The Living Legends of Comedy." I was the publicist for the tour, and had to handle all the print, TV, and radio coverage for its promotion. We needed Sid to record a radio commercial for a San Diego station, and I wrote up some text/copy that Sid was to read by phone so that the station could record it, then run it as an on-air commercial in their market.

Kim and I were out at a movie one night. When we came home, the light on my answering machine was blinking.

I pressed "play" and heard, "Dan, this is Sid Caesar. I got your copy for this radio spot. Do you honestly fucking expect me to fucking say, 'This is Sid Caesar. Join me and my fellow Living Legends of Comedy, Milton Berle and Danny Thomas, on such and such a date? In what fucking world would I call myself a fucking living legend? How could you write such a fucking piece of shit?! I won't do it, God damn it!"

The phone call then went "click."

I wish I'd saved that tape cassette. It was the greatest celebrity phone call I ever received in my life. Classic, and so very Sid!

The first time I ever met Jay Leno, we were peeing, side by side, at The Improv in West Hollywood at the tail end of 1980, shortly after I'd arrived in L.A. I knew somehow that he was from Boston. While relieving ourselves, I told him I'd attended BU.

"Emerson," he responded, "but I went to some great parties at BU."

Seven years later, I now found myself working as Jay's West Coast publicist. At the time, he was just about to be named as Johnny Carson's "permanent guest host." I wrote that press release. His managers then were Jerry and Helen Kushnick (now both deceased)-in their heyday, they were the most despised, horrendous and horrific human beings not only in Hollywood, but on all of Planet Earth itself.

Jerry and Helen would take turns calling me at my office, cursing and screaming at me, "Dan, who the fuck are YOU to be talking to the *New York Times* about Jay Leno?"

The duo treated Jay like he was the Queen of England. I feared those calls with a passion and had to then tell Lee Solters about them.

"Don't worry about it, just keep doing what you're doing, I'll handle it," he told me.

Once Jay was named the permanent guest host for *The Tonight Show*, Lee and I would drive up to NBC Studios in Burbank and hang out with Jay and Jerry Kushnick in Jay's dressing room. Jay would be in his underwear, completely unashamed. We'd discuss various upcoming PR and media opportunities by which to further his career through TV, radio, and print interviews to promote both *The Tonight Show,* as well as his dozens of live appearances across the country.

Jerry opened Jay's dressing room door one time, allowed just Lee inside, then abruptly and rudely slammed the door in my face! I was amazed. Seconds later, Jay opened the door, said, "Come on in, Dan, don't worry about it, everything's fine" and I entered. Jerry never spoke to me during these meetings–he simply pretended I didn't exist.

This continued until one day Jerry called me and said, "Dan you no longer represent Jay Leno."

I responded, "Really? Gee, thanks!" He then called Lee. Lee called me into his office and told me to stay the course. He was going to arrange for another publicist in the office, Peter, to "front" the account by dealing with Jerry and Helen directly. I was to continue to handle all of the media relations, working behind-the-scenes.

The sad part of this story is that for two years, I did the heavy lifting to promote Jay Leno, while Peter (in spite of this weird situation then, and still today, one of my best friends) got all the glory and affection from Jerry Kushnick. Jerry LOVED Peter! Jerry HATED me! Jerry never knew that Peter was "The Front" for my efforts during that whole period of time.

From '87 to '89, I got Jay amazing press coverage in the *L.A. Times, New York Times, USA Today,* magazine covers, and countless radio and TV interviews coast-to-coast. He was always incredibly nice to me.

Years after I repped Jay, a book and accompanying HBO movie called, *The Late Shift* (1996) came out. The story covered the fight for *The Tonight Show* after Johnny Carson announced his upcoming retirement. Both Leno and David Letterman were competing for the same coveted post. I enjoyed the book and movie a great deal, having personally "survived" some of the early part of that story myself, as I had to deal with the Kushnicks, those insane, non-human beings who once haunted me in my sleep.

Another of my clients was Matty Simmons, the publisher of *National Lampoon* magazine, the executive producer of the *National Lampoon's Vacation* (1983) movies, and the guy who essentially discovered Chevy Chase, Bill Murray, John Belushi, Dan Aykroyd and Gilda Radner. Matty was a super nice guy. I booked him at various colleges to give lectures about the state of comedy. He and I had several meals together and he told me wild stories about the "heyday" of the *National Lampoon Radio Hour* (1973) and the early days of the magazine. I even told him about my screenplay, *Carrots*, which he read and gave me notes on.

During my time repping Matty, he told me he was selling out his shares of the company to Tim Matheson, an actor and one of the stars of *Animal House* (1978). I once had a meeting in Tim's office, and his assistant brought me a tall glass of ice water. After maybe two minutes, I accidentally knocked the entire glass of water onto the carpet in his office. I spent the rest of the meeting hiding the massive reservoir with my foot.

I was assigned to serve as the Unit Publicist for a new TV series called *Buck James* (1987), a short-lived program which aired on ABC and starred Dennis Weaver. I attended numerous shoots of that show, both interiors (on the Sony-formerly MGM-lot) and at a ranch out in Newhall. Dennis wasn't particularly nice to me, so I never bonded with him, but I did get along well with the rest of the cast, especially the two attractive female cast members, Shannon Wilcox and Elena Wohl.

Actor Robert Englund is known around the world as "Freddy Krueger" from the *Nightmare on Elm Street* films. In real life, Robert was a super fun character, always hyperactive and alert, filled with a nonstop barrage of Hollywood gossip and interesting tidbits. Robert was evolving his craft into directing at this time ('87 through '89) and was just completing a movie called *976-EVIL* (1988)–a "horrific" take on the then becoming-popular "976" telephone sex lines that were popping up across the country.

I attended several night shoots for that movie and hung out with Robert and the cast for several weeks. He would invite me afterward to his home up in the hills off Laurel Canyon, where we would drink endless amounts of coffee. He'd tell me tall tales, and we commiserated with each other over our recent hernia surgeries! I mentioned to him that I also represented Sid Caesar and when I did, he shot off his chair, ran into his office, and returned to me in the living room with a *TV Guide* magazine cover of Sid dated July, 1953.

"Danny, you GOTTA get me Sid's autograph on this!" he demanded. "I'm the biggest Sid Caesar fan in the world. (I did get the autograph for him–if memory serves me, it was in a men's room for some reason.)

At this time, Robert was a huge fan of Howard Stern. As it happens, I had recently met Gary Dell' Abate, Howard's longtime producer, infamously nicknamed "Baba Booey," at a personal appearance event (along with Comic Artie Lange and Stern's "Stuttering John"), so I had direct access to Howard through Gary. During those days, Howard would come to Hollywood from New York a few times a year to broadcast his live radio show from the Hollywood Roosevelt Hotel. I booked Robert Englund on a Stern show–probably late '87. Robert and I chatted for a time with Howard and Gary. I told Howard that I also attended Boston University while he was there.

"Oh, yeah?" he said, "When did you graduate?"

I told him '78, and he said, "Oh, you're a few years younger than me–I guess we didn't hang out together then." (I took a photo of Robert with Howard but neglected to get one including me! Howard wasn't famous then – of course, I regret that 'no photo' decision now.)

After Robert did the Stern show, he treated me to a lunch at the legendary Hollywood restaurant, Musso and Frank. It was the first time I'd ever been there. I've been in love with the place ever since. (MORE about Musso's to come!)

Another of my clients during my era at Solters/Roskin/Friedman was a new cable TV network called SHOP TV or STV, for short. The producers of this new network created a huge, indoor "shopping mall" setting inside a large Hollywood soundstage. The hosts of the network's programs were Pat Boone and Juliet Prowse, both nice people with whom I had a few lunches during breaks in production.

One day while at my office, Lee Solters called me into his and told me he'd booked Milton Berle as a guest for the STV network to help Milton in his efforts to sell his new biography: *B.S. I Love You*. It was well-known to me that "Uncle Miltie" was important–he essentially put television itself on the map between 1948-1954, when people in the U.S. began purchasing their very first TV sets.

There was great excitement on the STV set, while the cast and crew were anxiously awaiting the arrival of the living legend himself–Milton Berle. I greeted Milton at the back door to the stage and was rather shocked to see an ancient old Jewish man hunched far over, with a hat on his head and his hands trembling.

"Hi, Milton, I'm Dan. Lee Solters wants me to take good care of you today," I said in greeting.

"Oh, okay, that's fine," he whispered.

I escorted Milton to his dressing room and told him everyone was excited by his presence. He nodded to me and then slowly crept into the room, quietly shutting the door. I must have waited there for perhaps 15 minutes, when suddenly the same door BURST OPEN, Milton was dressed in a beautiful grey suit, no more hat, no more trembling hands, and sporting a huge, freshly lit cigar.

"Here I am, Dan!" he announced. And suddenly, I found myself standing with an ENTIRELY DIFFERENT MAN!

I wanted to ask him, "WHAT DID YOU DO TO MILTON BERLE?" I ushered Milton into the specially designed living room set that had been constructed for his interview and book promotion; it was gorgeous. White couch, beautiful plants and flowers everywhere, decorative touches throughout the space. It was picture perfect.

What did Milton do when he arrived on set? Did he greet the cast and crew warmly and shake hands with everyone? No, he started SCREAMING at them all!

"This set is terrible! This won't work for me! I need the couch over there, those plants over here, the lights are all wrong, this spotlight needs to be aimed over here, those follow lamps need to go over there, that coffee table is too small! Get me a new one, NOW!"

I never in my life saw anything like it, nor had anyone else on set that day. For the next 45 minutes, the crew at STV had to, quite literally, rearrange everything, numerous times, to please the remarkably obstinate Uncle Miltie.

Finally, Milton settled down, did his interview, hawked his book, and all was well with the world. He posed for a photo with me in which he is squeezing my cheeks with one hand while his ever-present cigar was still prominently displayed in the other. When I arrived back at my office, I bumped into Lee Solters in the men's room and began telling him how incredibly annoying Milton had been to everyone at STV.

"Dan, DON'T <u>YOU</u> TELL <u>ME</u> ABOUT MILTON BERLE!" Lee shouted. "I've known him since the '40's! Whatever you saw him do today, I've seen myself, a thousand times over!" Lee then flushed and quickly scurried away.

Working at Solters/Roskin/Friedman, I had several other "close encounters" of the celebrity kind while attending a variety of events that the company was handling PR for. These included: a fundraiser at Chasen's for the United Negro College Fund, in which Sammy Davis, Jr. and I, standing side by side, took turns piling jumbo shrimp onto our plates; the introduction of a 10-act live show coming to the U.S. called, The Imperial Bells of China, hosted by Gregory Peck at the Beverly Hills Hotel; the announcement of the "Monsters of Rock" tour by rock band Van Halen, held just below the massive King Kong attraction at Universal Studios (I got Eddie Van Halen's autograph that day for my brother, Mike, a guitarist who cites Eddie as his idol); a backstage pass for a *Monkees* concert at the Greek Theatre, where I stood next to Davy Jones (but was unable to meet him); and a party for a potential new client/movie producer who was dating Michelle Phillips from The Mamas and The Papas. I danced with Michelle for a song or two and couldn't believe I was with a woman whose voice had dominated much of the radio airwaves during the better part of my pre-adolescence.

My wife, Kim, and I were living in Century City back during this time frame, and we shopped at a terrific grocery store called Gelsons. There, I had a number of close celebrity encounters— Ray Manzarek of The Doors; Carnie Wilson (Wilson/Phillips); Belinda Carlisle (The Go-Go's); Ruth Buzzi of *Laugh-In* (1967); and Audrey Meadows of *The Honeymooners* (1955), whom I told while we were standing in the same check-out line: "Miss Meadows! You are a living legend!"

She replied, "Thank you–and yes, I know!" She had less items to purchase than I did, so I even let her cut in front of me.

Other celeb sightings included riding an elevator with Ruta Lee and Jack Warden–during which time I told him about my "fun" days at Columbia Pictures in New York, helping to promote his film, *Used Cars*, by sending greasy dipsticks to movie critics in the mail.

He laughed and said, "Sorry, that must have sucked." I also: advised Nicholas Cage while he was buying some tropical fish at an aquarium store on Third Street; gave Eric Roberts directions to Hollywood after he pulled his car next to mine at a red light and asked me the way, as he was many miles in the wrong direction at the time; and re-met Zsa Zsa Gabor in the emergency room at Cedar Sinai Hospital while I was there with my wife Kim, when Kim needed urgent gall bladder surgery.

Zsa Zsa came up to us, held Kim's hand and said, "Oh, Dahlink, you are much too young to be sick! You need to get better soon so you can take care of your very handsome husband."

I didn't bring up the fact that a few years earlier, I'd almost broken the valuable antique chair in her living room!

One of my Solters/Roskin/Friedman clients was a feature film production company called CineTel. They were rather prolific at this time, cranking out one low budget movie after another. The celebrities I met during this period included Christian Slater at a screening of his movie, *Beyond the Stars* (1989); Tommy Chong of Cheech & Chong fame, and his daughter, Rae Dawn Chong, with whom I spent a day on the Griffith Park set of a film he was directing called *Far Out Man* (1990); and Actors Paul Bartel and Divine (the legendary transvestite actor), who I accidentally caught watching a hardcore gay porn film in a hotel room together when I was asked to bring them onto the set for a film being shot called *Out of the Dark* (1989).

FYI: A few weeks after filming this scene, Divine died, on March 7, 1988. So I wound up promoting "Divine's Last Movie"–a mixed blessing as it felt morbid to me to capitalize on someone's death, although it did generate some media attention.

Another *Out of the Dark* story: Actress Karen Black of *Easy Rider* (1969) and *Five Easy Pieces* (1970) fame, was the star of that movie, but at the time she didn't have a car, so the producer of the film asked me if I wouldn't mind driving her from her home in Hollywood to the set and back again every day, for one week. I was glad to do so since I always thought she was quite sexy in an off-kilter way.

One morning I arrived a few minutes early at her home and knocked on the door. No answer. I entered, calling, "Karen, it's Dan! Are you here?"

At that moment, the door to her downstairs bathroom flew open and a very naked–and dripping wet–Karen Black walked out. She saw me–I saw her–both of our mouths were agape, and then she screamed so loudly, I thought the police were going to arrive. She ran up the stairs, then shouted, "Give me a few minutes, Dan!" before vanishing into her upstairs bedroom.

I drove her to the set that day and the naked "incident" was never discussed. I liked her very much and have a nice photo of us together on the set–the film happened to be produced during a record-breaking cold spell in Los Angeles. In the picture we are wearing hats, gloves, scarves and heavy winter coats.

I helped to produce an event in the parking lot of *The Hollywood Reporter* magazine for which a number of noted celebrities would "Feed Hollywood's Homeless." One of my clients was the financial sponsor of this event, which took place the week of Christmas, 1988. I stood in a long serving line (I was assigned the baked yams) and dished out food to over 1,000 hungry homeless people.

Standing in the same line right next to me that day, were Monty Hall of *Let's Make A Deal* (1963); Harvey Korman of *The Carol Burnett Show* (1967); Mike Farrell of *M*A*S*H* (1972); Zsa Zsa Gabor yet again; Singer Donna Summer; and Valerie Harper, star of TV's *Rhoda* (1974). I met them all briefly, but I enjoyed talking the most that day with Valerie, as I was positioned right next to her.

The last major event I covered while working for the Solters/Roskin/Friedman PR firm was the 1989 Grammy Awards, held at the Shrine Auditorium. I was assigned to handle the "radio room," which was one of the backstage rooms designated for radio reporters who wished to interview Grammy Award winners after they came offstage. The radio room was the last–and least prestigious–of the backstage media rooms, coming after the TV room, the Photographers/Wire Services room, and the Print Media room (there were no digital/social media rooms back then). On that night, February 22, 1989, I very briefly met in the radio room Linda Ronstadt; Bobby McFerrin ("Don't Worry, Be Happy"); Tracy Chapman ("Fast Car"); Composer Danny Elfman; Amy Grant; Anita Baker; and for a second time, Weird Al Yankovic, who won a Music Video Grammy for his Michael Jackson parody, *Fat* (1988).

Gary Dell' Abate was in the radio room, covering the event for *The Howard Stern Radio Show*. My favorite–and most memorable–story from that night is when Olivia Newton John, one of the presenters at that evening's Grammy Awards, was asked by Gary, "Olivia! How are you planning to celebrate Black History Month?"

Clearly a comedic question, Olivia was horrified. She had no response and turned to me, her face drained of color, nearly pleading with me to do something!

"Gary, that's a really great question," I shouted, "but I think Olivia needs to get back to her seat now!" Gary and I laughed at each other, as a much-relieved Olivia Newton John whispered "Thanks!" to me, hurriedly fleeing the scene.

My last major Solters/Roskin/Friedman client was a guy I happened to meet at a party for the launch of a new toy line from Mattel during the fall of 1987. Robert Short was a special effects artist who was currently finishing up a new movie called, *Beetlejuice* (1988). I met Bob and his wife, Barbara, at the Mattel party and told them I was a publicist.

They hired me on the spot, saying, "We think this crazy movie, *Beetlejuice*, might get a lot of attention, and we'd like to capitalize on the publicity."

Over the next months, I spent a great deal of time in Bob's workshop, where he showed me not only the funny/weird props he contributed to *Beetlejuice*, but also E.T.'s "heart-light," a James Bond gun, a "pod" from *Cocoon* (1985), and the mermaid costume worn by Darryl Hannah in the movie, *Splash* (1984).

I got Bob Short dozens of print newspaper and magazine articles, in which he'd pose with the wacky *Beetlejuice* characters. I even booked him on the *David Letterman Show*, and his appearance remains, to this day, one of the most awkward and wonderfully hilarious moments in Letterman history. (Bob had rigged an "alien" to explode out of Dave's chest and then cover him with squirting blood. Letterman looked like he wanted to kill someone. When I watched that videoclip, I laughed so hard, I was crying.)

When *Beetlejuice* came out, none of its top stars were doing ANY PR! Michael Keaton, Alec Baldwin, Geena Davis, and Director Tim Burton were busy doing other projects, so a great deal of the promotion that Warner Bros.' PR Department undertook was enlisting ME to help THEM publicize the film by using MY CLIENT, Bob Short, and his crazy little creatures for media interviews!

About a week after the film opened big, Warner Bros. invited me to attend a media event for international press, and that was where I met Wynona Ryder, a lovely girl who was only 15 at the time. Of course, meeting her reminded me of my days with Brooke Shields in New York, also 15 back then.

Another week later, Warner Bros. PR invited Bob Short, his creatures, and me to a photo shoot for *Rolling Stone* Magazine. While the feature article was primarily about the up-and-coming new Director, Tim Burton, Bob and his props were also photographed for the piece.

When I met Tim Burton that day, I was rather taken aback by his slovenly appearance. He was dressed head to toe in black, very rumpled clothes, and his hair looked like it hadn't been washed or combed in a decade. After meeting him, I turned to the Head of Warner Bros. PR and said, "THAT's Tim Burton?"

She replied, "Yep, I know. He looks like a homeless person, but we have big plans for him. He happens to be a genius. You'll see."

That Warner Bros. executive was certainly right. Tim Burton's next film was *Batman* (1989), and his remarkable and extraordinary success was thereafter forever secured.

The next year, on March 29, 1989, Bob Short was one of three Special FX Makeup Artists to win an Academy Award for their work on *Beetlejuice*. I was home that night watching the Oscars on TV, along with Kim and our one-year-old son, Jordan. When Bob's name was announced, Kim and I screamed so loud that Jordan started crying from fright. As Bob Short was the last one of the three people to make his acceptance speech, his "talk time" was very limited, plus he was naturally a painfully shy person to begin with. I was afraid he'd be too nervous to say anything at all. He did manage to thank his crew and his wife, Barbara, but he didn't get a chance to thank me on national television.

The next day, he called me to say he HAD PLANNED to thank me during his speech! But the music started playing and he simply didn't have the chance. He was going to say, "and a very special thank you to my amazing publicist, Dan Harary."

That's as close to an "Oscar shout-out" as I ever got.

<u>Coda</u>: The next day at work, Lee Solters came into my office and stared at me. It was the first and only time while I worked at his PR agency that he ever came into my office.

"Dan," he said, "You did amazing work with Bob Short. Amazing. I don't even know what I would have done with him. Great job." He then left.

In the two years I worked there, it was the one and only time the man, an infamous curmudgeon, ever gave me a genuine compliment.

Chapter Seven

1989-1996

SCRAPPING LASSIE'S STAR / SEINFELD REMEMBERS / STING GOES THE WRONG WAY / CROSBY, SLICK, NASH & DAN / TWO MOON MEN / JERRY LEWIS WINKS / INSULTING MERYL STREEP / BLINDED BY MICHAEL JACKSON / MARKY MARK'S PECS / JULIA'S DRESS HAS A TAG / THE WHO'S PRIVATE CONCERT / MARY TYLER MOORE IN VEGAS / SAM KINISON'S LADIES / JEAN SMART GIVES A HUG

After two years working my ass off for Lee Solters, whose remarkable temper could explode at any moment without warning, I'd begun thinking it might be time for me to move on. Two of my co-workers from Solters/Roskin/Friedman had recently left the agency. Both of them joined a rival agency just about a half-mile west on Wilshire Boulevard. They told the owner of that agency about me. He called me in for a meeting and hired me on the spot.

When I returned to Solters/Roskin/Friedman from that interview, I knocked on Lee's door. He looked up at me from his extraordinarily cluttered desk, studied my face, and simply said, "When and where?"

He knew I was leaving by pure intuition. I told him. He said, "Why are you going to that press release factory? You'll learn much more from me if you stay here."

I replied that the new position would pay me quite a bit more, and as I'd just had a child, it was time for me to make some real money.

I left Solters/Roskin/Friedman with no hard feelings and Lee's partner, Monroe Friedman, said to me, "Dan, if you ever want to come back, the door will always be open."

Note: Since the owner of the new agency was a man I'd come to despise with a passion, I will not mention the name of this agency, nor his name. I will refer to him only as "the Duck," a nickname I gave him because he was a short, squat person.

On my first day working for the Duck, I was told I had a meeting that morning up at Universal Studios, where I would become the publicist for a new, syndicated TV series called, *The New Lassie* (1989). An hour later, I found myself at a photo shoot with the cast of this new show. They included Dee Wallace, best known as the mother from Steven Spielberg's *E.T. the Extra-Terrestrial* (1982); Christopher Stone (Dee's husband at the time); Jon Provost (who played "Timmy" on the original *Lassie* (1954) series; and a few child actors who never went anywhere further. I also "met" the new Lassie, the most gorgeous collie imaginable and the actual 7th generation descendant of the original Lassie. (The Weatherwax family owned and raised all of the Lassies, and I would work with Bob Weatherwax whenever I needed the famed dog to do some publicity or promotional activities.)

For the next two and a half years, I would spend countless hours on both indoor and outdoor sets with *The New Lassie* cast members at Universal Studios. Along the way, I also met and worked with two guest stars: June Lockhart, a wonderful woman who played the mom on the original *Lassie* series, and Roddy McDowell, who played a young boy in the very first *Lassie* project, a film called *Lassie Come Home* (1943), in which he co-starred with Elizabeth Taylor. I also worked, in addition to those guest stars, with two guest directors of episodes of the new series–Tony Dow, the iconic "Wally" from *Leave it to Beaver* (1957) and Ted Lange, who portrayed "Isaac" on TV's *The Love Boat* (1976).

The single person I became closest with from *The New Lassie* was Dee Wallace. After I'd been working with the cast for a few months, Kim, my wife, became pregnant with our second child–a daughter who would become my beloved Anjuli. However, while she was pregnant, Kim became incredibly ill and could not get out of bed or eat any food due to her overwhelming nausea. During several quiet lunches I had with Dee, I would tell her about Kim's condition and Dee confided in me that she, too, had had a terrible experience during her pregnancy with her and Chris Stone's daughter, Gaby. Dee told me the only way she was able to get through it was with the help of a fantastic acupuncturist who gave her treatments at home while in bed. She said the nausea went away and her daughter was born healthy and strong.

One night while I was home with a very ill Kim, who I'd moved into the living room and onto a rented hospital bed, an IV drip implanted into her arm, the phone rang. It was Dee Wallace, calling to tell me she had hired her acupuncturist to come visit Kim for the next several weeks AT HER EXPENSE, as she was such a strong advocate for his healing powers.

The man came over to treat Kim a number of times and cured her pregnancy illness. My daughter, Anjuli, was born healthy and happy in April, 1990.

Dee's completely altruistic act of kindness was, by far, the nicest thing any celebrity would ever do for me.

<u>Funny story</u>: During my time representing *The New Lassie* series, I suggested to the producers and cast that we "re-dedicate" Lassie's star on the Hollywood Walk of Fame. (The original Lassie had received that honor back in 1960.) Johnny Grant, the (now deceased) "Mayor of Hollywood," had given me his blessing for a re-dedication ceremony. Once I got that okay, the producers and cast were all onboard.

We selected a date for the Hollywood Star Event, and arranged for the cast, the producers, and even the new Lassie dog, to attend. With Johnny Grant at a small podium, and the cast, producers, a huge horde of photographers and TV news crews surrounding original Lassie's Hollywood star, a long white limousine pulled up and the new Lassie hopped out of the car. The media was flashing photos like mad and all seemed right with the world, until I happened to glance down on the original Lassie's star and realized there was a huge blob of BUBBLE GUM covering the capital letter "L" from Lassie's name! It looked like "Assie!" I quickly pulled out my keys, got on my hands and knees, and scraped the gum off the star.

I have to admit, in retrospect, that being on my hands and knees on a filthy dirty sidewalk in a suit, scraping bubble gum off of a DOG'S STAR on the Hollywood Walk of Fame had to be, without question, the lowest point of my entire Hollywood career.

One of the Duck's clients was a company called DIR Broadcasting. They specialized in major, live, pay-per-view TV events across America. The only such event I worked on during my tenure with the Duck was for DIR's presentation of the rock band The Who, performing "Tommy" at the Universal Studios Amphitheatre. The event was designed to raise money for a children's charity.

I was invited to attend The Who's rehearsal the night before the live pay-per-view event. As I entered the amphitheater which was virtually empty at the time, I happened to glance over to my left side to see Roger Daltrey and Pete Townsend standing about six feet from me, having a quiet conversation. Since The Who was one of my all-time favorite rock bands (the concert of theirs which I saw with my brother Bob at Madison Square Garden in early 1976 was the best rock performance I ever saw in my life), I stopped in my tracks. For about 20 seconds, I simply stared at these two rock idols. They stared back, certain I was a lunatic.

The Who gave me-and only a very few others, including Whoopi Goldberg sitting a few rows ahead of me-a private show. At one point, while I was still sitting alone in a seat inside the huge, empty arena, the band took a break. Roger Daltrey hopped off the stage, up into the seats, and sat directly in front of me.

Daltrey's blonde hair was inches in front of me! "Tommy," himself, was close enough that I could have combed his curly locks!

An assistant brought Roger a hot cup of tea with lemon and as he sat right in front of me, sipping his beverage, a million thoughts ran through my mind. "What do you say to one of your all-time rock music heroes?"

Finally, after a tortuous 10-minutes, I managed to tap him on the shoulder. When he turned his head back toward me, I said, "Hey Roger, I'm Dan. I'm doing some PR with DIR Broadcasting. I just wanted to say--"

I froze for a few seconds, then continued: "I just wanted to say, 'Thank you' for your wonderful, amazing music."

Daltrey smiled, nodded his head, and replied, "Cool, mate. You're welcome."

The Who's performance would be the next night, and a few hours beforehand, I found myself backstage mingling with various agents, managers, and Universal Amphitheater employees. While strolling about, I happened to quickly turn to see Phil Collins, holding his newborn daughter Lily (today a movie star), standing quietly in front of me. I can honestly say, as a longtime drummer myself, that Buddy Rich and Phil Collins were the two most innovative and fantastic drummers I ever saw live in concert. I'm staring at Phil, he's staring at me, and I simply said, "I've seen almost every famous drummer ever, including Buddy Rich, and you are without question one of the world's all-time greats."

Phil smiled and said, "That's nice to hear. You play?"

I told him I started playing drums in 1966.

"Welcome to the club," he added, at which point little baby Lily started crying. "Sorry man, gotta dash," and then off he went.

In addition to Phil Collins, The Who's guest stars during their "Tommy" show included Elton John, Billy Idol, Steve Winwood and Patti LaBelle–I met none of them. The concert was spectacular, although I still think the show I saw back in '76, which included the since deceased drummer Keith Moon, was actually better.

After the concert ended, there was an industry party on a back-lot at Universal Studios for the band. Almost instantly, I ran into The Who's bassist John Entwistle, who chatted with me for a bit and gave me an autograph on the concert's official program. I was hoping to get Daltrey to sign the same program for me, but he was ensconced by a huge throng of industry folks, and I couldn't get near him. Then I realized that sitting quietly in a corner, Pete Townsend and his mother, Betty, were talking at a small table. There was a line of about six attractive women standing in front of the table, all eagerly awaiting an autograph. I joined the line and stood at the very end. Without ever once averting his eyes from his mother, Townsend signed everything those fine ladies presented in front of him without hesitation. When it finally became my turn, however, a huge bouncer appeared out of nowhere, stuck out his arm and said, "Sorry, Mr. Townsend won't be signing any more autographs."

I was literally the VERY LAST PERSON in the line! I looked at Pete, he looked up at me, and I said, "Pete, really, are you serious, man?" while showing him the program which Entwistle had already signed.

Townsend stared blankly at me with his crystal-blue eyes, then went back to his intense conversation with his mother.

While I will forever be a huge fan of Townsend and his musical genius, would it have killed the guy to take five seconds out of his life to sign my program? Geez!

In conjunction with Earth Day (April 20, 1990), TimeWarner Media, then the owners of Warner Bros. Studios, was producing a special TV program about how Americans could better protect the environment. It was entitled, *The TimeWarner Earth Day Special* (1990). One of the Duck's clients was Warner Bros. Television, so I was asked to attend a photo shoot in Century City. The photo session was to produce a promotional image that would be used to advertise the program.

As soon as I entered the photo studio, I saw Kevin Costner posing in front of a large slate grey backdrop, holding a small sapling tree. The photographer was snapping away, and I watched.

Note: This was months before Costner's *Dances with Wolves* (1990) came to theaters, so while he was not yet a superstar, he had first become famous just two years earlier with his popular hit, *Bull Durham* (1988).

After a few test images, Kevin walked over to me and we started talking. At the time, he had a little ponytail. I told him about how, 15 years earlier, my hair was halfway down my back.

"You're kidding, right?" he said. "That's so cool. I never did that but always wanted to."

More and more people showed up during the photo session, and a large buffet style luncheon was set up on a table. While eating, I met a number of programming and publicity executives, both from TimeWarner and from ABC, the network that would be airing the special. I also reconnected with a woman named Carla, a Warner

Bros. TV publicist, who I'd known a few years earlier when we both worked together at Columbia Pictures Television.

As we were eating, someone shouted, "She's here! She's here!" and everyone immediately began to position themselves in a long line. I asked Carla, "Who's here?"

She said, "Meryl Streep."

I was stunned. Meryl was just eight years out from having won a "Best Actress" Oscar for *Sophie's Choice* (1982). My heart started pounding and my hands became a bit sweaty. As I stood at the very end of the long line that formed to greet her, I kept repeating to myself, "Meryl Streep is coming! Meryl Streep is coming!" I have no idea in retrospect why this made me nervous–I was not then, nor have I ever been–a fan of Meryl Streep.

Finally, the outside doors opened, and there she stood, appearing as a silhouette inside a blast of intense, white-hot sunshine, her arms spread wide as though she were Mother Mary blessing the "little people" standing in awe beneath her.

Meryl made her way to the start of the long line and everyone there, while waiting to introduce themselves to her, put out his or her hand for the great lady to shake. It appeared to me like the Queen of England was slowly making her way down a processional and these top TV executives were her subjects. My friend, Carla, stood to my right. I kept whispering to her, "What should I say to Meryl Streep?"

Carla simply "shooshed" me each time I asked.

Finally, Meryl came up to Carla. "Hello, Ms. Streep, my name is Carla Princi from Warner Brothers Television. It's so wonderful to meet you!" While these two women shook hands just inches to my right, my heart began pounding out of my chest, and I went into a daze.

Then, as perhaps the most famous women on Planet Earth presented herself before me, I said, "Hello, Carla! It's so great to meet you! My name is Dan, I'm a publicist."

Yes, you read that right! I ACTUALLY CALLED MERYL STREEP, "CARLA!"

While our hands were still intertwined in a handshake, Meryl slowly turned her head to the side and studied my face. She looked exactly like the RCA Victor dog. Finally, she retrieved her hand, walking away toward the buffet in silence.

"Dan, I can't believe you just did that!" Carla said.

"Did what?" I asked.

"You just called Meryl Streep, 'Carla.'"

"I did?" I responded. "I have no recollection of that!"

That was, without question, my greatest "close encounter of the celebrity kind" fuck up! It would take a great deal of effort for anyone to ever top that story!

Duck's PR Agency handled the American Film Institute's "Lifetime Achievement Awards" dinner/events during my time there. I worked three of those events in this era–the award dinners for Kirk Douglas (1991), Sidney Poitier (1992) and Elizabeth Taylor (1993). My role at each of these events–for which I had to wear a tuxedo– was to greet the celebrities as they arrived at the entrance to the Beverly Hilton Hotel lobby, and then to announce them into a walkie-talkie to the rest of my fellow publicists who were working with the media gaggle arranged in the nearby bleachers, so they would know which famous people to expect next.

I don't remember all of the celebrities I "greeted" for the Kirk Douglas dinner, but a few do stand out:

** <u>Sylvester Stallone</u>: When I met Stallone at the front door, I shook his hand, and said, "Hey Sly, what brings you out tonight?"

His reply: "The man (referring to Kirk Douglas) is Spartacus! How can you NOT honor Spartacus!" We laughed, and I also led him to CNN–there is a videoclip of us together there, as well.

Later at the event, Sly and I ended up side-by-side in the men's room, peeing together. Flashing back to my days with Oscar winning director Robert Wise, I said, "Hey Sly, we simply have GOT to stop meeting this way!" Big laugh–always funny.

** <u>Michael Landon</u>: As soon as the *Bonanza* (1959) and *Little House on the Prairie* (1974) TV star Michael Landon entered the Beverly Hilton Hotel lobby, he asked me, "Hey buddy, where's the men's room?" He looked like his bladder was about to explode. During those few seconds of time, a photographer from *PEOPLE Magazine* happened to click a shot of Landon, his wife, Cindy, and me together. That photo-which appears in this book-ran in print in the next week's issue. I have a copy of it framed on my wall. The poor man died of cancer just four months later!

** <u>Kevin Costner (again)</u>: For some reason, I hadn't caught Kevin at the front door of the hotel but about an hour later, I saw him standing alone toward the back of the banquet hall. I approached him and we talked about our "long hair" conversation from the year before. I said, "Hey, what happened to your ponytail, man? That looked so cool."

His reply: "Yeah it was fun, but a guy's gotta grow up eventually, I guess."

As I was speaking with him, I saw to the right of me a secretary named Sharon from Duck's PR agency whom I'd recently met. I could tell she was simply staring holes through Kevin Costner, so I motioned for her to come over to us. She did and turned bright, bright red in the process. "Hey Kevin, this is Sharon. She works with me."

Kevin shook Sharon's hand and I kid you not, Sharon started to breathe so rapidly and loudly that it appeared quite obvious: the poor girl WAS HAVING AN ORGASM!

Kevin and I looked at each other in awe as this was happening. He tried to stifle a laugh and I felt bad for poor Sharon, who never said one word. Once her cum-session subsided, she simply turned, utterly humiliated, and fled.

The next year's dinner was for Sidney Poitier. I again served as celebrity door greeter. The only person I remember meeting this time was:

** <u>Tom Hanks</u>: I not only met Tom Hanks at the front door, but I also walked him inside on the red carpet and led him up to the news crew from CNN, who asked me earlier to please be sure they were able to talk with him. Somewhere in my archives, I have a videoclip of Tom and me standing side by side, laughing.

And during the celeb arrivals for the AFI Award dinner for Elizabeth Taylor (1993), I met: Michael Jackson. Michael had recently broken his ankle and arrived in a huge maroon, chauffeur-driven Bentley. The car pulled up to the front door of the hotel and Michael hopped out, skillfully working a pair of crutches. The paparazzi photographers who lined the hotel's exterior red carpet were flashing their lightbulbs like mad–here was the biggest star in the world! I walked outside onto the red carpet to help usher Michael inside and away from the glare of all those horrible pop-flashes.

For a few seconds, Michael and I were alone together on that red carpet. The flashbulbs were so numerous and intense, I honestly could not see or breathe. I grabbed one of his arms and helped him hobble inside the hotel lobby where he could, at least for a few seconds, escape the madness.

Once inside, we looked at each other, took a deep breath and chuckled. I said, "How on earth do you deal with that every day, Michael?"

He replied, "You get used to it."

I meant to talk with him about my cousin Franz, the magician, who was one of his best friends at the time, but I simply forgot because I'm a yutz.

I felt bad when Michael died years later. I remain concerned to this day about the terrible allegations made against him by many young boys during the final years of his life.

Another of Duck's clients was the Environmental Media Association, better known as EMA–a group of high-profile Hollywood industry members, including Norman Lear, who created an organization by which to encourage "environmentally friendly messaging" within movies and TV shows.

At the kick-off luncheon event for EMA, I sat at a table with Julia Louis-Dreyfus of *Seinfeld* (1989) and *Veep* (2012) on one side of me, and Mel Harris of *Thirtysomething* (1987) and her husband, Cotter Smith of *L.A. Law* (1986) on the other. I had a nice chat with Julia about the very, very early days of *Seinfeld* and she couldn't have been sweeter. She told me she was concerned about the environment for her future children and she seemed truly committed. Mel and Cotter and I talked about how disposable versus cloth diapers impacted the environment–they just recently had a child and my daughter, Anjuli, was still in diapers at the time.

I had a meeting with Duck and the heads of the EMA a few weeks later inside Duck's conference room. The EMA people wanted to hold some kind of an awards event, but they also wanted to do an entirely separate fundraising dinner for VIPs. I simply said, "Combine them–do the awards event AND the fundraising dinner AS ONE, AT THE SAME TIME!"

Thus, I am the man who gave birth to the annual "Environmental Media Awards Dinner," which kicked off in September, 1991.

The "First Annual Environmental Media Awards" event was a massive media and celebrity-filled occasion, held at the Sony Studios lot (formerly the MGM Studio lot) in Culver City. I was solely in charge of media attendance, and I can honestly say we had every major media outlet based in Los Angeles there that night.

The red carpet for that first awards show saw almost as many celebrities as the Oscars. I met, greeted, and led along to the various TV camera crews many celebs, including Shirley MacLaine, and Jane Fonda and Ted Turner (a couple at the time).

I said, "Hey Mr. Turner, CNN would like to interview you. You're probably familiar with them, right?"

"Good one, kid," he replied.

Also in attendance were Jamie Lee Curtis; Ted Danson; Robert Redford; Diane Sawyer, and Dan Aykroyd, marking the fourth & final "Ghostbuster" I'd met. Memorable stories from that evening:

** Chevy Chase: I'd gotten a call on my walkie-talkie from the security guards at the front Sony Studios Gate that I was needed there. A quick walk-over and I saw Chevy Chase alone in a convertible behind a guard gate, which was blocking his entrance onto the studio lot–he was fuming. A security guard came up to me and said, "This guy says he's supposed to be one of the awards presenters, do you know him?" Shocked to my core, I said, "Are you kidding me? That's Chevy Chase! Yes, of course, let him park his car, please." The guard, having received my "blessing," raised the closed gate so Chevy could move his car. "Next time, I'll have a cheeseburger and a blow-job instead," Chevy snarked at the man, clearly annoyed beyond words.

** Sting: Rock superstar Sting was one of the presenters for the EMA Awards, but he was on a plane back to the USA from Ireland and ran a little bit late. When he finally arrived at the studio gates, I got a call on the walkie-talkie to "Come get

Sting!" I raced over there, shook his hand, and said, "Sting, please follow me." We jogged back over to the awards stage. For Sting to appear ON the stage itself we had to enter a fairly complex, under-the-stage labyrinth with enough twists and turns to make you nauseous. We both entered the tunnels but after about 10 seconds, I realized Sting was no longer behind me. Shouting out to him in a loud whisper (so as not to disrupt the events taking place directly above us on the stage) I said, "Hey STING! You're going the WRONG WAY! Take a left, Sting! TAKE A LEFT!!"

He heard me, corrected his direction, and I was finally able to deliver him to the proper entryway onto the stage.

** Julia Louis-Dreyfus (Story # 2): This is one of my favorite-ever celebrity stories. As mentioned, I'd already had lunch with Julia, so I kind of knew her. When she arrived on the red carpet for the First EMA Award event, she was the very last celebrity to appear. She was wearing a beautiful light blue dress that was clearly SO BRAND NEW it had a SALES TAG STICKING UP INTO THE AIR and out from her right shoulder! She was a few yards away from the world's press corps! I ran up to her, grabbed her by both shoulders and shouted, "Julia! You've got a SALES TAG on your dress!"

Horrified, she looked me deep in the face and cried, "Are you kidding me? For God's sake, DO SOMETHING!"

In a maneuver I am still quite proud of, even today, I managed to yank the plastic stem at the base of the sales tag from her dress WITHOUT ripping it! Did it with my bare hands. In any other universe, I would have ripped her dress to shreds and caused Julia to have to turn and flee for her life.

After I showed her the tag, Julia and I looked at each other and laughed so hard, we almost started crying. "Julia!

Every media outlet in the world is right over there!" I said, pointing.

"Can you even imagine?" she replied. (25 years later, I would meet Julia again and recount this story for her and her husband, Brad Hall. It didn't go well. More on that in a later chapter.)

While I simply do not recall the 2nd Annual EMA event (perhaps it was because I was getting divorced at the time), the 3rd EMA Awards show took place in September 1993, and was held at 20th Century Fox Studios. There, the most memorable moment for me was meeting:

** Al Gore: Vice President Al Gore was the special guest speaker for the 1993 EMA Awards. After the event ended, I managed to corral him for a quick chat and to shake his hand. A photographer popped off a photo of us together. I thanked the man for "speaking to us today, and helping Hollywood spread the word."

"It's important," Gore replied. "Hollywood has a big megaphone and the creative people here are crucial in including environmentally responsible messaging into their storytelling. The best thing we can possibly leave to our children is a cleaner Planet Earth."

I felt a bit of a high, having just met the second-most-powerful-man in America.

Backing up to 1992: I flew to Houston to oversee the publicity for the grand opening of Space Center Houston, a brand-new, multi-million-dollar NASA Space Museum that was designed by one of the Duck's clients.

There were dozens of media members from around the world at the opening of this new venue. I was especially proud of the coverage I helped generate that appeared on CNN and in *Newsweek* magazine.

At one point while scurrying around during the opening ceremonies, I literally bumped into Buzz Aldrin, the second man to walk on the Moon. Startled, I said, "Mr. Aldrin? Wow! Hey, I'm Dan. I'm handling the PR for today. It's such an honor to meet you."

He shook my hand and, clearly annoyed, replied, "I'll bet it is."

Not exactly the response I'd hoped for.

A few hours later, I ran into Eugene Cernan, the 11th man to walk on the Moon. He was friendlier to me, but he began every sentence with a reference to his famous journey. "You know, when I walked on the Moon," or "You know, when you're on the Moon, there's a lot of dust flying around," or "Stepping on the Moon, you find yourself thinking about how small Man really is." He basically gave me an unrequested peek into his world of self-glorification.

The Duck called me into his office around this time period to tell me his agency was now handling MTM Studios–the famed home of *The Mary Tyler Moore Show* (1970), *Rhoda* (1974), *Phyllis* (1975), and *Lou Grant* (1977). An executive of MTM then was our client, Bill Allen, whose father happened to be the late-night television pioneer, Steve Allen.

Steve Allen had decided to release all of the episodes of his decades-old series, *The Steve Allen Show* (1956), which originally aired on NBC from 1956 to 1964. Steve made a deal with the new HA! cable TV network to air those shows. (HA! would later merge with The Comedy Channel to form the current "Comedy Central" Network.)

Steve wanted to hold a press conference to inform Americans that they would soon be able to view these long-lost episodes of his iconic comedy series for the first time in nearly three decades. I was the guy who had to produce the press conference.

Cut to maybe two weeks later: Steve Allen and I are standing at the front doors of MTM Studios (in Studio City, California) waiting for the hordes of press to arrive for the conference. The event was slated to start at 11:00 am, and it was now about 10:57 am. There were ZERO members of the press anywhere to be seen for miles. A bead of sweat ran down from my forehead.

"Where are they, Dan?" Steve asked me. "Where's all the press coverage you promised me?"

Nauseous and feeling feint, I lied and told him, "They're coming, Mr. Allen. I'm sure they'll be here at any minute."

10:58 am–nothing. 10:59 am–nothing.

Then a true PR miracle occurred. About five TV news trucks showed up from thin air, along with perhaps a dozen print journalists and four or five still photographers. They all arrived EXACTLY at 11:00 am –to the second! Their magical appearance was a huge relief to both Steve and me, and we looked at each in awe. Neither of us could believe what had just happened.

The press conference went very well. We generated a lot of TV stories and newsprint articles about Steve Allen's "lost episodes."

At the end of the event, Steve walked me off into a hallway and said, "You did a fine job, Dan. As a thank you, I'd like to invite you to my party at the Beverly Hills Hotel this weekend."

So now I also became the publicist for Steve Allen's "lost episodes" release party. It was the first time I'd ever been to the Beverly Hills Hotel. I drove up to the valet parking in my 1976 Honda Civic, utter piece-of-shit station wagon with its blue paint badly rusted from the sun. Clearly, I was the poorest person who'd ever arrived there.

I entered one of the hotel's ballrooms and found myself amidst a quite literal "Who's Who" of celebrities from the '50s and beyond. I worked closely with the photographer I'd hired to commemorate the event. Together we shot photos of Steve Allen and Jayne Meadows; Esther Williams; Louise Nye; Shecky Greene; Jack Carter; Shelley Berman, and others I can't recall.

The highlight of the night for me was when Bob and Dolores Hope entered the ballroom as "special surprise guests." I shook Mr. Hope's hand when he walked into the room, but I was too tongue-tied to say anything. "Hiya, kid," he said to me.

I have a photo of Bob and Dolores Hope standing side-by-side with Steve Allen and his wife, Jayne Meadows, from that party–my "very small head" appears just behind and over Bob Hope's right shoulder. It's one of my favorite career photos. My tiny head looks like either a mistake or a special effects moment gone horribly wrong.

One other enjoyable moment from the Steve Allen party: while standing adjacent to the large prominent food display on a banquet table, I heard to my immediate right a very low, deep voice say, "God, these shrimp are so fucking good." I turned to see Bea Arthur of *Maude* (1972) standing beside me. "You're right, they're fucking great!" I replied. She and I stood shoulder-to-shoulder for several minutes, chatting, and inhaling the biggest, freshest jumbo shrimp I'd ever seen in my life.

Duck assigned me to become the publicist for a hit ABC/Disney television comedy series called *Empty Nest* (1988), which was a spinoff from the show, *The Golden Girls* (1985). *Empty Nest* starred Richard Mulligan as a widowed pediatrician named Harry Weston. The show's storyline: "Dr. Weston is a miracle worker when it comes to dealing with his young patients, but he's more challenged by the other people surrounding him: daughters Barbara (Kristy McNichol) and Carol (Dinah Manoff), his wisecracking office assistant, Nurse LaVerne Todd (Park Overall), and his enormous dog."

I would attend the Friday night tapings of the series before a live audience, and during breaks would flirt with Actress Dinah Manoff. I kind of felt some sparks between us. Had she not been a rich, famous actress and had I not been the driver of a total piece-of-shit car, I might have considered asking her on a date, but I never did. (I should note, I was divorced by then.)

I met all of the cast members several times, along with Gil Junger, one of the producers. In fact, I wrote a spec script for an *Empty Nest* episode that I handed to Gil. He later said it was "pretty good, but not quite something we'd use here."

One day Duck called me into his office and told me I'd been fired from *Empty Nest*. I asked him why. He told me my suggestion to the show's producers–to have actress Park Overall pose for a *Playboy Magazine* profile-was "a brilliant PR idea," but "totally out of character for a TV show that's being produced by Disney Studios."

I repped the show only for about six months. For me, the experience was no loss, no gain.

Another TV series I handled for the Duck was a syndicated show based on the movie, *Harry and the Hendersons* (1987). The show starred Bruce Davison (later of *X-Men* fame -2000), who played the role of "George," the head of the Henderson family. Co-stars included Molly Cheek of *American Pie* (1999), Gigi Rice of *Frazier* (1993) and *Two and a Half Men* (2003), Noah Blake–son of actor/alleged murderer Robert Blake, and Kevin Peter Hall, the originator of the "Harry" bigfoot creature from the movie.

I fucked up on a radio interview for Bruce Davison early on while I was repping *Harry*, and he never forgave me. I'd arranged for him to appear on a local radio station on a Saturday morning to promote the *Harry* series, but when he'd arrived, the DJ had no idea why he was there or that he was even coming! Bruce called me at home, totally pissed off. He and I never spoke to each other again.

During this era, Noah Blake and I would have lunch together on a regular basis, and I'd ask him about his famed father. He told me they were never close and he was doing his best to "make it in showbiz on my own merits." He was a good kid and I liked him.

Kevin Peter Hall had to wear the huge, heavy "Harry" fur costume. While appearing under the heavy lights required for filming, he'd remove his "Harry" head from time to time to reveal a remarkable amount of sweat pouring down his body. Alas, Kevin died of AIDS during the time I was the publicist for this series, but no one from the studio (Universal Studios Television) or Kevin's wife would allow me to tell the world the real reason for his death. We put out a press notice that Kevin died "of pneumonia." It would be several more years until his AIDS diagnosis became public knowledge.

One of the fun projects I had while working for the Duck was handling on-set publicity for a proposed new cable TV show called, *The Inside Track with Graham Nash* (1989). The show, originally known as *The Ring* and based on a Russian show of that same name, featured Crosby, Stills & Nash Singer/Musician Graham Nash, standing on a circular stage interviewing a singular guest while a live studio audience was situated in the round, in front of the stage.

I got to the set of *The Inside Track* early and met Graham right off–the nicest man on the planet. I introduced him to my photographer and we set up a beautiful backdrop for still photography backstage. Shortly after we finished setting up, David Crosby arrived. I met him and led him to the photo area so we could get some snapshots of Crosby and Nash together.

I had no idea that in a few more minutes, Grace Slick of Jefferson Airplane was going to arrive as another separate interview guest of Graham's. When she came into the soundstage no one else was around so I ran up to her, introduced myself, and asked her if she'd be willing to shoot some photos with us.

Grace took me by the hand and said, "Just let me know where you want me, Dan. I'm all yours."

Wow, that was so cool! The woman who sang "White Rabbit" and "Don't You Want Somebody to Love" was all mine!?

I posed the three legendary rock stars together and said aloud, "Here they are, ladies and gentlemen, please welcome Crosby, Slick and Nash!"

My three charges laughed and then Graham added, "And Dan!"

I came THIS CLOSE to posing for a photo with them. I should have and easily could have but for whatever reason, I couldn't bring myself to do it. After all, who am I to defile a photograph of three of the most iconic members of the Woodstock Era?

After the tapings of the two episodes (Crosby interview, then Slick interview), Graham invited everyone who'd been sitting for hours in the studio audience to come up onstage to meet each other and just "hang out."

On the stage that evening, I "just hung out" with Drew Barrymore, Bonnie Raitt, and Jackson Browne, along with the three singers previously mentioned.

One last moment of interest: During the dinner break for Graham's two episodes, I ate with Henry Diltz, probably the most prominent photographer of iconic 1960's era rock bands. Henry shot the legendary first album cover artwork for the Crosby, Stills & Nash debut album, along with album covers for The Doors (including the iconic *Morrison Hotel*), Neil Young, and many others. Super interesting guy. I still have his paper card in my Rolodex!

One of Duck's clients was GoodTimes Home Video, a company that produced their own VHS videotapes of original content. I've got four "close encounters of the celebrity kind" stories related to my handling of this account:

** <u>Cindy Crawford</u>: Supermodel Cindy Crawford shot two workout tapes for GoodTimes: *Shape Your Body Workout* (1992) and *The Next Challenge Workout* (1993.) I attended one of the video shoots for her *Shape Your Body* release and, of course, was taken aback by her natural beauty and charisma.

During a break in production, I went up to Cindy and introduced myself. We shook hands and spoke for a few moments about her goals for the project: "To help give women everywhere the ability to perform some simple exercises from home." While we were speaking, Cindy's personal photographer–who was standing across the room at the time–shouted, "Hey Cindy, wanna see these latest shots?"

Cindy's face lit up. She looked me straight in the eye, clapped her hands together, and said, "Oh, goody! More photos of ME!" And then, like a young schoolgirl, she skipped across the room to review them (like she'd never seen photos of HERSELF before?)

** <u>Mark Wahlberg</u>: Before Mark Wahlberg became a legitimate movie star, and after his initial rise to fame as music rapper "Marky Mark," Mark shot a GoodTimes Home Video release called, *The Marky Mark Workout* (1993).

I was on the set the day of the shoot. When Mark appeared inside the studio and removed his shirt to begin lifting weights from a bench press, an audible gasp spread across the building. Mark's muscles were so remarkably PERFECT that everyone there, men and women included, nearly swooned. (Myself included!)

At the break, Mark put his shirt back on and that's when we met. I told him I had a TV crew that was about to arrive at any moment from the show *Entertainment Tonight*, and they were coming to interview him about his career. Mark looked me dead in the eye and said, "No, I don't wanna do that." Then he walked away from me, entered his private trailer, and shut the door.

When the crew from "E.T." arrived, I was at a loss. I had to explain to them that Mark "was resting now" and "maybe, hopefully" he'd be coming out of his trailer soon.

I knocked on Mark's trailer door a number of times in desperate hopes that he would change his mind and do the interview (which I'd "cleared" with the producers of the exercise video earlier). I knocked probably five or six different times and each time Mark said, "No, Dan, no. You need to go away."

Finally, I approached the President of GoodTimes Home Video, who happened to have arrived on set, and informed him of the stalemate. "Let me see what I can do," he said. He knocked on Mark's trailer door, entered, and a few minutes later the two men come out, all smiles.

"Where do you want me, Dan?" Mark said, happy as a clam. I set him up with the crew from *Entertainment Tonight* and all was right with the world.

I later asked the GoodTimes President how he performed that magic trick.

"His contract," he replied. "I just reminded him that doing PR for us was in his contract."

** <u>Charlton Heston</u>: Legendary Hollywood movie star Charlton Heston recorded the voice for a GoodTimes Home Video release entitled *Charlton Heston Presents the Bible* (1992).

I never met him in person, but he and I worked together via telephone for a few weeks, as I arranged phone interviews for him with various members of the press to generate promotional articles about the new videotape.

One day, I arranged with Charlton to have a young female reporter from a local L.A. newspaper go to his home in Beverly Hills to do an in-person interview there. Charlton agreed to this and I had assumed it would simply take place as planned.

About 15 minutes after the interviewer had been scheduled to arrive at Heston's house, I got a call at my office from the woman. She was in tears. She told me that Heston had met her at the door, ushered her into his living room, and as soon as she started asking him some basic questions about playing Moses in the iconic *The Ten Commandments* (1956) movie, he yelled at her and tossed her out of his house.

I never worked with Heston again after that day.

** Richard Simmons: Richard Simmons, at this time, was a hugely successful exercise and fitness guru with a media empire that included television, videotapes, and uniquely branded products. Richard was producing a new tape with GoodTimes called *Disco Sweat* (1993), and I attended the taping.

For this production, Richard created a large Brooklyn-themed disco dance set on a Hollywood soundstage, and was surrounded by about a dozen overweight women, all in tights. Richard, too, was in tights.

I was at this shoot with Lynn, another publicist who worked for the Duck. She and I shared this GoodTimes account. When Richard was ready to begin production, he approached Lynn and I, put his arms around each of us and said, "Oh, you guys are just too cute! You must be in my video!"

That's how it came to pass that I can be seen in the introduction of the *Richard Simmons Presents Disco Sweat* home videotape. In the piece, Lynn and I both say, "How 'ya doing?" to the camera, which represented the point of view of a person physically walking into a Brooklyn-based discotheque. Not exactly a career highlight!

Duck's biggest client was the NATPE (National Association of Television Program Executives) Television Association. This is the industry group that serves as a marketplace for all of the networks, studios and production companies that produce and sell television programming. I attended a number of NATPE conventions during my years with Duck, and along the way I met: Kelsey Grammer of *Frasier* (1993); Burt Reynolds, who was giving my old pal, Milton Berle, a lifetime achievement award; Ron Howard, who was giving a Lifetime Achievement Award to Andy Griffith; Adam Carolla and Geraldo Rivera.

During one NATPE, I spent a day in New Orleans inside a limo with Ron Reagan, Jr., and Cristina Ferrare who, at the time, were co-hosts of a proposed national talk show. I don't recall that the show ever aired nationally, only locally in L.A., but it was a lot of fun riding around New Orleans, going from TV station to TV station to do press interviews with the pair.

I had a huge crush on Cristina back in the '60s when she'd appeared in a white fringed bikini in the David Niven film, *The Impossible Years* (1968). I told her about that, and she told me that "countless guys your age" had, over the years, relayed the same stories of having had "the hots" for her due to that sexy outfit.

Ron was a nice, sweet guy. I was surprised there were no secret service men protecting him while we were together. His father, Ronald Reagan, had been President just a few years before this. We spoke about his dad and he told me he was closer to him than many realized. It was pretty cool for me to be having a conversation about one of America's most beloved Presidents while discussing him as a person and a father rather than as a political icon.

I also spent a full day with another formerly popular TV personality, Graham Kerr, best known as *The Galloping Gourmet* (1968) during a NATPE conference. He and I also rode around New Orleans in a limo. He told me hilarious and rather raunchy stories that I only wish I could remember.

My most memorable NATPE moment by far took place in San Francisco in 1993. I was walking through the convention floor and came upon the Sony Television booth to see Jerry Seinfeld there, greeting fans. I first met Jerry in 1981, as I wrote earlier, at a car wash in West Hollywood when I told him I was his biggest fan. Now, here I was again with Jerry, 12 years later, his TV show *Seinfeld* having very recently become wildly popular.

"Hey Jerry," I said, approaching him. We shook hands. "I met you back in 1981 at the Sunset Car Wash. It was the day you made your debut on *The Tonight Show*."

Jerry studied my face for a few seconds, then said, "Oh, I remember YOU! YOU wanted to be MY FRIEND!"

As if he'd suddenly received a wild jolt of electricity to his spine, he withdrew his hand from our handshake, turned, and waltzed off quickly.

While I did happen to get a photo of this brief encounter, all I can say about it in retrospect is that Jerry probably thought I was GAY when I asked him, "Can we be friends?" back in 1981. After all, we met at a car wash in West Hollywood–a predominantly gay community!

I worked with a number of other celebrities throughout the course of my years with the Duck. Among moments that stand out:

** <u>Robert Englund/Sam Kinison</u>: Robert Englund was the host of a nationally syndicated TV special airing around Halloween called, *The Horror Hall of Fame* (1990). The show was shot before a live studio audience up at Universal Studios.

As I'd worked with Robert a few years earlier he, of course, remembered me and we shared some laughs during breaks in the taping of the program.

The special guest comedian for that special was Sam Kinison. He was simply hilarious.

After the taping ended, there was a private party for the cast and crew at a nightclub on Universal CityWalk. I was in charge of the guest list at the front door. When Sam Kinison showed up, he was with two very attractive women whom I later learned were his future wife and his future sister-in-law.

"Hey Dude, can you get me into this party?" Sam asked me, rather shyly. "Of course, Sam!" I replied. "Are you kidding? You were the star of the show. Why don't you and your two lovely ladies come right this way." I ushered in the trio and Sam thanked me profusely.

(Decades later, I would have a brief, romantic encounter with one of those women!)

** Stephen Stills: I was the publicist for a company that developed a new film format called ShowScan, which was essentially high-definition imagery shot on film instead of videotape. The company was years ahead of its time, and the format was never widely adopted by the motion picture industry.

During an event at ShowScan for investors, I met Stephen Stills, who apparently owned a good deal of company stock. I mention this quick meet so I can say, officially, that I have in fact met Crosby AND Stills AND Nash.

** William Shatner: "Star Trek" icon William Shatner wrote a book about the future called *Tek Power* (1994) and to promote its publication, he hired Duck's PR Agency to handle the press for a live event he would be hosting at Universal Studios.

By this time, Peter, my friend from the Lee Solters' days and the guy who fronted the Jay Leno account for me, was now also working for the Duck. He and I were in charge of generating as much Southern California media coverage as possible, since the PR would be solely responsible for bringing the general public/fans of Shatner's to the event itself.

Peter and I got Shatner major print articles in all the top local newspapers, as well as several high-profile radio interviews. We felt assured that we'd gotten SO much press, in fact, that the event at Universal might even be sold out.

Cut to: Peter and I are standing at the doors of the Universal Sheraton Hotel, expecting swarms of people to plow through in efforts to ensure the best seats. A huge ballroom had been rented out for the affair, and there were many hundreds of chairs awaiting asses.

In an almost exact repeat of my experience with Steve Allen, NO PEOPLE for MILES were visible, with about 10 minutes to go before the start of the talk. Shatner came up to Peter and I and simply said, "Well?"

"Um, oh, they SHOULD be here soon, Mr. Shatner," I said.

"I see," he replied, walking briskly away.

In another true miracle, a sudden burst of humanity arrived exactly at the start of Shatner's talk, but it couldn't have been more than maybe 50 people, tops. The room probably held enough seats for 500. While the turnout was pretty embarrassing, Shatner and his fellow guest speakers did their best, were asked dozens of great questions, and seemed pleased with the results.

As he left the venue hours later, Shatner approached Peter and me. "Great job, fellows," he said. "You do good work."

Another potentially disastrous project that became just a little too close for comfort.

Another of Duck's clients was Orion Television, which was then producing a nationally syndicated TV series called, *CrimeWatch Tonight* (1989). The host of that show was Ike Pappas, who had been a CBS News correspondent for 25 years.

I spent a good deal of time with Ike, setting up photo sessions for him in "gritty" L.A. scenarios, places that would give the impression that crimes would likely occur there in real life.

The best part of my hours with Ike was one time when we had lunch. He began telling me about his incredible days in Dallas just after the JFK assassination in November, 1963. On the afternoon of November 22, Ike was one of dozens of journalists standing inside the hallway of the Dallas Police Department, and was able to ask Lee Harvey Oswald a few times, "Did you shoot the President?" Ike also asked Oswald the same question that evening, when Oswald was paraded out before the media. Oswald repeatedly denied the allegation.

Ike told me that evening he met Jack Ruby, who was handing out coffee and sandwiches to the media. "I still have the matchbook he gave me," Ike said, "from his Carousel Club. It read, 'Jack Ruby, Proprietor' and included his phone number."

On the morning of November 24 that year, Ike was among the throng of reporters present at the Dallas City Jail for Oswald's transfer to the County Jail. Working for WNEW A.M. Radio in New York at the time, Ike began his report as Oswald came into view: "Now the prisoner, wearing a black sweater, is being moved out toward an armored car, being led out by Captain Fritz." (Car horn sounds.) "There's the prisoner." Ike held his microphone out toward Oswald and asked, "Do you have anything to say in your defense?"

Seconds after Ike asked Oswald that question, Jack Ruby stepped out of the crowd of reporters with a pistol, moved in front of Oswald, and fired one shot into Oswald's abdomen. Ike's infamous broadcast became: "There's a shot! He's been shot! Lee Oswald has been shot!"

Ike later testified during Jack Ruby's trial.

As I've been a longtime JFK assassination researcher, Ike was the only person I ever met who eye-witnessed a good chunk of that historic weekend, first-hand.

** <u>Mary Tyler Moore</u>: Mary Tyler Moore starred in a GoodTimes video release entitled *Every Woman's Workout* (1994), and she was appearing as a special guest at an industry event in Las Vegas called the Video Software Dealers' Association (VSDA) Convention. I was hired to serve as her personal publicist for that day.

Mary was wonderful–warm, sweet and kind. I arranged for a number of media members to interview her at our booth. If I recall correctly, her husband, Dr. Robert Levine, was with us that day.

During a break from Mary, I walked around the VSDA show floor and happened to notice that directly in front of me, JERRY LEWIS was sitting at a small table, alone, signing autographs for a very long line that had formed to his right.

I halted suddenly in my tracks. JERRY LEWIS! I religiously watched his telethons for Muscular Dystrophy with my grandmother during my childhood and always cried when he sang "Walk On" at the end of each telecast. I heard no mention of the fact that this living legend would be appearing at the VSDA show. In fact, he looked rather bored sitting there, alone, just signing one autograph after the next without another soul to really talk to.

As I stood gawking, my mouth open, Jerry looked up at me. I waved at him, he winked back. This was the best I could do. I wish in retrospect that I'd grabbed Mary Tyler Moore and brought her over to Jerry to get a photo of the two of them together. That would have been a great PR opportunity–but unfortunately, I was too star-struck to pull that one off. Jerry Lewis was too big a childhood hero of mine to annoy.

** Kim Alexis: Duck's agency handled the PR for a national association that oversaw regulations for the newly burgeoning infomercial industry and, lucky me, I was chosen to handle that account. As infomercials literally sickened me, it was the hardest client I ever had to deal with without vomiting.

The only fun thing that came from this assignment was my time with Supermodel Kim Alexis, who was asked to record some audio content promoting the informercial industry. At the time, she had a line of beauty products she'd been hawking on TV, so she was the ideal candidate for this task.

Kim and I spent a day together in an audio recording studio in Hollywood and took turns revising and re-writing the verbal text she needed to read and record. In addition to her remarkable beauty, she was super funny and sweet. I only wish I had my photo taken with her that afternoon.

** Lorenzo Lamas: Actor Lorenzo Lamas was the star of a low budget movie called, *Snake Eater* (1989), that was produced by one of Duck's clients, a company called MovieStore Entertainment.

At the photo shoot to create the PR image that would promote this film (called "key art" in the industry), I stood next to Lorenzo, perhaps the most incredibly handsome man I've ever seen in my entire life, to this day. He was 6'2" and simply towered over me.

While next to him, I said aloud to all assembled, "Lorenzo, you're so good looking, standing next to you, I'm not sure you and I are members of the same species!"

** Lois Laurel: GoodTimes Home Video was releasing the classic Laurel and Hardy film, *The March of the Wooden Soldiers*

(1934) to concur with the 60th anniversary of that movie's original release, but this time the film had been colorized instead of appearing in black and white. Stan Laurel's daughter, Lois, was my contact for this project. I spent a few days with her at her home in the San Fernando Valley. She had a small Laurel and Hardy museum in a separate building in her backyard, filled with remarkable L&H memorabilia. She was incredibly sweet and kind, and I enjoyed setting up interviews for her immensely. Lois alone represented the only 1930s era-related client project I ever worked on.

** Tom Hanks (again): I had to produce a press conference at the Four Seasons Hotel in Beverly Hills for one of Duck's clients, a company called Tribune Entertainment. The most prominent, L.A.-based writers who covered television would be interviewing the president of that company in a private meeting room. While I stood outside in front of the hotel, awaiting my media guests to arrive, Tom Hanks walked up to me.

"Hey Tom, are you here for the Tribune event?" I asked him, baffled.

"No, no, no. I don't know what that is," he replied. "I'm here to do some press for my new film."

I said, "That rock and roll movie? I saw the trailer–it looked great!"

He replied, "It's called *That Thing You Do* (1996), and thanks."

I added, "I played drums in the '60s and '70s, and your movie looks like it really captures the excitement of playing rock during that era."

Tom said, "That was my goal. I hope other music fans like you enjoy it as much."

Such a good guy.

Not all of the celebrities I met during those years were work-related. During my era with the Duck (1989-1996), I also encountered these famous folks:

- ** <u>Buddy Rich</u>: Buddy Rich was the greatest drummer who ever lived. Period. One day, Kim and I were shopping for a child's birthday gift at a little toy store on Melrose Avenue in West Hollywood. As we were browsing for gift ideas, I happened to see Buddy Rich by himself, playing a small child's xylophone with two small, elongated mallets. I was amazed. "Mr. Rich?" I said, "My name is Dan. I've seen you in concert several times. I'm a drummer, too. You're the most remarkable musician I've ever seen."

    His reply, "I know." He continued to tinker.

    I mentioned to him that a friend of mine named Dave had once been one of his trombone players and had written an arrangement for him of the song "On Broadway."

    "Dave? Yeah, I remember him. Good guy," Buddy replied.

    That was the whole encounter, but for me, those few seconds were hugely memorable.

    Buddy died shortly after that "meet cute."

- ** <u>Olsen Twins</u>: When my two kids were very small and after my divorce, I had them on weekends. It was always "fun time at Daddy's house." We went to the movies, the park, ate pizza and ice cream, rented a million movies, and often went bowling. One day at the bowling alley behind Jerry's Deli in Studio City, the three of us found ourselves standing next to the Olsen Twins–Ashley and Mary-Kate (Drew Carey was in the next lane over.) My daughter was a big fan of theirs, so I asked them for autographs for my little girl. One of them was super sweet; the other, not. I don't remember which was which.

- ** <u>Cheech Marin</u>: As mentioned earlier, I once spent a day with Tommy Chong. One morning at the Duck's agency,

I happened to walk into a colleague's office to see Cheech Marin sitting there, alone. I introduced myself and told him I'd seen he and Tommy perform live in concert at Asbury Park's Convention Hall in the early 70's.

"Wow, man, you go way back," he said, adding, "Were we funny?"

So, yeah, I met both Cheech AND Chong, and yes, they were very funny.

** John Landis: I took my kids to a "Three Stooges" Convention in Burbank and there, the audience members were shown various rare film clips of the Stooges in action. As my son loved Moe, he was particularly enthralled. Sitting next to us was Director John Landis of *Animal House* (1978) and *The Blues Brothers* (1980) with his kids, too. John and I spoke briefly about our mutual love for those wacky, zany guys who could destroy each other's faces with large tools without ever becoming physically harmed.

** Tawny Kitaen: I was sitting at a car wash in Hollywood waiting for my car to be finished, when sex symbol Tawny Kitaen sat next to me. I'd heard a rumor around that time that she was dating Jerry Seinfeld, so I asked her.

"Well, I'm not supposed to talk about him," she whispered. "We've seen each other a bit, but I think he's more into himself than he is into me!"

We chuckled and I got her a cup of hot chocolate to help pass the time.

I was sorry to hear of her recent passing.

** Max Weinberg: I met Bruce Springsteen's drummer, Max Weinberg, at a fundraising event being held at PickFair, the very famous and lavish estate in Bel-Air, California, once owned by Mary Pickford and Douglas Fairbanks. When we spoke, I told him that I worked with Bruce in '73 at The Sunshine Inn, to which Max responded, "Oh yeah? That's a year before my time." I continued, telling him that I learned (through my good friend Steve in New York, who in turn was good friends with Steve Van Zandt, Bruce's best friend and fellow guitarist with The E Street Band) that Max had one of Ringo Starr's bass drumheads featuring the words The Beatles framed on a wall in his house and that he had a small spotlight shining directly upon it.

"How on earth could you possibly know that?" Max asked me, stunned.

"My spies are everywhere," I jokingly replied.

** Jerry Springer: This one is Duck-related. Jerry Springer apparently had finished a meeting with the Duck and I happened to meet him inside the men's room down the hall from the Duck's offices.

We wound up peeing side-by-side, and all I could think of to say was "Jerry! Jerry! Jerry!" like the idiots who used to appear in his audiences would chant.

His response? "Is that really the best you can do?"

I replied, "Well it was either that, or 'We simply have to stop meeting this way.'"

Jerry answered, "Option # 2 is definitely funnier."

My last client at the Duck's agency was one I brought into the company myself. A long-lost friend of mine from the Playboy Channel days called me out of the clear blue sky and told me he was producing some new video content for Actress Dixie Carter, best known for her role as Julia Sugarbaker in the hit TV series, *Designing Women* (1986).

I met with Dixie, we hit it off instantly, and she hired me to become the publicist for her newly-launched television production company which she called, "Little Lambs Productions" -a reference to her term of endearment for her children.

I represented Dixie for several months. She was super nice and I enjoyed her greatly. One time she invited me over to her home for a holiday party. There I met her very famous husband, Hal Holbrook, and her dear friend and fellow *Designing Women* co-star, Jean Smart. Jean hugged me when we met, pressing her remarkable bosom hard against me. She said to Dixie, "This one's cute!"

I have to admit, I got a bit turned on during that luscious hug!

I'd be remiss closing out this chapter without talking about my friendship and collaboration with my fellow publicist, Peter, my "front man" with Jay Leno. Peter and I, while both begrudgingly accepting our plights as "Pub-la-cysts," have had to keep at bay, against our wishes, our true dreams and goals in life: becoming comedy writers for television sitcoms.

For the many years we worked side by side for the Duck, Peter and I cranked out a number of "spec" scripts for hit TV shows. A spec script is a writing sample based on the characters, premise and tone of a show that could possibly become an actual episode.

The first script Peter and I co-wrote was a spec for *Seinfeld* which, at that time, was NOT YET a popular show! During its first year, the series almost got cancelled.

Our script was entitled "The Pimple Problem." The premise was that Jerry gets a pimple on his nose and as long as that pimple remains prominent, Jerry "loses his funny." He is no longer able to make people laugh while doing standup comedy.

I sent that script to Sid Caesar's manager, who remained a friend of mine and who, I knew, was friendly with the executive producers of the *Seinfeld* series. He told me he would submit it for us, and he did. Peter and I were thrilled.

A few weeks later, Peter and I returned from lunch to find a phone message on my desk that said, "Please call back J. Seinfeld at such and such an 818-area code phone number." Since I knew that *Seinfeld* was shot in Studio City, which had an 818-area code, I felt my entire body quiver. Peter and I looked at each other and felt that THIS WAS IT! This was going to be our moment in time that would extract us from the misery of promoting the accomplishments of others and send us on our path to finally becoming TV comedy writing kings!!

I called the phone number back. It belonged to a guy named JOE STEINFELD, who had a banners and flags promotional company. He wanted to know if I needed any promotional banners and flags for any of my clients.

Peter and I considered weeping.

Peter and I continued writing more spec scripts during our years together, including those for the TV shows *Mad About You* (1992), *Herman's Head* (1991), *Wings* (1990), the afore-mentioned *Empty Nest,* and our own original concept called *Party of Two*, about two best friends who run a calamitous events production business.

Nothing ever happened with any of those spec scripts.

At the end of our time together with the Duck, Peter and I managed to get a phone interview with the Executive Producer of *The New WRKP in Cincinnati* (1991), which was an updated version of the earlier series of that name from the 1970s. This producer told Peter and I by phone that if we could pitch him "a bunch of funny ideas" for his remake program, he would offer us a writing contract!

Peter and I spent every waking moment of the next week cranking out storyline after storyline. We felt each would have been hysterically funny. I think we came up with 25 altogether. When we phoned this producer back, he told us he was going to fax us a letter of agreement BEFORE he could commit to either buying any of our storyline ideas or hiring us to become staff writers.

Since this was pre-computer days, Peter and I received a 20-page mega-fax that outlined the various possibilities this producer might be willing to offer us, IF he liked our original concepts.

Peter and I shed tears of joy as we both signed the massive fax and returned it to him for his approval. We truly believed this was going to be our exit from PR Purgatory and serve as our launching pad into TV writing fame and fortune.

Alas, we never heard back from that producer again. He dropped off the face of the globe. And since neither Peter nor I ever watched any episodes of *The New WRKP in Cincinnati*, we'll never know if that shithead stole any of our ideas outright.

Chapter Eight

1996-2009

ASBURY LAUNCHES / ARNOLD SNARLS / BIGGIE SMALLS GETS KILLED / JACK BLACK IS STONED / JENNA JAMESON GETS NAKED / JIMMY KIMMEL IS MY NEIGHBOR / A GO-GO WRITES LOVELACE / RENE RUSSO WANTS MY BONE

I'd surpassed seven years of working for the Duck—a Napoleonic little prick who once threatened to punch me in the head in the men's room when I neglected to mention to him that that same day was the birthday of one of his clients. I could barely stomach the thought of even looking at his heinous face any longer.

He had fired my friend Peter over a very minor incident in the recent past, and my hatred for him began building up to a climax; something big needed to happen soon. In June, 1996, a series of remarkable things took place that changed the course of my life forever. They were:

> ** I was dating a woman named Elyse who owned a ceramics company that crafted beautiful, customized dishes, plates, bowls, cups, etc., for her high-end clients. One night, while I was complaining about the Duck to her, she simply said,

"Why don't you start your own company?" At the time the notion was purely alien to me, as I didn't have a clue as to how to even begin that process.

** Elyse asked me, "Dan, how come you never smile?"

I replied, "I can't." My 40th birthday was fast approaching, and it was at this point in my life I realized there must be something wrong with me medically–I was incapable of smiling. I looked in the Yellow Pages (no Internet back then) and found a psychiatrist in the San Fernando Valley. I met with him, told him my life story, and he was stunned.

He said, "Dan, I'm incredibly impressed with you. You've had clinical depression for most of your life and in spite of that, you've accomplished so many big things. You're like a diabetic who never took insulin!"

The man handed me a prescription for Prozac. One week later, not only was I smiling, I felt like the weight of the world had been lifted from my shoulders.

** I asked the Duck for a promotion; he said, "Okay."

About two weeks later, I got my next paycheck and it was the same as it had been for the two years previous. I went into the CFO's office and asked her, "Where's my raise?"

She replied, "You got your title promotion to Senior Vice President," she snarled. "That's it. Now get the fuck out of my office."

I stood there stunned, staring at the woman with utter hatred. "Are you serious?" I asked.

"Yep," she replied.

While leaving her office, I vowed to myself in that moment that somehow, someday, I would get my revenge on them both.

** One early evening a few days later, the Duck and I were meeting with two executives from a local TV channel who were seeking PR representation for their nighttime newscast.

For what seemed like the one-millionth time, I had to listen to my short squat boss pontificate about his life story, his years on Wall Street, how he was "discovered" by some major Hollywood big shot, etc. I could have recounted his life story myself, as every time he told it, it was the same exact verbal vomit, verbatim.

As I suffered through this meeting in my suit and neck-constraining tie, I "heard" a "heavenly voice" emanating from the enormous chandelier hanging above us in the restaurant at the Beverly Hills Four Seasons Hotel. Truly, I did.

The "voice" spoke unto me: "DAN! START YOUR OWN BUSINESS!!"

"Huh?" I actually said out loud, staring up at the chandelier. The others at the table looked at me. "Oh, sorry," I said, "I just remembered something."

While my boss continued his masturbatory self-aggrandizing, my heart began to race. "Holy shit," I said to myself, "I've had a revelation from God." Pretending to take notes earlier during the meeting, I had now been "spun off" into an entirely new direction. I turned my notepad to a clean page and began writing down all of the clients I was representing, and what they were paying my shithead boss to be represented—by ME—through HIS agency.

I immediately realized if I simply represented these same clients FROM MY HOME, I could more than triple my income overnight! At this point, I stood up while Duck was still speaking, chuckled, then said, "Sorry guys, I gotta go," and dashed off without further explanation. It was one of the great moments of my entire life.

That night from home, I called each client I'd been representing. Every single one of them told me they would continue to utilize my services, regardless of where I was based.

Said one, "I'd follow you to Botswana."

The next day I lined up two business partners; one who provided start-up cash, the other an office building in Hollywood, along with phone lines, a computer system, an accountant and a lawyer.

In less than 48 hours, I'd conceived and was ready to launch, a brand-new company. When my partners asked what I wanted to name this new entity, I said, "I grew up in Asbury Park, New Jersey. I'm gonna call it 'Asbury Communications.'"

About to earn 100% (instead of 10%) of the same money that had been going to an asshole boss for far too many years, I now stood at the cusp of earning well over seven times the annual salary that my father—a genius who invented technology preventing World War III—ever made in his best year.

Before I could give the Duck notice that I was leaving, I had to plan carefully, as I knew that several of his previous employees who'd left to start their own PR agencies had been physically tossed out of his offices. I spent the next solid three months in preparation for my departure–I squirreled out of Duck's agency dozens of my work files, computer discs, office supplies, rolodex cards, reference books, etc., taking only a few items home with me at a time each night. More difficult was removing my personal artworks from the walls and my office chair–I had to replicate these items with others floating around so as not to raise any suspicion.

My favorite part of this time frame was when I would stay at the office late at night, photocopying lists of important media contacts. Doing this, I felt I was living out real-life scenes from the Tom Cruise movie, *The Firm* (1993), when he and Holly Hunter were nervously copying dozens of Mob clientele files from their law firm! I was building up a stash of important PR agency intel that I'd need once I was officially on my own.

Finally, the day came in mid-September, '96, when I was ready to tell Duck *adios*. I was supposed to go have lunch with Pamela Anderson right after I did that, in fact, on the set of *Baywatch!* (1989) True story! One of my fellow publicists from Duck's agency represented that show and invited me to meet the sex icon that same day.

Duck walked past my office. I called out to him, "Hey, Duck, can you come in here for a second?" He entered and I closed the door. I knew the only way I could get out of there unhurt would be to lie.

"Duck, I'm leaving. I recently met two men at my gym who want to start a new production company and they want me to run their PR. I'll be a full partner with them. It'll be far more money than I make here, now."

Duck was stunned. He stared out the window, speechless. He'd just lost two other longtime publicists a few weeks earlier. I was about to become Number Three.

After I'd worked there seven and a half years, giving this prick blood, sweat and tears, not to mention hundreds of thousands of dollars from MY clients, did he even ask me to stay? Did he even make me a counteroffer? No.

"Can you give me two weeks?" he asked, meekly. All I wanted to do at that moment was split, have lunch with Pam Anderson, then head over to my new office building in Hollywood which was already set up and awaiting my arrival.

For some God-only-knows reason, I said, "Okay, two weeks."

He left my office and I realized that in spite of my utter hatred for this guy, his pitiful reaction to my announcement still struck a chord in me. I realized giving him two-weeks-notice (not that he deserved it) was simply the right thing for me to do.

Clearly, I had Stockholm Syndrome.

I stayed in my office that day, and for the next two weeks I continued cleaning things up and training my assistant who would soon become my replacement.

I remain so pissed at myself! I gave up lunch with Pam Anderson for the Duck??

One of my new business partners had asked me to hire his brother-in-law and train him how to become a publicist. I had to agree to this caveat even before I met the guy, who'd soon become one of my best friends. Mikey at the time was a high school teacher, but he hated that profession and was desperate to play some role within the entertainment industry. He and I actually didn't meet until the very first day I launched my company, October 1, 1996, at a small but funky office building on Cole Avenue in the heart of Hollywood. The iconic Hollywood sign was visible through my new front window.

Mikey was a remarkable character, extremely funny and goofy, but he also had a dark side if crossed. He grew to love me like "the brother he never had." With my business quickly growing exponentially, I became enthralled and spiritually uplifted by my new life.

During the first months of Asbury Communications, I built up a client base that was beyond my wildest dreams. I had five of Hollywood's top special effects companies, one of the world's leading designers of theme parks, the world's most successful motion graphics/design company, film festivals, live performers, music studios, and a host of others. The workload was instantly overwhelming, and I quickly hired another five employees to share it all with me, including one publicist friend based in New York.

My first client under the Asbury banner was a videogame called "Creature Crunch," an interactive DVD that featured the voices of Martin Short and Eugene Levy as a boy and a mad scientist trying to evade a series of evil monsters. I spent some time with both of those comedy icons during their voice-over production sessions. Martin was sweet, funny and kind; Eugene was solemn, serious and a bit dark when he wasn't performing in character.

During our first month in business, Mikey scored an invitation for an event at the Beverly Hills Friars' Club in honor of Milton Berle, that would feature an appearance by Arnold Schwarzenegger. We went to the event together; all of the tables were arranged so as to be surrounded by a boxing ring in the center of the room. There was some kind of boxing exhibition that evening, for charity I think, but I can't remember.

My goal that evening was to get Arnold's autograph for my son, Jordan, age eight at the time, who loved *The Terminator* (1984) movies. I'd come prepared. I had with me a photo of Arnold from *Terminator 2: Judgment Day* (1991) and a white marking pen that would allow an autograph to appear legibly over the rather dark photograph.

After the boxing match ended, I stood and walked over to Arnold, who was sitting at a table at the polar opposite side of the room from me. There were two enormous bodyguards standing right behind him, each with small earpieces sticking out from their heads. I was a bit nervous but assumed since this was a very low-pressure environment, getting Arnold's autograph would be a snap and take two seconds.

"Hey Arnold, my name is Dan," I said as I walked up to and behind his left shoulder. "My son Jordan loves *The Terminator* and I was wondering if you'd be able to give him your autograph?"

Arnold's bodyguards moved in closer toward me. He backed them off with his hand, without a word. Arnold looked up at me and if looks could kill, I would have died on the spot. His face started turning red and smoke, almost literally, started to shoot out from his ears. He growled and snarled at me, "GRRRRR!!" noises I'd never heard emanate from another human being. He sounded like a wild animal about to be caged and knew it.

I wasn't expecting this. My palms started getting clammy and I was a bit worried about the bodyguards. "Please, Arnold, he REALLY LOVES *The Terminator* and it would mean so much to him to get your autograph. Please??" I was now begging.

Arnold's face, demeanor, and animal sounds didn't abate for one second. His upper lip was curled and it looked like he wanted to eat me.

I was now completely determined to accomplish this mission. "Come on, Arnold, it'll take you two seconds. It's for my son. He's eight years old! How hard could this be?"

Finally realizing I was a man on a mission, Arnold grabbed the white marking pen and photo from my hands. He wrote, "To Jordan, best wishes, Arnold Schwarzenegger" over the image of him as *The Terminator*, riding a motorcycle and holding a shotgun.

Handing the photo and pen back to me, he simply continued to growl. "Thanks man!" I said, gleeful that I scored the item for my son. "He'll love this!"

Arnold never said one English word to me. I never in my life saw anyone angrier at having to perform such a small task. My son loved the autograph, and today it hangs, framed, in his home in Anchorage, Alaska.

One year into the life of Asbury Communications, we got a call from a man who was creating and producing the Hollywood Film Festival and the Hollywood Film Awards. This guy turned out to become a colossal asshole, so I won't mention him by name, but Mikey and I met with him and he "hired" us (for NO fee, I might add) to handle the PR for the 1997 launch of those two productions. He insisted that our freebie participation in these high-profile events would help us generate a ton of new business.

It didn't, but I did get a few stories out of this work. And an ad in the *New York Times.*

The 1997 premiere Hollywood Film Awards honored Kirk Douglas with a Lifetime Achievement Award. The event was held at the Hollywood Roosevelt Hotel (rumored to be haunted by Marilyn Monroe's ghost).

The ballroom of the hotel was packed that night and as I made my rounds while awaiting the arrival of Kirk Douglas, I met Kirstie Alley of *Cheers* (1982); Bob Barker, who I wound up peeing side-by-side with in the men's room; and Graham Nash, again, who remembered me from the taping of his TV show a few years earlier.

I also met a beautiful blonde who I recognized—Lydia Cornell, one of the co-stars of the Ted Knight hit comedy TV series, *Too Close for Comfort* (1980). Lydia and I had instant chemistry and I felt sparks. I told her: "I'd really love to stay here and flirt with you all night, but I have to go get Kirk Douglas. Can I get your phone number?" She gave me her card and I was kind of high on that "score" for a while. (But when I called her days later, she blew me off, telling me she was going through a terrible divorce and had no time for dating.)

A long black limo pulled up into the parking lot of the Hollywood Roosevelt Hotel, and Kirk Douglas came out. Only 18 months before the first annual Hollywood Film Awards took place, Kirk had suffered a stroke, which greatly impaired his speaking abilities. Nevertheless, the great "Spartacus" himself walked up to me and I introduced myself, telling him what an honor it was to meet him.

I had to lead Mr. Douglas back behind the hotel and past the huge trash dumpsters, so he could make his appearance from a rear door of the banquet room and surprise everyone by walking onto the stage from that entryway. As we passed the dumpsters, the horrid smell was overwhelming.

"Sorry, Mr. Douglas for the stink!" I said to him.

He replied, "What are you saying?"

Again, I apologized for the rancid smell that greeted us during our short walk.

"That's okay, kid," the great man replied. "I've smelled worse!"

When Kirk entered the ballroom, he received an instant standing ovation. While his award acceptance speech was rather difficult to understand, it didn't really matter. One of Hollywood's greatest legends was with us, in person, and that thrill alone was enough to carry the night.

One year later, my agency again handled the PR for the Second Annual Hollywood Film Awards, which honored Shelley Winters with its Lifetime Achievement Award. For that show, Mikey and I escorted Shelley from backstage onto the stage itself. This time the event was being held at the much larger ballroom at the Beverly Hilton Hotel. As we escorted her, the famed actress promptly farted in our faces, before she strode to the microphone to get her award.

"Did you just fart?" I asked Mikey.

"No, I thought that was you!"

Realizing Shelley Winters gassed us, Mikey and I collapsed with laughter and had to run away from the stage, stifling our laughter so as to keep from interrupting the proceedings.

I was running around like a chicken without a head earlier that night, ensuring that all the media members in attendance were being taken care of, when a man I knew who worked in-house for one of my clients approached me and introduced me to his girlfriend, Actress Lesley Ann Warren. I knew who she was, of course, and found her even more attractive in person than I imagined. He asked me if I could walk Lesley through the press line so someone would accompany her while she was being interviewed. I agreed. We started off together doing a few quick radio interviews. However, I was suddenly needed backstage-one of my colleagues called me on a walkie-talkie to request my presence there. I had to apologize to Lesley for leaving her alone while I dashed off.

The next day Lesley's boyfriend called me, screaming at me for leaving her alone! I told him, "I'm not her personal publicist. I was there to rep the EVENT and I was needed backstage. YOU should have stayed with her, my friend."

That man and I never spoke to each other again.

The wife of the man who produced the Hollywood Film Festival and the Hollywood Film Awards was a lovely and beautiful model named Janice Pennington, whom I remembered from the '70s, having seen her layout in a *Playboy* magazine. During the second film awards event, I asked Janice if I could bring my two kids (then ages 10 and 8) to see a taping of the TV game show she appeared on, *The Price is Right* (1972). She told me yes, anytime, just let her know and she'd leave our names at the security gate at CBS Studios.

A few weeks later, I took my kids to a taping of *The Price is Right* and we got the VIP treatment. We hung out backstage with Bob Barker (there's a photo in this book of the four of us together) and we had a little tour of the set before the live audience entered the studio.

During the actual taping of that episode, my son, my daughter, and I were standing off to the side of the stage in the wings. Once when they went to a commercial break, Bob Barker asked my son Jordan and my daughter Anjuli if they'd like to come out onstage to "help him." They said yes, of course, so my kids were led to center stage, with microphones. If I recall correctly, they were asked to pull some tickets out of a bowl and read off the winning numbers. (I don't remember what the prizes were.)

It was a great thrill for me to see my kids, both big fans of *The Price is Right*, so happy. This became an instant classic Harary Family moment.

During the first 14 years of Asbury Communications, I was invited to attend numerous Hollywood events, and was also asked to handle the public relations for other such events. The list is long, but the highlights included:

** <u>VIBE Magazine Party</u>: A friend of mine who owned an event production company invited me to attend a huge party for Quincy Jones' *Vibe Magazine*, which was being held at the Petersen Automotive Museum on Wilshire Boulevard. Just moments after I arrived, I saw a short, stout, African American man walk past me. He had several enormous gold chains around his neck and two large bodyguards accompanied him. As he walked by, I knew he was "somebody famous" but, as I never followed hip-hop music stars, simply did not know who he was.

As far as I could tell, I was the only "white guy" at this party, which took up a few floors of the museum building. I never in my life, before or since, saw so many INCREDIBLY GORGEOUS African American women assembled in one place at one time! I felt like I'd entered Black Heaven.

When I was ready to leave a few hours later, the valet guy pulled up my car, I hopped in and drove off, listening to the news on my radio. Maybe about ten minutes after I'd left, I heard on the radio a report that rap music star Notorious B.I.G. had JUST BEEN SHOT AND KILLED while waiting for the valet to bring him <u>his</u> car outside of the Petersen Museum! The date: March 9, 1997.

The large Black man who'd walked past me when I first arrived was Notorious B.I.G., aka Biggie Smalls! I stood at the exact spot where he had been assassinated by a drive-by shooter JUST TEN MINUTES EARLIER!

His murder still gives me the willies, even to this day.

** The "Genii Awards": The wife of one of my clients had been elected to serve as the new President of the American Women in Radio and Television Association–now known as the Alliance for Women in Media–an organization that advances the impact of women working within electronic media. Each year, AWRT handed out their "Genii" Awards to outstanding women in the broadcasting industry.

For this particular event, two women I'd had "close encounters" with many years earlier–Brooke Shields and Victoria Principal–were both to be honored. While I was unable to spend any time with Victoria, I did chat briefly with Brooke and reminded her that she, her mother and I watched *The Blue Lagoon* together back during the summer of 1980, at Columbia Pictures in New York.

"Wow, really?" she replied. "You have some memory! I can't believe you remembered that!"

Ah, Brooke, you will always be memorable to me!

** The World Animation Celebration: In 1997, my agency was tasked to run the public relations for that year's annual World Animation Celebration, a huge gathering of members of Hollywood's animation production community and lovers of that art form. We ran the press room for that year's event, which was held at the Pasadena Convention Center, and during the course of that week I met both Matt Groening, creator of *The Simpsons* (1989), and Yeardley Smith, who performs the voice of "Lisa Simpson."

** "Star Trek: The Experience": One of my clients was a major designer of theme parks and attractions around the world. As such, I was involved in the PR for the grand opening of *Star Trek: The Experience* (1998), a new, highly interactive, Star Trek-themed attraction based adjacent to the Hilton Hotel in Las Vegas.

There was a black-tie, red carpet grand opening for this event, which generated a tremendous amount of television publicity. After arranging for my client to sit down for several interviews, I was able to schmooze around during the opening night party. My son, Jordan, who was about 10 at the time, joined me in his little tuxedo as we chatted with Nichelle Nichols ("Lt. Uhura"), LeVar Burton ("Geordi"), and Majel Rodenberry, widow of *Star Trek* creator, Gene Rodenberry.

** <u>Promax Conference</u>: Many of my initial clients with Asbury Communications were advertising, graphic design and/or marketing agencies that promoted television programs. Each year they attended the Promax Conference–a gathering designed for television marketing executives.

I don't recall the year, but during a Promax event at the New York Hilton Hotel, I was invited to a private party that featured musical performances by Christopher Cross and by the band America.

When Christopher Cross was leaving, I told him, "Every single time I hear you sing 'When you get lost between the Moon and New York City,' it brings tears to my eyes."

He stopped in his tracks, smiled broadly, hugged me so hard he lifted me into the air and said, "Really, man? Wow. Thank you for telling me that. That means so much to me!"

Nicest guy, ever.

When the two founders of *America*–Dewey Bunnell and Gerry Beckley–were leaving, I approached them and asked them who handled their PR.

Dewey said, "No one at the moment, why don't you give me your card?"

I did and they left. I never heard from them again but for a moment in time, I thought perhaps, maybe, I would become the PR guy for a group that enjoyed so many hit songs during the '70s.

** Israel Film Festival: I was hired to handle media for the 1998 Israel Film Festival, held each year in Beverly Hills. One of that year's honored guests whom I met was Actress/Singer Lainie Kazan, telling her, "My mother loves you."

She replied, "Tell your mother, I love her, too!"

** Race to Space: I had a client who built costumes and props for outer space movies, basing their materials on real-life NASA specifications. The company, called WonderWorks, supplied a Space Shuttle interior for a motion picture called *Race to Space* (2001), starring James Woods. I was invited to the premiere of the film, met James, and took photos of him standing with my clients next to a mounted poster of the film in the lobby of the theatre.

** Visual Effects Society: Many of my earliest clients were top companies working within Hollywood's visual effects industry. As a result, I was asked to handle the PR for the launch of the Visual Effects Society's very first, annual "VES" Awards dinner. Among the honorees that evening was legendary filmmaker Ray Harryhausen, whose stop motion animations brought life to such famous movies as *Mighty Joe Young* (1949), *The 7th Voyage of Sinbad* (1958), and *Jason and the Argonauts* (1963), to cite a few.

After the dinner, Mr. Harryhausen asked me to help him carry many of the small, fragile, iconic props he had on display during the dinner. There were several paper bags filled with these irreplaceable little models. I actually prayed to God while walking them to his car that I wouldn't trip and smash any of them along the way!

** Groundbreaking Ceremony for the "MarvelMania" Restaurant: I was hired to help embellish the PR efforts of Marvel Comics Creator/Legend Stan Lee in his role as a special advisor for a first-of-its-kind new restaurant called "MarvelMania." Located at Universal Studios in Hollywood, the new themed entertainment venue was going to enthrall diners who ate there by presenting them with the experience of "living inside a comic book" while interacting with characters like Spider-Man, The Hulk and some of the X-Men. I helped entice media to attend the groundbreaking ceremony for the site of the new building. Stan Lee and others were photographed with shovels digging dirt. Stan seemed like a very genial fellow–I only spoke with him for a few minutes. We generated a good deal of media coverage for this ceremony. Once the restaurant opened, about six months later, it didn't do well. It closed a few years later. Of course, this was long before the huge explosion in pop culture that the modern day "Marvel Universe" of characters has bestowed upon the world. Now, Marvel films regularly gross over one billion dollars each from the global box office.

** *Battlestar Galactica*: One of my clients built and sold exact replicas of every famous robot featured in movies and TV shows, beginning with "Robbie the Robot" from *Forbidden Planet* (1956), and including others such as "B9" from *Lost in Space* (1965) and "R2D2" and "C3PO" from *Star Wars* (1977). His name was Fred Barton, but he was known throughout the entertainment industry as "The Robot Man."

The Robot Man was asked to provide one of his large "Cylon" robots to appear on the red carpet during a media and fan event for the cast of the hit TV series, *Battlestar Galactica* (2004). The event, a new season premiere, was being held at a famous L.A. landmark, the Cinerama Dome theater on Sunset Boulevard.

The entire cast of *Battlestar Galactica* showed up that night and, while standing adjacent to Fred's "Cylon" robot, I met Edward James Olmos, telling him how much my son, Jordan, loved his show. He was intrigued that my son moved to Alaska and asked me questions about Anchorage.

I also spoke with Mary McDonnell, to whom I said, "I used to have a girlfriend who looked very much like you!"

She replied, "Well, lucky you!"

I next met series star Katee Sackhoff, who stopped to pose next to the "Cylon" robot for photos. I tried "flirting" with her for a while and told her how much I enjoyed her as an actor, asking what upcoming projects she had. She told me about her soon-to-air episodes of *Nip/Tuck* (2003) and *24* (2001), two additional shows I greatly enjoyed.

While I was talking with Katee, blonde bombshell Trisha Helfer, another *Battlestar Galactica* star, left her limousine and walked directly in front of us, neither stopping to pose with the "Cylon," nor to talk with Katee. Trisha was so REMARKABLY attractive, Katee watched as I simply gawked at her while she sashayed past us. I found it hard to breathe, and gasped (Celebrity Woman Gasp # 3.) The assembled paparazzi photographers also went wild, flashbulbs blinding everyone in their wake.

Realizing I'd stopped talking to her, Katee said, "I know, she's hot. I get it. What am I? Chopped liver?"

I replied, "Katee, the two of you are equally stunning."

She knew I didn't really mean that, but she seemed to appreciate the gesture.

** The "Saturn Awards": Every year, Hollywood's Academy of Science Fiction, Fantasy and Horror presents their annual "Saturn Awards" event, honoring films, TV shows, performers and others who work within those three genres. The Robot Man invited me to attend the 2008 event, where I met gorgeous brunette Actress Claudia Black, star of TV's *Stargate SG-1* (1997); and the very lovely Summer Glau, then starring in TV's *Terminator: The Sarah Connor Chronicles* (2008). I got Summer's autograph for my son, Jordan, still a huge fan of all things *Terminator*, as I'd mentioned earlier.

** <u>Another Hollywood Film Festival Awards</u>: I bumped into the founder of the Hollywood Film Festival Awards at a restaurant, years after I first met and worked with him. He invited me to attend the next such event. I remember there were a number of major movie stars there that night, including Leonardo DiCaprio and John Travolta, but I did not meet them.

I did, however, literally bump into Scarlett Johansson at the end of that evening, while people were leaving the Beverly Hilton ballroom to retrieve their cars. Scarlett was so incredibly sexually alluring she caused me to gasp, literally gasp, while I shook her hand. (For those of you counting: Bo Derek, Gasp One; Shannon Tweed, Gasp Two; Trisha Helfer, Gasp Three; Scarlett Johansson, Gasp Four.)

I asked Scarlett what she was working on. She told me about an upcoming film called, *The Island* (2005), in which she co-starred with Ewan McGregor. We spoke for several minutes, but I couldn't really focus on her words. Her charisma was so powerful it was hard for me to simply keep a straight face (although she did reek of cigarettes).

** <u>"Smile"</u>: One of my clients was an advertising agency that handled promotional campaigns for motion pictures. This agency had been assigned the campaign behind a small, delicate art film called *Smile* (2005). The premise of *Smile* follows a young teenage girl named Katie (Mika Boorem) who learns about "Doctor's Gift"–a program that provides worldwide medical assistance to those in need. She is then informed about Lin, a Chinese teenager in need of facial surgery to repair a severe deformity. Katie joins the program on one of its trips to China and convinces Lin to have the life-altering surgery she so desperately needs.

A few days before that film's premiere, I spent several hours with *Saturday Night Live* Comedienne Cheri Oteri, an adorable and wonderful woman who was one of the film's stars. I booked Cheri for a live radio interview with Tim Conway, Jr., at KLSX FM radio, and after the interview, we chatted for a bit about her role in *Smile*. A few nights later, we held the premiere of *Smile* at the ArcLight Theatres in Hollywood, in conjunction with the real-life charity Operation Smile. On the red carpet that night, I met the film's stars Linda Hamilton (icicles–not an especially warm woman); Sean Astin (the only star from the cast who insisted on being paid to attend the premiere and having a limo sent for him, round-trip); and young teen actress Mika Boorem, while also grabbing a quick "hello" with Cheri Oteri once again. Later in the evening, during the after-party, I met Neil Giraldo, Pat Benatar's husband and the famed guitarist with her band, along with the couple's cute young daughter, Hayley Giraldo, age 20 at the time. I told Neil he was one of my very favorite guitarists from the '80s, and we spoke of his musical contributions to *Smile's* score.

** <u>*Jesus Christ Superstar: Original Cast Reunion* (2006)</u>: An Asbury client was producing and directing a one-performance only, live theater play of *Jesus Christ Superstar* (1971), reuniting the original cast members of the 1973 movie. Jack Black, as special guest star, portrayed the role of King Herod.

During rehearsals for the show, I spent some time chatting with Ted Neely, Yvonne Elliman and Ben Vereen– all wonderful people. Just a few hours before the live show began, Jack Black pulled me aside. With red, watery eyes, he was clearly stoned when he asked me to please ensure that his sister would be allowed entry into the after-party to be held upstairs at the theater. He told me her name, and I assured him I would take care of it.

The show itself was mesmerizing and the cast got a standing ovation at the end. In the audience that night were

Hollywood moguls Jeffrey Katzenberg and Mark Burnett, along with Burnett's wife, Actress Roma Downey of *Touched by an Angel* (1994). I met all three. I later heard that Janet Jackson was also in the audience that night, but I did not see or meet her.

At the after-party, I hung out with Jack Black and an attractive woman who had worked the ticket counter. Hoping to date her, I got her phone number, but nothing came of that. There is a photo of the three of us together. During that party, I also met acclaimed Hollywood film director Bryan Singer who was, at that time, just finishing up production of *Superman Returns* (2006). This was many years before severe sexual allegations against him surfaced in Hollywood, besmirching his reputation forever.

** <u>Jazz Event</u>: I was hired to lure media to an event honoring longtime jazz pianist, composer and arranger Mike Melvoin, who was receiving an award from a prestigious music organization. Mike had served as chairman and president of the Recording Academy, and worked as a prolific studio musician, recording with Frank Sinatra, John Lennon, The Jackson 5, Natalie Cole and The Beach Boys, to name some artists. That evening I spent some time talking with Mike and also met his "lady friend," Actress Theresa Russell, renowned for her work in *Whore* (1991). I also spoke with Mike's daughter, Wendy Melvoin, a member of Prince's band, The Revolution. I told Wendy I'd love to be her publicist and gave her my card. She said she would definitely call me but, alas, she never did.

** <u>The Hayworth Theatre</u>: I was dating a woman named Jodi, who was best friends with a guy who acquired a long-abandoned live theatre house called the Hayworth Theatre, on Wilshire Boulevard, just past Koreatown. Since I was beginning to greatly enjoy live theatre, following my work with the *Jesus Christ Superstar* project, I agreed to represent the Hayworth at no charge. This would grant me access to all of their upcoming plays, as well as rehearsals and after-parties, for free. Two projects from this time frame stand out:

** <u>The Catskills Sonata</u>: Acclaimed movie director Paul Mazursky produced and directed this play by Michael Elias. The show allowed its audience to take a journey back to the year 1957 and to the Mountainview Hotel in the Catskill Mountains. In the play, the Mountainview Hotel serves as a place for performing artists to share their art.

My mother had come to L.A. to visit me. I picked her up from LAX and then together we had to race to the Hayworth in time for the premiere of *The Catskills Sonata* (2007). Once inside the theater, I was asked to check in media members and VIPs. Early on that night, a very cute young blonde approached me with her ticket. I had to write down everyone's name who would be in attendance. I simply asked her, "Name please?" and she was instantly insulted.

"Don't you know who I am?" she demanded. "I'm Kaley Cuoco!" I'd never heard of her before in my life and had never watched either of her hit TV shows, *8 Simple Rules for Dating My Teenage Daughter* (2002) or *The Big Bang Theory* (2007), I simply nodded my head at her and said, "Oh, okay. Come on in." I believe some steam came out of her ears as she passed by me.

Also, before the show began that night, Mel Brooks entered the lobby. I knew he was going to show up, as he and Mazursky were longtime friends. I kept this secret from my mother, though, because I wanted to surprise her. During a moment in time when Mel was alone, I ushered my mother along with me and we introduced ourselves. "Hey Mr. Brooks, my name is Dan Harary, I'm the publicist for this theater."

Mel started singing, "Dan Harary! Dan Harary men have named you!" to the tune of "Mona Lisa." Very funny.

Then I introduced him to my mother, saying, "Mr. Brooks, this is my mom, Joan. You and she both went to the same high school!"

Mel was rather intrigued by this and spent the next 15 minutes chatting with my mother about Eastern District High School in Williamsburg, New York. Even though the two of them realized that Mel was eight years older than my mom, they seemed to have a great conversation.

I have a photo of my mother and me with Mel Brooks from that lobby. It looks like I'm with my parents in that picture, and that Mel is my father! (It appears in this book.)

At the after-party for the premiere of this play, upstairs in a small ballroom of the theater, I also met Laraine Newman, Michael Chiklis, Dan Lauria, and Amy Smart. I was speaking with Laraine about her time during the first few legendary years of *Saturday Night Live* and she told me she was writing a book about her experiences there. I told her I would love to do her publicity for the book when it was completed and gave her my card. She promised me she would contact me in the future but, of course, she did not.

Michael Chiklis was a super nice guy. When we met at the food table, I asked him what it was like to appear in those *Fantastic Four* (2005) movies wearing such an enormous, cumbersome outfit playing the role of "Thing."

He said, "It really sucks wearing that costume. It's 60 pounds of Hellish latex. The worst part is when I have to pee. You have to hold it in for a really long time. I got a few urinary tract infections!" While he was joking to me about this, I could sense there was more than a bit of anger behind that brave face.

Actor Dan Lauria, best known as the "Dad" on *The Wonder Years* (1988), told me he was moving his career further into directing and hoped to be able to direct a show soon at The Hayworth. I also told adorable blonde actress Amy Smart that her frantic sex scene in the film *Crank* (2006) with Jason Statham was remarkable. In that film, she had to have sex with Statham's character to keep his heart alive.

"Really, did you think so?" she asked, naively. "I know a lot of guys say that to me, but I never thought of myself as a sex symbol before."

** <u>Lovelace</u>: The biggest live show ever presented by the Hayworth Theater was *Lovelace* (2009), an original musical based on the biography of *Deep Throat* (1972) star Linda Lovelace called, *Ordeal*. The music for this show as written by Charlotte Caffey, a member of the legendary all-female rock band, The Go-Go's. I spent many hours at the theater during rehearsals for *Lovelace*, and had the opportunity to chat with, albeit very briefly, the star of that play, Katrina Lenk. Notably, Katrina would go on win a 2018 Tony Award as Best Actress in a Musical for *The Band's Visit* on Broadway.

Charlotte was a joy to work with. We talked a great deal about her life and her time with The Go-Go's, and I especially enjoyed her stories about Ringo Starr. I generated a tremendous amount of press coverage for *Lovelace*, including seven different mentions of the show in the *Los Angeles Times*. That play was incredibly dramatic, powerful and intense, and the songs were truly extraordinary.

** <u>Adult Superstars Action Figures</u>: I got a phone call from out of nowhere from a guy who owned a toy company that manufactured action figure dolls based on famous movie and TV characters. He had become personal friends with porn star Jenna Jameson, and told me he was going to create and market an adult figure doll based on her likeness. Would I be interested?

Although I am an occasional aficionado of porn, I never heard of Jenna at that point in time–this was the summer of 2002. My client, Jerry, invited me to a hi-tech computer place in the San Fernando Valley to watch Jenna get her body "scanned" for use in the design of the new action figure based on her image.

When I arrived at the scanning place, there were about 10 men standing around a machine that resembled those X-ray type devices you find at airports before you board a plane. While we were waiting, Jenna Jameson appeared, wearing a white bathrobe. She introduced herself to me. She then took off the robe, stood totally nude, and entered into the scanning machine.

I joked, "Hey, Jenna, you really should work on getting over your remarkable shyness!" That got a decent sized laugh from everyone there.

We watched as Jenna stood, slowly rotating her body, as laser lights scanned every curve of Jenna's terrific figure. After this process was completed, she put her robe back on and walked off and into a private dressing room.

Jerry called me a few weeks later and told me he was ready to put Jenna's action figure toy on the market, and did I have any ideas on how to promote that news to the general public?

I suggested I meet him in person at his toy shop to discuss. When I arrived at his shop, I looked around and saw the realistic little action toys he had based on so many famous comic book characters. Suddenly, I came up with a brainstorm idea.

"Let's do a live event with Jenna at the Hustler sex store on Sunset Boulevard and have her debut her toy, live, in person. She can pose for photos and sign autographs. We can promote that in print in the local papers and on the radio. We can call it 'Jenna Jameson Day in LA.'"

Jerry instantly loved the idea. He got Jenna on the phone and we ran it past her. She agreed, immediately. I then had to make arrangements with the manager of the Hustler store itself. Through a friend I tracked down the manager, who happened to be *Hustler* founder Larry Flynt's daughter, Theresa.

A date was set. I persuaded Jerry to take out a full-page print ad in the *L.A. Weekly* newspaper to herald Jenna's upcoming appearance. I arranged for Jenna to do an in-studio interview with a top AM radio news/talk station a few days prior to event day. I also hired a photographer and security for the event itself.

Hours before our "Jenna Jameson Day in L.A." event was to begin, there was a very long line of men–and some women– queued up for several blocks down Sunset Boulevard. It was very exciting. Once Jenna arrived, I seated her at a small table in front of a large banner that had her name and photos of the toy on it. We then opened the doors and for the next three hours, many hundreds of people came through the store, dozens buying the toy right then and there, and others simply posing for photos or getting autographs from Jenna. (I had my photo taken with her at the end of the event.)

The NEXT NIGHT, Jay Leno, during his opening monologue on *The Tonight Show*, talked about the Jenna Jameson toy! And the next week, *NEWSWEEK Magazine* ran a photo and caption of Jenna holding the product also! Jenna called me up to tell me she couldn't believe I'd gotten her into *Newsweek Magazine*. I told her she was poised to become a very big star.

She replied, "In the next two years, I'm going to earn $100,000,000.00." I asked her to repeat that line a second time. She did.

A few days later, Jenna's personal manager, Linda, phoned to ask me if I wanted to become Jenna's personal publicist. I told her YES and then, stupidly, proposed an enormous monthly retainer fee of $7,500.00, based on the "$100-million" line Jenna shared with me. The bottom line: my fee was far too high, I didn't get the gig, and I never heard from Jenna or Linda again.

A few months later, Jerry called back to say he made over $1.5 million in sales of Jenna's toy, and he was now going to expand the line, called "Adult Superstars," to include several additional top porn stars.

Knowing that doing a live, in-store event at Hustler was the way to go, we once again took out a full-page print ad in the *L.A. Weekly*. I also accompanied four top porn stars–Kylie Ireland, Nikita Denise, Houston, and Julie Meadows–to do a live, in-studio radio interview with KLSX evening host Tim Conway, Jr. (son of comedian Tim Conway from the iconic *Carol Burnett Show*-1967).

This time entitled "Porn Star Day in L.A.," we, once again, had a huge line of men and women lined up and down the block from the Hustler store. We had paparazzi press photographers there and the girls posed for photos. Jerry made another small fortune. He later introduced me to another top porn star, Jasmin St. Claire, whom I represented for one year, getting her an endorsement deal as a spokesmodel for a guitar company, and a role in the movie, *National Lampoon's Dorm Daze 2: College at Sea* (2006).

In addition to handling events, I also experienced a variety of encounters with these other notables:

- **John K**: Within the earliest years of Asbury Communications, I received a phone call from a producer who was the right-hand man to John Kricfalusi, known as John K, the animation genius and creator of the *Ren & Stimpy* (1991) cartoon series. I met with John at his shabby office in Hollywood, and realized he was about as odd as a person could be. I sat in a chair in his office, directly in front of him, while he was seated behind his desk. He never once looked up at me, even when he shook my hand. He simply drew little cartoons on pieces of paper while we talked.

    He told me, "I am going to launch a cartoon series on the Internet. If I hire you for PR, what can you do for me?"

    By coincidence, I had-just the week before-befriended a woman writer with the *New York Times* who was interested in writing about content for the Internet. "John, if you hire me, I will get you an article in the *New York Times*," I boldly declared.

    John actually looked up at me. He stood, shook my hand and said, "Deal."

    As promised, I got John a huge profile story in the *New York Times*, as well as in many other major media outlets, including *USA Today*, the *L.A. Times*, and even the CBS *Sunday Evening News*.

    I repped John K for about a year, then he flaked, but the press I got him was truly remarkable.

- **Andy Summers**: Another early client of mine at Asbury was a company called Megatrax Music. This company specializes in creating background music of every conceivable genre for insertions into TV shows, feature films and commercials. One day after a meeting at Megatrax, I stopped by their recording studio to watch whatever happened to be going on. There, I met Andy Summers, the renowned guitarist from The Police, who was recording a solo album. Nice guy.

** Kiera Chaplin: I hired a friend of mine from New York, Mitch, to be my assistant around 2005. He had met the gorgeous Model/Actress Kiera Chaplin at a party. Kiera was one of Charlie Chaplin's granddaughters. Mitch brought Kiera into the fold, and we repped her for about two years. Mitch got her a few product endorsement deals with some high-end brands. We also arranged for Kiera to attend a few Hollywood events on the red carpet and to be a guest at a Playboy Mansion Halloween party.

** Hollywood Center Studios Office: During the early 2000s, I moved my office into a production building based on the Hollywood Center Studios in the heart of Hollywood. My office neighbors in that building were Jimmy Kimmel and Adam Corolla, who I met a number of times. Their company, called JackHole Productions, was producing *The Man Show* (1999) at that time. One day I gave Jimmy a collector's item sweatshirt from "The Fox," a man famous for singing dirty songs at a Santa Monica Bar while drinking huge mugs of beer while standing upside down on his head. "The Fox" was a recurring character on *The Man Show*, and Jimmy was most grateful.

Another of my office neighbors inside that building was actor Sean Astin, today best known as Samwise Gamgee from *The Lord of the Rings* (2001) film series. (This was a few years before I met him at the *Smile* movie premiere.) Sean and I spent several hours talking one day about his famous parents Patty Duke of *The Patty Duke Show* (1963) and John Astin of *The Addams Family* (1964).

Alas, that Hollywood Center Studios office building suffered a terrible fate when it caught fire on Christmas Eve

2002 and almost burned down to the ground. We all lost a tremendous amount of office equipment and furniture, along with memorabilia items that were irreplaceable.

Everything about the aftermath of that fire really sucked! It took me a while to get myself back together again, both mentally and financially.

During 1996-2009, I had many celebrity run-ins just from real life. Among these encounters:

** <u>Kirsten Dunst</u>: My good friend from Hebrew school, Eric, got married in San Diego and during the course of his wedding reception, I met Kirsten Dunst and her mother, Inez Rupprecht. This was just BEFORE the premiere of the first *Spider-Man* (2002) movie in which she co-starred. I knew she was in that film–having seen the promotional trailer–and I spent some time flirting with her at the reception. At the time, I was 46 years old and she was 20. When I asked her to dance, she hemmed and hawed, until her mother came over to rescue her.

Inez said, "She's far too young for you!" and scooped her up, waltzing Kirsten away. I did manage to get a photo of us together, however, before that embarrassing moment took place.

** <u>Jennifer Love Hewitt</u>: I had a new business meeting in a building on Robertson Boulevard in West Hollywood. I entered an elevator to return to my car afterward, and the beautiful actress, Jennifer Love Hewitt, walked in. We spoke briefly during the short elevator ride and I told her my PR agency had done some promotional work on one of her early films, *Can't Hardly Wait* (1998). She was a lovely lady and her smile could really light up a room, not to mention a small elevator car!

** <u>Henry Winkler</u>: A female friend of mine invited me and my two small kids to a huge charity event/outdoor BBQ being held in West Hollywood on a Saturday. I don't remember the cause, unfortunately, but I do remember Henry Winkler, aka "The Fonz" was there, working one of the BBQ grills. He was super funny and nice, and spoke with my kids and me for a while.

** <u>Jeffrey Tambor</u>: I was dating a tall, attractive redhead who was handling PR for the hit children's TV series, *Mighty Morphin Power Rangers* (1993). One evening, after we dined at a cool little Chinese restaurant in West Hollywood, we started walking out of the place when I saw Actor Jeffrey Tambor of *The Larry Sanders Show* (1992) and, years later, *Transparent* (2014), sitting at a nearby table. When he saw my girlfriend, he scanned her body up and down with his eyes. He then looked at me, smiled, and gave me a "thumbs up" sign, as if to say, "Nice job, buddy!"

I was flattered by that until, just recently. His compliment soured after Tambor was fired from his own show, *Transparent*, for a number of serious sexual harassment allegations.

** <u>Hillary Swank</u>: I was having dinner with a date at one of my favorite restaurants in Hollywood, when I realized two-time Oscar winning Actress Hillary Swank was seated at the booth right next to me, along with a male companion. During our respective meals, I kept turning my head to look at her, and she was doing the same to look at me.

Finally, I turned and said, "Hillary! We have to stop flirting like this! Our dates are gonna get jealous!"

She smiled and laughed, and that was just fine by me.

** <u>Micky Dolenz</u>: My childhood friend, Steve Walter, had become close friends with The Monkees' Drummer/Singer

Micky Dolenz, as Micky had performed musically at Steve's club a number of times. Once while Steve was visiting me in L.A., he invited Micky to join us at the Sunset Tower Bar, high above Sunset Boulevard. The three of us met for many hours, and Micky "kinda" remembered meeting me 20 years earlier at Columbia Pictures Television. I was peppering him with questions about The Monkees.

Micky finally said, "Dan, what is this? An interview? Can't we just relax?"

We laughed, got drunk and I finally got my photo taken with him.

** <u>Harvey Keitel</u>: After the Hollywood office fire, I relocated my business office into a terrific building within the "Golden Triangle" area of Beverly Hills. The downstairs restaurant, Trilussa, was very popular and I ate there often.

One lunchtime, actor Harvey Keitel was sitting next to my table. After our lunches, I shook his hand and said, "So great to meet you, man. Keep up the good work!"

A stupid thing to say, and he looked at me with disdain. I thought he wanted to hit me.

** <u>Ryan Stiles</u>: A bit out of chronological order: Just before New Year's Eve 2000, many people feared the "Y2K" computer bug was going to shut down electricity and cause airplanes to fall from the skies. That night, I had my two young children and their little dog, "Sumi," with me. I also wanted to watch a performance by a comedy improv group based in Sherman Oaks–The L.A. Connection. For that historic New Year's Eve, I took my kids and their dog (in a little portable cage) to watch this comedy group perform. They were hysterically funny. The cast included Ryan Stiles of *Two and a Half Men* (2003) and *Whose Line Is It Anyway?* (1998), who picked out my son from the audience and included him in a skit on the stage. In addition to being comedically gifted and remarkably tall, Ryan was a great guy. We chatted with him briefly after the show was over.

PS: No planes fell from the sky that night!

** <u>Lou Diamond Phillips</u>: I was having lunch with my longtime friend, Caryn Richman (*The New Gidget*) in Hollywood, and Actor Lou Diamond Phillips was seated at the next table. The three of us ended up in a long conversation over coffee. I told him how incredible he was in the *La Bamba* (1987) movie, when he portrayed Ritchie Valens. Very nice man, and surprisingly funny.

** <u>Charo</u>: I was having drinks with a client of mine who was in Los Angeles from Nashville. He was a prominent music producer/composer. We were sitting at the outdoor patio of the legendary pink Beverly Hills Hotel. As we got up to leave, I noticed that Charo, the Latina singer/dancer/performer, was sitting alone at a nearby table.

A little drunk and wanting to impress my client, I approached her and said, "Hey, Charo! How's my little 'Coochie-Coochie' Girl doing tonight?"

Without missing a beat, Charo replied, "Listen my friend. That 'Coochie-Coochie' made me A LOT of MONEY!"

She was dead serious.

** <u>Pat Sajak</u>: I was with my cousin Franz, the magician, at the famed Magic Castle in the Hollywood Hills. He was telling me about his idea for an upcoming one-man show in China. We then noticed that Pat Sajak of *Wheel of Fortune* (1975) was standing near the bar. We spent some time chatting with him and discovered he had a real passion for the magic arts.

** <u>Jason Statham</u>: I was shopping at the fine Bristol Farms grocery store (formerly the site of the legendary Chasen's restaurant) near my home in Beverly Hills, when I almost bumped into actor Jason Statham. I told him I was a huge fan of his *Transporter* (2002) movies and asked him if he planned to make any more.

"Man, I'm fucking TIRED!" he responded. "Maybe I will, who knows, but right now I just need a fucking REST!"

I kind of felt bad for the guy.

** <u>Keanu Reeves</u>: I had a meeting with a female Chinese actress at a restaurant in West Hollywood. She had just signed me as her publicist to promote a new HBO movie in which she was co-starring. Sitting at the next table was superstar Keanu Reeves. Keanu left the restaurant a few minutes before I did. After my meeting ended, I left the venue, got into my car, and started driving along Santa Monica Boulevard.

While stopped at a red light, I heard a loud, powerful motorcycle engine pull up just to the left side of my car. Sitting atop it was Keanu Reeves. I waved at him; he waved back. I gave him a "thumbs up" sign; he returned the gesture to me. We both started to laugh until the light turned green, and we continued along our separate ways.

** <u>Patti Davis Reagan</u>: I was shopping in a Santa Monica hardware store for a few supplies for my house. As I was walking toward the checkout cash register, I saw a very attractive brunette woman in front of me looking at cans of paint. She then dropped a small can of paint onto my foot! She quickly bent down, scooped up the can and replaced it on the shelf. "I'm SO, SO sorry!" she said.

Recognizing her instantly, I replied, "That's okay, Nancy! You can drop paint on my foot anytime!"

Her response? "My <u>mom</u> is Nancy. I'm <u>Patti</u>."

I'd just inadvertently called Patti Davis Reagan, "Nancy!" Another dyslexic "Meryl Streep" moment!

** <u>Jeremy Piven/Anthony Anderson</u>: I met another attractive woman one day while at a Mercedes Benz dealership getting my car adjusted. It turns out she was the personal assistant to actor Jeremy Piven, who was riding high in his career at that time due to his portrayal of "Ari Gold" in the HBO series *Entourage* (2004). The woman and I spoke at length, and she invited me to a private party in Hollywood where Jeremy was going to be playing the drums with a small band. I attended the party and watched Jeremy play. He was pretty good. After he was finished, I introduced myself and told him about my years as a drummer as well. He was intrigued by my 1968 Vintage Ludwig drum set, and even asked if I would sell it to him.

"No, sorry, man," I replied, "it was a Bar Mitzvah gift from my father."

While we were talking, comic actor Anthony Anderson took to the stage and began pulling ticket numbers out of a hat; apparently, there were "prizes" to be given away to attendees that night. When a woman standing next to me shouted out, "That's my number," Anthony tossed an enormous pink dildo through the air and in this woman's direction. The toss went a bit astray and the sex toy almost conked me in the head! I ducked just in time, but it did smash into the face of the man standing behind me.

** <u>Danny Masterson and Bijou Phillips</u>: A new client of mine, a newly-launched advertising agency, was throwing a party at a West Hollywood nightclub to celebrate their grand opening. When I walked into the room, I saw Danny Masterson, star of *That '70s Show* (1998) sitting in a booth with his then girlfriend (now wife) Bijou Phillips, daughter of The Mamas & The Papas star, John Phillips. I sat with them for a few minutes, sharing a drink. They were very nice, and very young. Recently, Danny, a Scientologist, has been accused of raping four women and faces criminal charges. Yikes!

** <u>Carmine Appice</u>: I met legendary rock music Drummer Carmine Appice at an Italian restaurant in Valencia,

California, where my kids moved to live with my ex-wife. I'd seen Carmine perform at the Sunshine Inn during the '70s in a band called *Cactus*. He had first become famous with the band, Vanilla Fudge. In later years, he'd become much better known as the drummer for Rod Stewart's hit song, "Do Ya Think I'm Sexy." I knew Carmine had befriended my buddy Steve back at the Cutting Room in New York, so we had a number of things to discuss while waiting for our respective tables to be ready.

** <u>Patricia Kalember</u>: I'd taken my kids to a park in Studio City one day. While they were playing, I noticed that Actress Patricia Kalember was standing next to me, watching her daughter. I knew her from her role on *Thirtysomething* (1987) and as the tragic figure who dies a terrible death in the movie, *Signs* (2002). We talked about being busy working parents and we introduced our children, who played together for the rest of that afternoon.

** <u>Rene Russo</u>: I'm ending this chapter with one of my all-time favorite celebrity encounter stories. I was on a date with a female photographer I'd met at a Hollywood event/party for one of my clients. We were eating at a fine steak house in Santa Monica. The date was going just fine. As our meal was winding down, a party of three men and one woman sitting adjacent to our table got up to leave. The men walked by first and then the woman, a VERY beautiful lady, stopped, stood to my immediate left, leaned over to me and asked, "Can I have YOUR BONE?"

She was referring, of course, to the giant T-bone that was left over from my steak meal.

Recognizing that it was Actress Rene Russo, I quickly responded, "Rene! You can have my bone ANYTIME!"

Rene loved my sexual innuendo and sat down right next to me! I introduced her to my date, and the three of us began talking about our love of dogs. Rene requested the bone for her German Shepard. Then the conversation continued, and I asked her if she had any new films coming up. She did; a movie with Tim Allen called, *Big Trouble* (2002). I told her I thought she was a fine actress, not to mention a true Hollywood beauty.

She replied, "Thanks, that's very kind. I'm glad you like my films. I NEVER watch them myself, EVER. I cannot stand the way I look on a large screen."

This story illustrates that even beautiful, talented women in Hollywood can have insecurities about themselves.

<u>Coda</u>: The woman I was on a date with was arrested the following week for fraud! It seems she had been posing as a Wedding Photographer for many months, pretending to be shooting pictures at dozens of weddings, when all she was doing was getting paid for "clicking" an empty camera.

Boy, I sure know how to pick 'em!

PHOTOS

Richie Havens' Autograph, Asbury Park, 1972

Bruce Springsteen Poster, Asbury Park, 1973

Joan Rivers' Autograph, Boston, 1976

With Hugh M. Hefner, Playboy Mansion, Bel Air, 1984

With Playmate Lynda Wiesmeier, Van Nuys, 1984

With Playmate Kym Malin, Van Nuys, 1985

With Alice Cooper, Columbia Studios Burbank, 1986

With Cast of "What's Happening Now!" Hollywood, 1986

FLIRTING WITH FAME • 157

With Sid Caesar at Larry King Radio Studio/Culver City, 1987

With Bob "Gilligan" Denver, Hawaii, 1987

With Caryn "New Gidget" Richman, Hawaii, 1987

With Alan "The Skipper" Hale, Jr., Hawaii, 1987

With Robert "Freddy Krueger" Englund & Steve Walter, Hollywood, 1987

With Karen Black, Studio City, 1988

With Milton Berle, Hollywood, 1988

Jay Leno's Autograph/Backstage "Tonight Show," Burbank, 1988

FLIRTING WITH FAME • 161

With Bob Hope & Steve Allen, Beverly Hills Hotel, 1990

With Steve Allen, MTM Studios/Studio City, 1990

With Dee Wallace, Jon Provost, June Lockhart, Bob Weatherwax and Lassie on set of *The New Lassie*, Universal Studios, 1991

With Michael Landon, Beverly Hilton Hotel, 1991

With Sylvester Stallone, Beverly Hilton Hotel, 1991

With Tom Hanks, Beverly Hilton Hotel, 1992

With Jerry Seinfeld, NATPE/San Francisco, 1993

With Vice President Al Gore, FOX Studios/LA, 1993

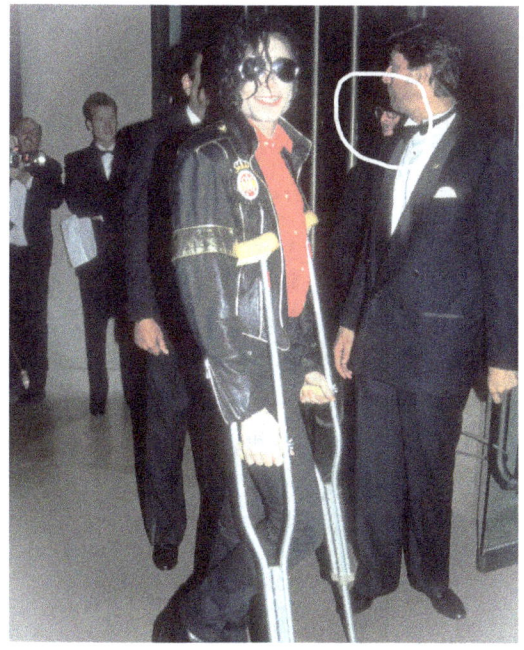

With Michael Jackson, Beverly Hilton Hotel, 1993

With Lois Laurel, San Fernando Valley, 1994

With Kirk Douglas, Hollywood Roosevelt Hotel, 1997

With Bob Barker, Jordan & Anjuli Harary, CBS TV City, 1998

With Ray Harryhausen, Culver City, 1998

With Victoria Principal and Brooke Shields, Beverly Hills, 1999

With Kirsten Dunst, San Diego, 2002

With Porn Star Jenna Jameson, West Hollywood, 2002

With Cheri Oteri, KLSX Radio Station/Los Angeles, 2005

With Jack Black, Ricardo Montalban Theater, Hollywood, 2006

With Oscar Winner Robert Short, Beverly Hills, 2006

With Mel Brooks & Joan Harary, Hayworth Theater/Los Angeles, 2006

With Jason Alexander, The Improv/West Hollywood, 2007

With Steven Spielberg, Universal Studios, 2010

With Supermodel Amber Smith, Hollywood, 2012

With Monkees Drummer Micky Dolenz, West Hollywood, 2015

With KISS Guitarist Paul Stanley & MCZ/Japanese Singing Group, Downtown Los Angeles, 2015

With The Cowsills & Steve Walter, Sirius XM Radio Studios, NYC, 2015

With Queen Guitarist Brian May, Disney Studios, 2017

With Dr. Ruth, Beverly Hills Hotel, 2017

With Chef Robert Irvine, Anjuli Harary, Mike & Kim Garfinkel, Calabasas, CA, 2017

With Ann-Margret, Downtown Los Angeles, 2019

With Drew Carey, Musso & Frank Restaurant/Hollywood, 2021

With Jim James/My Morning Jacket, Beach Boy Brian Wilson, Rolling Stone Editor Jason Fine and Filmmaker Brent Wilson, Musso & Frank Restaurant/Hollywood 2022

Chapter Nine

2009

HELP! I'M IN LOVE WITH A SUPERMODEL!

I'm not sure why I'm donating a full chapter here, but this "close encounter" was different than most and personally affected me deeply. Here goes:

One night in early 2009, I stood in my living room, channel surfing on my large, hi-definition TV, when I came upon a program featuring an incredibly beautiful blonde woman sitting on the floor, vomiting into a trash can. Fascinated, I stood watching the rest of the show, *Celebrity Rehab Presents Sober House* (2009), which aired on VH-1.

I'd never heard of the series, which presented eight "celebrities" (most of whom a far stretch from that word) going through withdrawal from their addictions to drugs and alcohol, on national television. There was a marathon of *Celebrity Rehab* episodes that day, so I sat watching half a dozen in a row.

Quite simply, I was mesmerized by this blonde woman, who was coming off a 20-year addiction to painkillers. As I watched her puking, sobbing, and wiping tears from her Goddess-like face, I HEARD A VOICE that whispered into my right ear: "You need to reach out to this woman. She needs your help." I swear to God, I really did!

Her name was Amber Smith. Go ahead, Google her photos. I'll wait.

I'd never heard of Amber before, so I looked her up on the Internet, and found her website. There, I saw photographs of perhaps the most stunning blonde sex-bomb model ever. I discovered she'd appeared on the cover of more than 300 magazines around the world, including a 1985 issue of *Playboy* that had been published when I was working there. Amber was a tall, extremely attractive blonde from Florida who, in the *Playboy* layout, had posed with large yellow feather-fans, and very dark red lipstick.

At the bottom of Amber's website was a phone number as a contact. I called and left the following message: "Hello, Amber, my name is Dan. I'm a publicist in Beverly Hills. I've been watching your show, and I simply have to say that it's breaking my heart. Your story has touched me, deeply. If you need some help re-starting your career, I'd be glad to try to help you. I know this sounds kind of crazy, but I simply felt compelled to call and reach out to you. If you'd like to have lunch with me sometime to meet, please let me know. My phone number is XYZ. Either way, I wish you the best of luck with your sobriety and I hope you're able to stay away from drugs in the future. Clearly, they're NOT your friends. Take care."

A few days later, I got a call. "Dan? This is Carol Smith. I'm Amber's mother. We were very touched by your message, and we'd like to meet with you."

I was taken aback. I'd actually gotten a response!

Over the course of the next few days, I researched everything I could find on the Internet about Amber Smith. I also developed a list of possible publicity, promotional, and marketing ideas for her, such as potential product endorsements, public appearances, speaker's bureaus, talent agents to meet with, etc. I wanted to be prepared for this meeting with my "Damsel in Distress."

I'd chosen my favorite Hollywood restaurant, Musso & Frank, for our lunch meeting. Arriving in an old, loud, junk-heap of a car, Amber and Carol got out. We sat at a plush red leather booth (Amber in the middle) and for the next two hours, I told them about myself, my career, and my ideas for Amber to pursue, now that she was sober. She revealed a good deal to me about her struggles with drugs—an addiction she shared WITH HER MOTHER—for over 20 years! Carol had become clean, also, but now the two women faced an even more prominent problem: poverty.

"I'm broke," Amber told me. "I had everything—a house, cars, clothes, money in the bank. It's all gone. My problem got really bad about five years ago, and my mother and I were almost homeless. We were living in a tiny Hollywood hotel room, and I didn't know where my next rent check was gonna come from. Then, I heard about the *Celebrity Rehab* TV show, and I called the producers, begging them to help me. I didn't do that show for the fame, or the money, or the publicity. I did it because without it, I knew I was gonna die."

Amber's ability to articulate her struggles with drug addiction and the devastation it left behind in her personal life, were extremely powerful. I sat on the edge of my seat. I'd never, in my life, met a hardcore drug addict before.

I told Amber that "a voice" told me to help her, and that I'd like to be both her personal publicist and her manager, for free. "I'm not here for money," I told the women. "I'm here because I'm supposed to help you." I picked up the check for lunch and walked the two back to their shitty car.

Later that week, I invited Amber to have dinner with me. I wanted to discuss our new relationship and have her sign a management contract. I picked her up and drove her to a Mexican place. She looked stunning. As we entered the restaurant, I noticed that the head of EVERY SINGLE PERSON (both men AND women) turned, to watch her simply walk across the room. When we sat at the booth, I said, "Wow. Everyone stared at you walking in here. What's that like?"

She replied, "It's been happening to me since I was 15. I don't even notice it anymore."

Amber and I had a fun meal. Our "relationship" was fresh and brand new. We talked about our childhoods, our careers, and our lives, in broad strokes. The fact that she had been a true supermodel in the 1990s (*Maxim Magazine* once voted her "One of the Sexiest Women Alive"), never entered into the conversation. We were just "a guy and a girl" having dinner and bonding as friends.

During dinner, Amber told me she'd been invited to participate in another VH-1 TV show, this one called *Sex Rehab with Dr. Drew* (2009).

"Are you a sex addict?" I asked.

"Oh God, no, not at all," Amber told me. "I'm not even a big fan of sex, at all. Actually, I'm a LOVE ADDICT. It's something entirely different."

She went on to explain that during the course of her life, she'd had "a lot of sex with a lot of men," but other than the "15 seconds of cumming and then, so what?" she never enjoyed it. She confessed she'd never had a "real" boyfriend, had never been married, and had never experienced "true love." The concept seemed alien to her.

Her affliction in this area was a mental, romantic "disconnect." She'd meet an extremely good-looking man at a party or a nightclub, speak with him briefly, and then become completely and totally smitten with him, beyond anything resembling normalcy. She would start stalking these men, finding out where they'd be and when, and show up, unannounced, just to stare at them from a distance. Amber told me the "high" she felt from doing this was even more powerful than the high she got from drugs.

"Wow," I said. "I did that with a girl I couldn't talk to in college. I called her 'Long Red.' I never knew there was a name for that condition."

Amber replied, "Most people don't know anything about love addiction. It's not been discussed within popular culture. I'm hoping that my appearance on the new show will help spread the word about this disease to others."

For the *Sex Rehab* TV program, Amber, along with seven actual sex addicts comprised of rock stars, porn stars, models, and film-makers, would be confined to the Pasadena Recovery Center for three weeks. She would have limited access to a telephone, and none to the Internet. During those weeks, I began reaching out to a variety of potential business partners for us, including talent agents, modeling agents, nightclub promoters, marketers of new products, ad agencies representing iconic brands, etc.

However, I quickly came to learn that because of her recent national "celebrity" on the TV shows that had aired the year previous (*Celebrity Rehab* and *Sober House*), Amber had earned a reputation for herself as, perhaps, the country's most beautiful drug addict. One noted talent agent actually told me, "She's probably the most stunning woman I've ever seen in my life. Unfortunately, she has the 'stink' of drug addict on her. I don't think that's something she'll ever be able to shake off, certainly not in Hollywood."

During her second week at the rehab center, Amber called and invited me to come for a "family and friends" BBQ visit, asking if I wouldn't mind picking up her mother along the way. During that car ride, Carol told me how sad it was that Amber just couldn't find the "right guy," had never been in love, and had never even had a real boyfriend. When we arrived at the clinic, Amber (and a TV crew) approached us. She looked especially sad.

"What's wrong?" I asked.

Amber replied, "The therapy here has been really tough. This is so much harder than even drug withdrawal." She explained that since she was now drug-free for the first time in 20 years, she was beginning to "feel again," and was delving into long-hidden feelings about her father's abandonment and guilt over his death. (Amber's dad, who left when she was five, drank himself to death. His body, along with hundreds of empty alcohol bottles, was found aboard a boat he owned. Amber, who was on the set of a low-budget movie at the time, blamed herself for "not being there" for him the day he passed away.)

After Amber was done with the three-week stint filming the new TV series, she and I, for the next four months, took meetings all over town with agents. Amber once turned down an offer for her own reality TV show (much to my dismay) because the powers that be wouldn't name her an executive producer! We also met for lunches at least a few times a week, visited each other at our respective apartments and spoke by phone at least four times a day.

I threw a birthday party for myself that June; my closest friends attended. About an hour late, Amber walked in, bringing all conversation to a screeching halt.

My friend, Jamie, pulled me aside. "Danny, I'm so NOT a lesbian, but for HER I'd make an exception!"

Jamie's husband, Andy, added, "God, she's so good-looking, it's off-putting."

Amber instantly eclipsed the attention of my gang, but it meant a lot to me that she showed up at all. When she left, she handed me an oversized birthday card. It read: "I know the going hasn't been easy so far, but I really appreciate all you have done to help me, and all of your selfless sacrifices. I honor our friendship and have had a lot of fun! You have quickly become a great friend and confidant to me. Here's to a wonderful, prosperous future. Happy birthday, and may this year be unforgettable for us both. Love, Amber."

Amber was invited to sign autographs at a booth at "Comic Con" (the biggest science fiction and comic book show in the world) that summer in San Diego. I suggested that she and I drive down together and stay at a (cheap) area motel. I'd help her set up her station at the booth. "Sounds like fun," she said.

From that Friday morning until that Sunday evening, Amber and I were inseparable, although I'd injured my right ankle dancing at my niece's wedding the weekend prior, and was forced to walk with a cane the whole time! We drove down to San Diego together, picking up a wacky, model girlfriend of hers along the way, checked into our little motel rooms (side-by-side), and set up shop at the booth of her sponsor, a top comic book company. Amber was among at least eight other "Booth Babes" sitting there, including several former *Playboy* bunnies, rock stars' wives, indie film "scream queens," and one red-haired, WWF wrestler to whom I said, "You re-invent the word 'Hot.'"

While the attendance for the show was record-breaking, guys who wanted to shell out good money for photos of pretty girls weren't amongst the crowd. (These geeky guys wanted autographs from "Mr. Spock" from *Star Trek*, and "Captain Adama" from *Battlestar Gallactica*, not from half-naked babes.) Amber and I lost money that weekend when we factored in gas, motel rooms, food, and "bike taxis." After parking the car incredibly far from the convention hall, we had to ride, sitting closely together in little bike taxis, pedaled by incredibly muscular men and women. Laughing and talking incessantly, we had tremendous fun during those trips, with fees of $25.00 in each direction. Those costs mounted quickly.

One night after her appearance, Amber and I shared some fast food in her hotel room. I chomped down fries, as I watched her remove her makeup, kick off her high heels, and change into her casual clothing (averting my eyes on purpose).

"I wish I didn't have to do these appearances anymore," she lamented. "I've been doing them forever. Girls my age don't make much money from autograph shows these days."

I said, "I only wish I was still making the income I made up until last year. We could start a business together."

Amber: "What happened?"

Me: "Wonderful George W. Bush fucked the world and killed the economy. I'm only making about 12-grand a month now, down from 30-grand a month, which I made for years."

Amber stopped eating, rolled her eyes, said, "$30K a month?" and pretended to faint, actually dropping to the floor. We laughed. "God, I wish I was making that kind of money."

Me: "Didn't you make millions in your heyday?"

Amber: "A lot of people made a lot of money from me for a very long time, but during my very best year ever, I only made about $250,000. I was making good money for a while, but never 'Gisele Bündchen' money, even though I was her body double a few times."

Back in Hollywood, I helped Amber schlep her unbelievably heavy suitcases up to her apartment door. We hugged and then, as I turned to walk away, she said out loud, but perhaps more to herself, "I love you, Dan."

I froze in time. Did I just hear correctly? I turned around. Amber stood about 15 feet from me, staring. The moment was suspended.

Me: "Amber, I love you, too. You know that, right? You KNOW I love you, RIGHT?"

She smiled. "Yeah, yeah, I know. Thanks for everything. Good night."

We stared at each other for a few seconds more. Then I split. I didn't know what else to do.

For months that summer, I arranged public appearances for Amber around the U.S. at nightclubs, parties, autograph shows, and even at a college campus, where she spoke about overcoming drug and love addiction. While I was helping her generate a few thousand dollars a month (and constantly driving her to and from airports for those appearances), she hit a snag financially.

"Dan, I can't pay my rent. What am I gonna do?" she asked.

Deeply touched and completely smitten with her, I handed her $2,000.00. "You'll pay me back someday when you're making the big bucks again," I said.

Hugging me, she said, "You're the only man on the planet I can count on and completely trust. What would I do without you? You are truly my hero."

I arranged a meeting for Amber and myself with Neil Strauss, a multi-bestselling author who I was able to contact, as he was friends with my cousin Franz, the magician. This author (whose book *The*

Game-about picking up women-was an international bestseller) was instantly smitten with Amber and agreed to help us pursue a book deal with a major, New York-based publishing company for rights to her autobiography. Then things took a strange turn. Neil hired a "nobody," young, "potential hot new author" he discovered from Toronto to write up a few sample chapters of Amber's life after having spent just a few days with her, one-on-one. When this famous author presented us with those sample chapters, Amber and I were shocked and disgusted. "These chapters are not remotely in "Amber's voice," we told Neil and rejected them.

Once that happened the whole thing fell apart, plus the publishing house this author was associated with decided that, while Amber's life story would "certainly make for compelling reading," they just didn't feel there would be "enough of an audience to actually buy such a product." Amber and I, who'd literally performed a dance for joy in the street after our first meeting with Neil Strauss, were crushed when the deal, which seemed like a sure thing, eventually fell through.

We decided to drown our sorrows over our lost book fortune at a killer Indian food restaurant in Beverly Hills. As I slathered up a big piece of naan with raita, and was about to inhale it, she said something like, "Yada, yada, yada, blah, blah, blah, AND IF WE EVER END UP HAVING SEX TOGETHER, etc., etc., etc., yada, yada."

I almost choked on my naan. I wished at that moment that the previous two sentences had been videotaped, so I could have played them back. I wasn't paying close attention to her preceding thoughts, so I wasn't 100% sure if her "having sex together" phrase was in reference to <u>me</u> or to one of the "love addiction" guys she was obsessed with from afar. (I didn't ask, so I'll never know.)

Amber and I went to see the incredibly scary horror film *Paranormal Activity* (2009) together. We were so frightened during the course of that film, we took turns grabbing each other's legs, and turning to each other with fear. (She was so scared she had her eyes covered at the very end of the movie, the most unsettling moment of all.) After the film ended, we were so rattled, we remained in our seats for quite a while, until the feeling subsided.

Leaving the theater, we went to a nearby nightclub, where we watched one of her best friends perform stand-up comedy. I hadn't felt this close to any woman in years. A Martian observing the two of us together would have said that Amber and I were on a date. (In heels, Amber was <u>very</u> tall. I used to insert "lifts" into my shoes to add some inches when together.)

Amber was invited to tape an appearance on *The Oprah Winfrey Show* (1986), along with Dr. Drew Pinsky, and two other fellow "sex addicts" from VH-1. I worked with Oprah's team to make Amber's arrangements (the show taped in Chicago.) Weeks later, when that episode of Oprah's show aired, my daughter was home from college and Amber came to my apartment to watch. There I was, sitting on the couch with my beautiful daughter on one side and my beautiful best friend, the supermodel, on the other, as the three of us watched Amber chatting with Oprah about the differences between sex and love addiction. It was truly a surreal moment in my life. (Oprah really seemed to "spark" to Amber's plight, even confessing a case of "love addiction" that Oprah, herself, had experienced decades earlier.)

"I got a great booking in Vegas," Amber called. "Fifteen hundred bucks to show up at a club and sign some autographs."

"Sounds like fun," I replied. I then realized I had both a brand-new Mercedes Benz, and absolutely nothing to do with myself that weekend. "Let's go together. I'll drive," I said.

"Great," she replied, "Should we stay there overnight? The gig will end around 2 am."

Thinking quickly, I offered, "To save money, why don't I get us a room with two beds?"

Amber: "Perfect, thanks. Sounds like a plan."

I went online and arranged for a fairly inexpensive room with two beds, within walking distance of the nightclub in which she was to appear.

For the next four days, I was a nervous wreck. I was going to be sleeping in the same room with my best friend, Amber Smith, the supermodel. I wrote down a little speech I planned to deliver during that weekend. "Amber, I think I'm starting to have feelings for you, and I just felt the time has come for me to let you know."

I picked Amber up from her tiny dive apartment in Hollywood at 2:00 pm that Saturday afternoon and for the next six hours straight, we drove through a good deal of traffic to Las Vegas. We never once played the radio or the "positive thinking" CD she brought along for the road. We talked about everything under the sun, neither repeating a stream of conversation nor ever running out of stories to recount.

We arrived at the front desk of the Vegas hotel. I gave the female clerk my info and credit card, and she pulled me up on her computer. "Here you are," she said.

"The room's got two beds, right?" I said.

The woman slowly looked at me, then the blonde goddess standing beside me, then looked back at me. She said, "Yeah, sure, right." (Only in retrospect did I realize she was being sarcastic.)

Amber and I got upstairs and, you guessed it, there was only ONE BED in the room. We both stood, frozen. "Amber, there's only one bed in here."

Amber: "Yeah, I see that."

Me: "You KNOW I ordered two beds, right? I just want you to be sure that you KNOW I did that, okay?"

Amber: "Yes, I know. Don't worry, I believe you. What should we do? Should we go back down and switch rooms?"

Realizing she only had about two hours to eat dinner, get dressed, and walk over to the nightclub, I said, "You know what? I'll sleep on the floor. Don't worry about it, it's not a big deal. I really don't care."

Amber: "Thanks, Dan. I appreciate that."

For the next 90 minutes, Amber and I sat side-by-side on the bed, ate a really shitty room service meal (ice cold French fries and greasy burgers), and watched an old comedy movie.

"God, I have NO INTEREST in doing this appearance tonight," she said.

Me: "I know. I would do ANYTHING if you and I could just stay here on this bed all night and watch movies."

Amber: "Me too! That sounds like heaven! I WISH we could do that and nothing else!"

The time came for Amber to prepare for her appearance. Watching her stand in the bathroom in just bra and panties, putting on her makeup, installing her hair extensions, and slinking into her skin-tight sexy costume, I was greatly surprised to find myself not turned on! In all honesty, I actually felt like Amber was my wife and we were simply a married couple getting ready for a night out on the town.

We arrived at the club and Amber was asked to pose for some photographs with the owner in front of the entryway signage. The promoter handed me Amber's check for $1,500.00, which I pocketed, then led us inside. The place was packed, and the DJ's music was deafening. (I have custom-made ear plugs for such occasions.) The club owner then brought us to the VIP table, sat down with Amber and me, and had two very sexy waitresses bring us round after round of Petron tequila. Amber, a recovering alcoholic, said, "I SO shouldn't be drinking tonight."

"I know," I answered, "but I don't think there's much of anything else to do here right now."

Amber: "You're right. A little tequila won't kill me."

The club owner split, and Amber and I sat on our big fat asses for the next four hours, drinking. Occasionally, a club patron or two would approach her for an autograph or a photo but, by and large, we were on an incredibly loud "date," for which she was being paid solely for her wondrously luminous presence.

A club photographer came by at one point and snapped a Polaroid picture of Amber and me hugging. The SECOND I saw that photo I said to myself, "Oh My God! I'm IN LOVE with AMBER SMITH! What the fuck am I gonna do now?"

Every rap music song the DJ played that night sounded something like this:

"Gonna fuck you in the ass, in the ass, in the ass,
Gonna fuck you in the big black ass, fuckin' bitch.
Back it up, back it up, and let me fuck that big black ass.
Gonna fuck that ass that ass that ass."

Amber and I, now both drunk, were laughing hysterically, taking turns reciting the unbelievably nonsensical words to these horrific rap songs. "John Lennon must be spinning in his grave right now," I screamed into Amber's ears. She fell against me, laughing, her lovely breasts pressed against my shoulder and her long blonde hair flowing everywhere.

Finally, 2:00 am arrived, and the promoter "sprung" us from this hellhole. He walked us back to our room, shook my hand, hugged Amber goodbye, then split. We entered the room, drunk, and were both instantly reminded that there was just one bed.

Not wanting to let the tension last too long, I simply said, "Amber, I need to ask you a HUGE FAVOR right now."

Amber: "What's that?"

Me: "I really don't want to sleep on the floor tonight. Can I share the bed with you?"

"Yeah, sure, of course, that's fine," she said.

I popped on my PJs and slid under the covers, while Amber entered the bathroom to "de-supermodel" herself. She returned in sweat pants and a loose-fitting T-shirt with no bra.

Amber got under the covers and turned off the lights. I was now lying in bed with one of the most beautiful women on Earth, at 3:00 am in the morning, drunk. Just inches apart, I realized if I didn't do SOMETHING just then, I'd regret it for the rest of my life.

I next did something so spontaneously stupid, I truly surprised even myself. I got onto my hands and knees, straddled Amber, and positioned myself directly over her face. "Amber, I need to kiss you right now," I declared. I stared into her eyes with love.

Her eyes were those of a deer caught in the headlights. She was horrified!

I slowly leaned my mouth down to press my lips against hers. She quickly turned her face. I got "the cheek." Truly surprised, I lifted my head back up, looked again into her shocked face, then went back down for a second try, this time kissing the other cheek. I lifted my head, looked directly into her face for a few seconds, then said, in hasty retreat, "Well, goodnight then." I got off my hands and knees, crawled under the covers, and instantly passed out, snoring just seconds later.

My friends have since asked me, "Why didn't you just ask her for sex?" The truth is, I knew instinctively that Amber simply had ZERO physical attraction toward me before I even went in for that first kiss. No amount of friendship-style love was ever going to change that, and it was just a fact of reality I was going to have to accept.

The next morning, my gal pal and I awoke about the same time. "Hey Amber, I just realized I can tell all of my friends I SLEPT WITH A SUPERMODEL!"

"Yeah, I guess that's true," she chuckled, and I knew she was not in the least offended by my reprehensible actions the night before.

We drove back to L.A., and again chatted non-stop for six consecutive hours. Amber brought up the "I've never had a real boyfriend, never been in love" theme she mentioned the day before, and I replied, "You know what? I actually find that hard to believe. Take me through the history of your love life, and let's be honest."

Hours later, Amber realized that there were a number of men she'd known in her past that truly DID love her. While most of them dumped her for becoming too clingy and needy, she did admit that she even dumped a few of them herself, when THEY became too clingy to HER.

"Wow," she said, "I never realized that before. I have loved some men, and some men have loved me."

"Of course," I said, "who could possibly date you and NOT fall in love with you?"

Then, the killer part came up. She said, "These days, it's so hard for me to find someone to date, because I'll only go out with extremely good-looking men, over six feet tall, who remind me of my father. My dad resembled Superman. I can't possibly be attracted to anyone else, for some reason." I believe this was Amber's cryptic way of telling ME that I simply would never make the "cut" within her stringent dating criteria.

I'd written my little "Amber, I think I'm starting to have feelings for you" speech on a yellow sticky post-it note, which was pasted to the left side of my steering wheel. I promised myself that at some point during our time in Vegas I was going to spill my guts, and let her know how I really felt. After the "I only date extremely good-looking, tall men who look like Superman" speech, we stopped off for gas. I surreptitiously tore off the yellow sticker from the dashboard and tossed it in the trash. "It's just NEVER GONNA HAPPEN," I said out loud to myself, as I filled the tank, preparing for our long drive back home to L.A.

A few weeks later, Amber met a multi-multi-millionaire at one of the Texas nightclub appearances I booked for her. This recently-divorced guy made his fortune by inventing some kind of unique dental implants. He bought a mansion in the Hollywood Hills solely to allow Amber to live there so she would be available to him at his beck and call. At this point, my relationship with her faded into history. My family and friends said to me, "God, she used you SO BAD," to which I, unfortunately, have no defense.

I became extremely disappointed that the minute Amber got involved with a mega-wealthy man, she was unable to find the time to maintain our friendship, dropping me like a hot potato. I honestly and sincerely believed that we'd become REAL honest-to-God friends, having shared so many intimate moments during our 10 months together.

With regard to our short relationship, I feel Amber's biggest flaw was simply her extraordinary inability to appreciate and nurture the love of a true friend. Her TV mentor, Dr. Drew Pinsky, once said of her, "Amber Smith is an empty person and she's struggling. She has a lot of emptiness and she doesn't even know sometimes what she's feeling." For me, those sentiments sum it up best.

I reflect back on Amber as my penultimate "Carrot on a Stick"—a woman with brains, beauty, honesty, sexuality, and mystery—whom I truly loved, or thought I loved, but could never quite "attain."

Today, she will no longer return my phone calls, emails, or texts. So close and yet so far!

Chapter Ten

2010

HOLLYWOOD & VINE / MEETING SPIELBERG / GEORGE LOPEZ IN WAX / SKINNY BARRY MANILOW / JONAH HILL GETS STUNNED / BILLY BOB IS RUDE

To begin this chapter, I need to backtrack a bit to the end of 2008. Just entering December of that year, my business was doing great. I was working from home, alone, making good scratch, and sending my two kids through college. About one month after Barack Obama was elected President, the worst recession in almost 100 years hit the United States, and between December 1 and December 15, two-thirds of my clients dropped me without warning.

"You're a great publicist and we love you, Dan," went the party line, "but the economy is tanking and no one knows what's gonna happen with this new President. We can't afford staying with you for our PR right now."

I was living pretty high on the hog at that time. I had a huge, three-bedroom apartment in Beverly Hills with a home gym. I had a 100-gallon saltwater fish tank filled with expensive tropical fish and a home gym. I had my drums (now a collectors' item) set up in my living room, along with a set of electronic drums in the bedroom (to keep the noise to a low roar for my neighbors) and I was driving a brand-new Mercedes Benz, not to mention the fact I was pursuing (but rarely "getting") attractive women who I would wine and dine at the most expensive restaurants in town. On top of all that, I was still supporting my ex-wife and I had to send two kids through college!

When my income suddenly plummeted to one-third of normal, I panicked. I knew I had to make many drastic changes quickly. As such, I moved into a new, smaller apartment, broke the lease on my Mercedes and simply turned it back into the dealership, sold my fish tank, my electronic drum set and my home gym. I also cancelled one of my life insurance policies, cashed in another, and pulled some money from my retirement account.

By the time early 2010 arrived, I'd downsized and was learning (finally) how to start living within my new means. I also had to declare bankruptcy for my agency, as well as for myself. I realized that after having to swallow that bitter pill, it might be a good time for me to partner up with another PR agency to strengthen my position, so as not to remain solely an independent publicist.

I had lunches with a few prominent publicists I knew in town who ran very successful PR agencies. I offered to "sell myself" to them; in other words, I asked them if they would consider buying my company outright. While they knew I was a killer publicist and had a great reputation, I wasn't billing enough money from my clients to make that idea viable for them.

Just about to give up all hope, I had one final lunch with a longtime, prominent, and quite old-school Hollywood publicist I never met before, but had known about for many years. His name was Jerry. Once he told me he was gay, he became known to me, forevermore, as Gay Jerry.

Gay Jerry ran a tiny three-man PR operation out of an office building located at the famed corner of Hollywood Boulevard and

Vine Street (Hollywood & Vine). He had, during the course of his many decades in the PR industry, represented everyone from Ray Charles to Bob Newhart to Bozo the Clown. We had a nice lunch, he suggested we partner up, meaning I would work out of his Hollywood office, and would split the income of any clients we managed to jointly lure into his agency. "We can play in the same sandbox," he said.

I accepted his offer and soon found myself inside the WORLD's SMALLEST OFFICE on Planet Earth. The room was essentially a glorified closet. An interesting side note about this office; it was the last one used by my late boss, Lee Solters. Gay Jerry and Lee had worked together, on and off, for many decades and Jerry allowed Lee use of that room during his final months alive.

The first time I left my house to go to Gay Jerry's agency (a schlep from Beverly Hills into Hollywood that, with traffic, took close to an hour each way, twice a day), I got a phone call from a woman named Helen. She was the founder of the annual Vision Awards, an event that honored men and women who helped raise funds to find cures for a variety of eye-related illnesses and diseases. Helen asked me if I could come and meet her as soon as possible at her home in the San Fernando Valley. I told her I'll "check with my new partner, Jerry" and get back to her.

I might note that Gay Jerry was the KING of handling PR for events. He and his team had the uncanny ability to lure virtually every single media outlet in Southern California to every one of his clients' events, whether or not those events even warranted that kind of media coverage (some did; many did not).

Once ensconced in my new shoebox office, I told Gay Jerry about Helen. A meeting was arranged and Helen hired the two of us in her living room, "sight unseen." (A cruel joke there. You see, Helen herself was blind.)

The KEY reason Helen hired Gay Jerry and I was because Jerry promised her that he had amazing contacts with high profile celebrities and, with him onboard, we would be sure to secure one BIG STAR for her so she could present to that celebrity a top honor. The event was slated to be held that fall in Beverly Hills.

Before I get to what ultimately happened with Helen and the Vision Awards, however, I would like to recount several celebrity stories that took place for me during the seven months (February through August) in which I was teamed up with Gay Jerry:

** Steven Spielberg: Gay Jerry represented the Universal Studios Tour and CityWalk. Back in 2008, a large portion of the Universal Studios backlot had been destroyed by a fire. It took the studio two years until that backlot had been restored to its former glory. Gay Jerry and his team–and me–were in charge of handling the media attendance for a Rededication Ceremony to mark the return-to-use of the fire-damaged backlot. In addition to several heavyweight Universal Studios executives, the special guests for that ceremony were going to be California Governor Arnold Schwarzenegger and superstar film director Steven Spielberg.

I'd known, instinctively, since I worked at Columbia Pictures in New York in 1980 and discussed the *Close Encounters of the Third Kind Special Edition* (1979) movie with publicist Marvin Levy, that I would, somehow/someway/someday, meet Steven Spielberg.

It was drizzling rain on the morning of the big Universal press event, so I came prepared with a hat and an umbrella. Gay Jerry and his cohorts managed to assemble a remarkable group of media. TV camera crews from all over the world were set up on two long bleachers. I was on hand to help corral these crews, as well as individual photographers and print journalists, and to ensure they had their proper credentials and they were placed in the right spots.

The sun broke through the clouds, the rain stopped, and the event began. Ron Meyer, then the President/COO of Universal Studios, spoke first and welcomed everyone. He recalled both the tragedy of the fire and the resilience of the fire crews, and of select members of the Hollywood community who came to the rescue to ensure the backlot would be reconstructed financially.

Steven Spielberg spoke next. He recalled how he'd first come to the studio back in the late 1960s, when he used to sneak around the various buildings, pretending to work there. He even once placed his name on the door of an empty office before anyone else knew who he was! He spoke of his long history of filmmaking on the Universal Studios lot and that, since his company, Amblin Entertainment, was headquartered there, he'd always considered Universal Studios "his Hollywood home."

Arnold Schwarzenegger was the sitting Governor of California at the time of this event, and had a phalanx of bodyguards everywhere. I chuckled when he spoke, reminded of the time I'd asked for his autograph 14 years earlier and recalling how he growled at me without ever once saying a word in English.

After the speakers spoke, the media crews came down from the bleachers and were lined up in a long row, behind a series of metal stanchions with red velvet ropes.

Virtually EVERY press member and media crew wanted to interview the Governor. "Arnold, Arnold! Over here! Over here! Can we talk with you Arnold? Arnold! Arnold!!"

What utterly amazed me by this display was that STEVEN FUCKING SPIELBERG, the most brilliant and successful director in the HISTORY OF MOTION PICTURES, was also there but standing alone, virtually in a shadow. It appeared to me as though he was almost hiding!!

I saw Marvin Levy standing not far from Steven. I knew the proper etiquette for me to introduce myself to Spielberg would be to go through Marvin, as Marvin had been Steven's publicist for 40 years (as of that moment in time). Just before I approached Marvin, though, a still photographer called me over to the red velvet rope.

"Hey, Dan, can you bring Steven Spielberg over here for me to shoot?" the guy said. "I'd love to get his picture."

Thinking quickly on my feet and realizing it would, in fact, take a good amount of chutzpah for me to pull this off, I responded, "I'll tell you what, my friend. IF I bring Steven Spielberg over here and IF he poses for a photo for you, you have to PROMISE ME you will ALSO take a photo of Steven AND ME TOGETHER! You have to also swear to me you'll email the photo of me tonight or tomorrow. Do you swear?"

The guy responded, "Sure, of course, I swear!"

Now a man on a mission, I waltzed over to Marvin Levy. I had during the course of the past 40 years bumped into him a few times here and there, mostly at a Gelson's grocery store in Studio City. He recognized me immediately and we shook hands. "Hey Marvin, would it be cool if I introduced myself to Steven?"

"Sure, of course, no problem," Marvin said.

I next had to make this important decision: What do you say to Steven Spielberg? He'd heard: "I loved *E.T.*" (1982) and "*Jaws* (1975) scared me to death" and "*Schindler's List* (1994) was a masterpiece" a hundred thousand times. I knew whatever I was going to say to him would have to be truly novel. I walked up to Spielberg who, again, was standing totally alone in life, in a shadow, looking like a man who didn't have a friend in the world.

"Steven?" I said, "my name is Dan Harary." We shook hands. I continued, "YOUR MOTHER makes the BEST BLINTZES I"VE EVER HAD IN MY ENTIRE LIFE!"

I should side note here: Steven's mother, the late Leah Adler, owned and operated a Kosher dairy restaurant, The Milky Way, two blocks from my home in Beverly Hills for many years. In fact, I'd taken MY mother there several times when she came to visit and each time, my mother, Leah and I would sit together at a booth. Leah would regale us with tales of her special Hollywood moments with "my brilliant son, Steven."

While still shaking hands, Steven said nothing. He then looked deeply into my face. I could see his gears spinning, and replied, "You know what? You're right! My mother DOES make the best blintzes in the world!"

It was a great moment. One of my all-time favorite celebrity close encounters.

I went on, "Steven, there's a photographer over there who is dying to get your photo. Would that be okay? If you don't want to, of course no problem, but he asked me to ask you. What do you think?"

"Sure, why not?" Steven replied.

He then followed me for the 20-step walk to where that specific photographer was positioned. "Steven, this is Lee. Lee, this is Steven Spielberg."

The two men shook hands and then Lee took his photos. Snap, snap, snap. When he was done, Lee then said, "Steven, is it cool if I get a photo of you and Dan together also?"

For a second, I almost puked, not wanting to embarrass this living legend.

"Sure, why not?" Steven said.

That night, Lee emailed me a photo of Steven Spielberg and me standing side-by-side, my hat and umbrella clearly in hand. Today, my mother has that photo proudly displayed via magnet on her refrigerator door. It appears in this book.

** <u>Jonah Hill</u>: Comedic Actor Jonah Hill also happened to be attending the Universal Backlot media event. After I left Spielberg, I walked over to him and told him the trailer for his upcoming movie, *Get Him to the Greek* (2010), looked especially funny.

"You liked it? Cool man, thanks," he said. "We're hoping it does well when it opens this weekend."

Mere seconds later, Steven Spielberg approached us, a small camera in his hands. "Hi, Jonah, I'm Steven," he said, extending his hand for Jonah to shake. Jonah had a look in his eyes that was indescribable.

"Of course, I know who YOU are," he responded, returning Steven's handshake.

Steven next said, "My daughter is a HUGE fan of YOURS! Can I get a photo of you and me together?"

Jonah Hill's mouth opened to the ground. "YOU want a photo with ME?" He was gob- smacked, a word I've never used, said or written before in my life. Here was the most famous director EVER wanting to pose for a photo with a young up-and-coming comedic actor who, in 2010, had not yet become as famous as he later would.

"Sure, of course, I guess," Jonah whispered. Steven handed the small camera to me, and I shot a picture of the two men together. Steven then thanked Jonah, shook his hand again, retrieved the camera from me and walked away.

Following that encounter, Jonah and I just stood there in silence. We were each bathed in the awe and the light that radiated brightly from one of the world's most remarkable creative geniuses.

** Barry Manilow: Gay Jerry had been retained to handle the media coverage for an event being held at the Dorothy Chandler Pavilion in downtown Los Angeles. The event was a musical tribute to Singer/Songwriter Barry Manilow. I helped corral the media reporters who stood behind the velvet ropes while the attendees walked the red carpet. The only celebrity that night I can recall was Barry Manilow himself. One of the TV crews standing behind me did not have their On-Air Reporter present. Apparently, she had car trouble *en route* and never made it there in time, so this cameraman asked me to hold a microphone out to Barry and to "just ask him any questions you can think of," and I did. I interviewed Barry Manilow for that local TV station, asking him a series of quick questions about his career, his songs and the honor he was going to receive that night.

I can't remember anything Barry said to me, but I did notice the man was remarkably skinny!

** Brendan Fraser: I was hired to handle the press for the First Annual 3D Society's "Lumiere" Awards. This was the kickoff awards event for the 3D Society, a non-profit Hollywood group that promoted the emergence of 3D filmmaking. The host for that awards event was Movie Star Brendan Fraser of *The Mummy* (1999). Years earlier, my kids and I used to watch (over and over again on DVD) a movie of his called, *Blast from the Past* (1999). In that film, Christopher Walken played Brendan's father. When I met Brendan, I asked him if he had ever seen the hilarious bit on *Saturday Night Live* when his movie "dad"–Christopher Walken–was portraying the manager of the rock band Blue Oyster Cult while they were recording their hit song, "Don't Fear the Reaper." In that skit, Walken kept insisting that the band "Use more cowbell!" (Watch it on YouTube, it's hysterically funny.)

Brendan's face lit up when I asked him this. "Have I ever SEEN IT? Are you kidding? Watch this!" He then pulled out his iPhone from his pocket and played me the "ringtone" from his phone. The ringtone was Christopher Walken's voice saying, "Fellas! I GOTTA have more cowbell!"

Duly impressed, I told Brendan that was awesome. We both had a good laugh over it.

** <u>Wayne Brady</u>: For a separate event at Universal Studios, Gay Jerry was in charge of handling the media attendance for the grand opening of a new attraction, "King Kong: 3D." There was a ton of press there that day and dozens of (non-memorable) stars walking the red carpet. For me, I was "in charge" of escorting comedic actor Wayne Brady and his family along the red carpet and introducing him to the various TV camera crews covering the event. I was a big fan of Wayne's brilliant comedy and singing skills from his appearances on Drew Carey's show, *Whose Line Is It Anyway?* He was a terrific guy and we spent a highly enjoyable afternoon together.

** <u>Mark Moses</u>: Mark, best known as "Duck" from the hit TV series, *Mad Men* (2007), was also in attendance at the "King Kong: 3D" event. After I finished handling media for Wayne Brady, I went to the banquet table to eat lunch and Mark was standing next to me. We spoke at length about *Mad Men* and I enjoyed meeting him very much.

** <u>George Lopez</u>: Gay Jerry represented Madame Tussauds Wax Museum, located on Hollywood Boulevard, one block from the legendary Grauman's Chinese Theater. Apparently, every time the museum was going to unveil a new celebrity in wax to the world, Jerry and his team corralled the press to attend. During my time teamed with Jerry, Comedic Actor George Lopez was to make his world debut as a wax figure. As I did with Barry Manilow, I was asked by a TV camera crew to hold a microphone and interview George about his thoughts on "this honor." He was witty and fun, and, although I'd never seen him on TV or in a movie before in my life, I was still impressed that Lopez was able to answer so many basic, inane questions with such instant humor.

** <u>Barney Burman</u>: I got a call from Special FX Makeup Artist Barney Burman. He told me he'd just been Oscar nominated for "Best Makeup" for his work on the J.J. Abrams-directed *Star Trek* (2009) movie. He wanted me to generate some articles about his work prior to the Academy Awards event. I generated several media stories about Barney in a relatively short period of time, and he did end up winning a 2010 Oscar for his contributions to *Star Trek*. Barney did not mention me by name when he won his award on TV, but he did mention me during his backstage/post-event interview which was streamed live over ABC TV's website.

** <u>Raquel Welch (Almost)</u>: This story will pain me forever! One day I was stuffed inside my closet of an office when Gay Jerry happened to come into my room for a quick visit. He asked me how things were going, etc., just small talk. Then he said, "Oh, by the way, I just had lunch with Raquel Welch."

I stood up from my chair, stunned. "What did you say to me, Jerry?"

He repeated, "I just had lunch with Raquel Welch."

I was so incredibly miffed that he hadn't invited me! Raquel Welch was my dream girl sex goddess all through adolescence! "Jerry! You're GAY! YOU met Raquel Welch and you didn't invite ME? I cannot believe this!!"

Jerry chuckled and walked away. He thought I was making a joke.

I wasn't.

** <u>Julia Louis-Dreyfus' Star</u>: Julia was getting a star on Hollywood Blvd.'s Walk of Fame, just in front of the building

I was working in with Gary Jerry, on Hollywood and Vine. There was a huge crowd there, so I couldn't get to talk with her. I just watched as they unveiled her star and she gasped. They had MISSPELLED her last name! When she spoke, she seemed clearly annoyed about that major "typo." Also, Larry David spoke during the ceremony. He walked right past me, but, again, I couldn't say hi due to the size of the crowd. His memorable line was: "Congratulations, Julia, on getting this immortal Star on the Hollywood Walk of Fame. Now the great 'unwashed' from around the world can walk all over you and find a convenient place to spit out their chewing gum!"

Now back to the Vision Awards: As I wrote earlier, I'd teamed with Gay Jerry to hopefully broaden my client base while splitting new business with him 50/50. When we secured Helen's Vision Awards account, I fully expected Jerry and his guys to help me handle all of the day-to-day activities needed to arrange for all of the pre-event publicity necessary to sell advance tickets. We also had to guarantee one BIG STAR's appearance and pull together a VIP guest list of additional attendees, including their representatives' physical business addresses for snail mailed invitations.

There was a lot of work to be done between February and September of 2010 for this upcoming event, and Helen was paying Gay Jerry and me $5,000.00 a month. Splitting that, I was getting only $2,500.00 a month. I mention this because Gay Jerry and his two aides DID LITERALLY NOTHING on this account the entire time I was there! I did EVERYTHING and they did NOTHING. I was giving Jerry half of my hard-earned fee for no gain and for no apparent reason, just like my dark days (and years) with the Duck.

During 2010, I reached out to dozens of very famous people through their reps, but none of them would commit to an appearance at the awards event itself. I do recall getting close with CBS Newsman Dan Rather and legendary Hollywood producer David Geffen. I ended up developing an email relationship with both men but, alas, neither was able to clear his calendar.

One day while pondering what to do, I saw an article in the *Los Angeles Business Journal* (weekly news magazine) about a man named Dr. Patrick Soon-Shiong, who was the richest man in Southern California at the time with a fortune of $9-billion, gleaned from two bioscience/pharmaceutical companies he founded.

I called Helen and ran the idea past her. She'd never heard of Patrick but said I could give it a try. I contacted Patrick's people, met with them in person, explained about the Vision Awards and the media attention they would attract, and after short order, he committed to be the special VIP Guest for our event. (Today, Patrick Soon-Shiong owns *The Los Angeles Times*.)

With just one month to go before the September date of the Vision Awards event, I decided to cancel my "partnership" with Gay Jerry. As he contributed nothing to the project and he was getting $2,500.00 a month for literally doing nothing, I had no desire to continue the arrangement. I told him I was leaving on a Friday, and over that weekend I retrieved my computer, my files and my office furnishings. Moving my office back into my home was a godsend and I promised myself I'd never make a mistake like that one again.

Finally, the night of the Vision Awards event arrived. I escorted on the red carpet: Lily Tomlin and George Schlatter (the creator of *Laugh-In*-1967); Black Eyed Peas Founder/Singer will i. am; Dr. Patrick Soon-Shiong, to whom I said, "I'm the guy that got you here!" to which he replied, "Very nice, thank you!"; Buzz Aldrin–this time he was very polite to me, unlike our first encounter; and Sherry Lansing, the iconic, first-ever female head of a movie studio (Paramount).

Also, Actor Billy Bob Thornton showed up late and the media gaggle wanted to interview him, but when I asked him if he'd do some interviews for me, he replied, "Sorry, man. I don't do that shit."

Gay Jerry, who'd made thousands of dollars from the Vision Awards for months doing nothing, didn't even bother to attend the event.

I finished out the rest of 2010 working from home and loving every minute of it.

Chapter Eleven

2011–2017

ASBURY AGENCY ARRIVES / WRANGLING KISS / THE COWSILLS' 50TH / BILLY CRYSTAL LIKES CHINESE / ANNOYING NANCY SINATRA / SPIRITUAL CARLOS SANTANA / KIM KARDASHIAN HAS BIG BOOBS / DIRECTING YOKO ONO / SEXY TIMES WITH DR. RUTH

At the start of 2011, I realized not having a corporation for income tax purposes was going to kill me, so I decided I would have to rise like a Phoenix and start a new one. Wishing to build on the good "brand name" I established for many years with Asbury Communications, I wanted to keep the Asbury part. My new corporation became The Asbury PR Agency, Inc. For exactly one year–March 2010 to March 2011–I'd been "unattached" to a company, even though I was still fortunate enough to handle several clients and maintain a steady income. When my new Asbury agency opened, I felt a sigh of relief. I could now, once again, use my corporation as a tool (and a shield) by which to write off a great number of related work and business expenses.

Another good thing about working from home again in 2011 was that my building was just a quick 15-minute walk up to the fantastic Kate Mantilini Restaurant, located at the corner of Wilshire Boulevard and Doheny Drive in Beverly Hills. I started using "Kate's," as we locals called it, as a regular lunch destination for client and new business meetings, and in the evenings for dates with very expensive and unattainable women.

Alas, poor Kate's went out of business around 2016, but during those five years, I had these memorable celebrity close encounters there:

** <u>Don Rickles</u>: As I was about to leave the restaurant one afternoon, I was heading toward the front door when I literally collided into Don Rickles! The man was rather ancient-looking at the time.

"Oh my God, Mr. Rickles, I'm so sorry!" I said. "Are you okay?"

He replied, "I'm fine, Sonny, but where's the fire?"

I apologized profusely and opened the door for him (from the inside) so he could leave the restaurant first. "Here you go, sir," I said, as he walked through the door.

"Thanks Sonny," he said.

I replied, "Anything for you, Mr. King of Comedy." He liked that remark and saluted me as he slowly shuffled away.

** <u>Alanis Morissette</u>: Another day at Kate's as I was heading toward the door to leave, I saw Singer Alanis Morissette sitting across the table from another woman. I knew I had to say something because my girlfriend at the time, Suzie, was obsessed with Alanis' record "Jagged Little Pill," so I simply walked right up to her. "Alanis! My name is Dan, and I have a girlfriend who I believe is more in love with YOU than she is with ME."

We shook hands and she replied, "Oh goodness, well I'm sorry to hear that, but at least you know she has good taste."

** <u>Yoko Ono</u>: Another day at lunch at Kate's, I was talking to a client and I saw from the corner of my left eye Yoko Ono, standing just to my left, appearing to be a bit lost. Like a shot, I stood. "Yoko! Hi, are you looking for someone?"

"Yes, the bathroom," she replied.

I pointed the way for her, she thanked me and walked off. I was tempted to say, "So sorry about John" in that moment, but those seconds were fleeting and she clearly really needed to go pee.

** <u>Mick Fleetwood</u>: As mentioned earlier, my friend Steve and I did lights for Fleetwood Mac at the Sunshine Inn back in the early '70s, so when I saw Mick Fleetwood again, now 40 years later at Kate Mantilini's, I felt a need to say a quick hello.

"Hey Mick, my name is Dan. I did stage lights for your band at the Sunshine Inn in Asbury Park, New Jersey in 1973."

He shook my hand and said, "My dear friend, if you remember 1973, then you weren't really PART of 1973." He patted me on the shoulder, then returned to his conversation with his lunch companions.

Backtracking a bit: the very first client I ever had for Asbury Communications, starting in 1996, was a brilliant and gifted Special Effects Makeup Artist named Todd Masters–a three-time Emmy Award winner. Todd's company, MastersFX, created special FX work for hundreds of movies and TV shows over the years, including *Star Trek: First Contact* (1996), *True Blood* (2008), *Six Feet Under* (2001), *The Handmaid's Tale* (2017), *The Good Doctor* (2017), *Tales from the Crypt* (1989), and dozens more.

For many of the years during our long relationship, Todd held an annual Halloween Bash at his large L.A. studio. That bash evolved into becoming THE Hollywood Halloween party each year, with entertainment industry people of all shapes and sizes attending and wearing costumes that redefined special FX. (I almost always went to these parties dressed as a Rabbi. And while it's been years since his last party, to this day, Todd still calls me "Rabbi Dan.")

Among the celebs I met at various MastersFX Halloween Bashes were: Charles Fleischer, best known as the "voice of Roger Rabbit." Charles was a very bizarre stand-up comedian and actor, and I ended up doing a small PR project for him on the side; Doug Jones, the tall, thin actor best known for portraying non-human characters. He appeared in a scaly fish-type costume in the Oscar-winning film, *The Shape of Water* (2017), and as the Faun in the movie *Pan's Labyrinth* (2006). I met James Gunn, the director of the massive hit film series, *Guardians of the Galaxy* (2014), long before allegations were made against him involving highly inappropriate sexual content he posted on social media; Nancy Allen was one of my favorite actresses from the '80s, appearing in *Blow Out* (1981), *Dressed to Kill* (1980), *RoboCop* (1987), and *Carrie* (1976). When I met her, she was still very attractive but now had silver/white hair. I complimented her on how beautiful she still was and confided I'd had a big crush on her back in the day; Lance Henriksen is an actor best known as "Bishop" the robot in the first *Alien* (1979) movie. We spoke briefly about his upcoming work; Robert Englund once again. Knowing Robert was going to be attending this party, I brought a color photocopy of the photo I'd taken of him and Howard Stern decades earlier. Handing it to him, he went silent and then hugged me saying, "Danny boy! I forgot this picture existed! Thank you!" He was still as funny and animated as I remembered him from years past; and Rick Baker, Oscar-winning makeup FX artist for films such as *An American Werewolf in London* (1981) and *Harry and the Hendersons* (1987). (I'd gotten Rick & Harry the cover of *Boys Life Magazine* years earlier.)

I'll add one last "celeb" into the list of those I met at various Todd Masters Halloween parties. Cynthia Preston was a beautiful blonde actress best known for her role on the soap opera *General Hospital*

(1963) and later on *Two and a Half Men* (2003). The night I met her, she was dressed like a sexy policewoman, wearing a black police uniform but with hot pants and black fishnet stockings. For that singular party, I was dressed as an escaped convict from Alcatraz (not as a Rabbi) and wearing black-and-white striped prisoner garb. Cynthia was so attractive, I went up to her and said, "I think you should arrest me, right here, right now." The line seemed to work; we spent the evening drinking and talking, and I got her phone number.

During our dinner the following week, we had a fantastic time together. I honestly thought I'd finally hit a home run–I'd connected with a true Hollywood beauty-one who also had brains and an actual personality!

Imagine my surprise then, when just after I paid the check for our dinner at Yamashiro Japanese Restaurant, located high up in the Hollywood Hills and featuring a romantic view above all of Los Angeles, Cynthia told me she had a great time with me and I was a "super nice guy," but she had started dating her divorce lawyer and, therefore, she would be unable to see me again.

Hollywood women–they never cease to amaze!

P.S. Todd Masters and I have been, and remain, close friends for 25 years.

One day, I heard a knock on my front office door. When I opened it, in walked Anthony Bongiovi, a director of music videos who just happened to be a brother of Rock Singer Jon Bon Jovi. Anthony heard about me through the grapevine and hired me on-the-spot to get him press coverage in the Hollywood trades about his various directorial projects. I generated several articles for him and then he vanished, as quickly as he'd first entered into my life.

My close friend Ron, who was now working within the On-Air Promotions Department at CBS TV, invited me to join him for an event being held at the Television Academy building in North Hollywood. The evening was designed to honor the cast of the comedy TV series, *How I Met Your Mother* (2005). During that event, I briefly met Neil Patrick Harris and marveled at how tall he was; inadvertently insulted *Mad Men* creator Matt Weiner, when I told him I was a big fan of his show but didn't remember a specific scene he asked me about; and swooned over the stunningly beautiful actress Cobie Smulders, a star of *How I Met Your Mother*. I had a few drinks and was flirting with her (or trying to) until she started telling me about her husband.

I had a crush on Cobie all during the run of that hit TV program.

I woke up on the morning of February 12, 2014, to hear the sad news that Sid Caesar, comedy icon and my former client, had passed away. I quickly phoned his former manager, Larry, and asked when and where the funeral service was going to be held. He told me and I went.

Inside the chapel at Forrest Lawn Cemetery up in Burbank, sat a virtual "Who's Who" of Hollywood's comedy industry–Mel Brooks, Richard Lewis, Norman Lear, Billy Crystal, Jack Carter, Shecky Greene, and Phil Rosenthal, co-creator of the TV series, *Everybody Loves Raymond* (1996), not to mention Jon Voight, Michelle Lee, and Connie Stevens.

Most of those I listed above spoke at Sid's memorial event, each praising the late comic as "one of the all-time greats," and citing specific moments in time he or she spent with Sid over the decades. Carl Reiner, one of Sid's best friends, happened to be sick that day, so he submitted a videotaped speech which we all watched, citing the importance of Sid's contributions to show business.

Mel Brooks gave the eulogy and it was stunning, essentially recounting the past 50-year history of television comedy. Mel told the gathered he owed everything in his life to Sid's having hired him when he was just a kid as a junior writer on *Your Show of Shows*. The best story Mel told was the time he and the rest of Sid's writers were at a restaurant in Times Square, waiting for Sid to show up for a dinner. When Sid did arrive, there was no parking spot for his car–a Volkswagen had parked in front of the restaurant's front door–a spot usually reserved for Sid. As Mel told it, Sid pulled his car up to the VW, got out, then physically LIFTED UP the VW with his bare hands and MOVED IT ONTO THE SIDEWALK! Sid then calmly parked his car in the now-open space, entered the restaurant, and sat down to eat as though nothing out of the ordinary had taken place.

I sat literally mesmerized by Mel's eulogy, as did everyone else in the chapel room that day. Mel took turns both laughing and crying while he spoke. He commanded the room with his stories. You could hear a pin drop.

As we each filed out at the end of the ceremony, I met Norman Lear and Phil Rosenthal, shaking their hands, and telling the men that "Mel's eulogy should have been recorded for posterity. We just heard the history of American comedy." Norman and Phil agreed!

I shook Jon Voight's hand, telling him I was touched by his shared memories of evenings he spent with Sid.

I finally met Richard Lewis, one of my absolute favorite comics, and thanked him for his wonderful reminisces. Richard recalled how he and his father never got along when he was a youngster, but when Sid's TV program, *Your Show of Shows*, came on the air, Richard's father would gather his family into the master bedroom and they, as a unit, howled with laughter. Richard said it was the only time in his entire life when he and his father got along without arguing.

I shook Mel Brooks' hand, reminding him we met previously (with my mother) and his eulogy was like "watching a historic document come to life." He, once again, sang, "Dan Harary, Dan Harary men have named you!" to the tune of Mona Lisa. The guy is consistent!

I introduced myself to Billy Crystal-I'd seen his one-man play *700 Sundays* (2013) the year before and was enthralled by his remarkable talents. I told him how much I had enjoyed that show. I also said I'd loved his line about "Jews know the best Chinese food in L.A. is at Twin Dragon on Pico." I'd been eating at Twin Dragon for decades.

He said, "Yeah, that place is great, right? The best kung pao chicken in the world."

Billy seemed like a nice guy and I could tell Sid's death affected him emotionally. When he'd spoken earlier during the memorial, his voice got choked up a few times.

My *alma mater*, Boston University, held a reunion for attendees of its School of Communications at the West Hollywood-based Improv comedy nightclub. Jason Alexander, a BU graduate and the iconic "George" from *Seinfeld*, was the special guest speaker.

After Jason spoke, we BU grads mingled amongst the crowd. I met Jason and told him I needed his opinion about something.

"Go ahead," he said.

I told him that in February, 1994, on the first day of its opening, I'd taken a date to see the movie *Schindler's List* in Marina del Rey. During the first few minutes of the film, my date hopped into my lap and started making out with me, furiously, much to my shock and utter surprise. So you can imagine MY shock and utter surprise when I watched the episode of *Seinfeld* which aired a few months later, in which Jerry Seinfeld was on a date to see *Schindler's List* and had HIS DATE start making out with HIM in the theater!

"Wow, is that true?" Jason asked.

"I swear on the lives on my children, Jason, that's a true story. That happened to me in real life MONTHS before you guys did an episode about it."

"Hmmm," Jason continued, "the only thing I can say is probably someone from our show SAW YOU in that theatre and told Larry David, or maybe it was Larry himself. Sounds like a remarkable coincidence otherwise."

In my gut, I know someone from *Seinfeld* was sitting behind me that night in that theater. It MAY have been Larry David, I'll never know. But to this day, I take pride in the knowledge that I "inspired" an episode of the iconic *Seinfeld* TV series.

I was hired to handle the media relations for the Animé Expo, being held at the Los Angeles Convention Center. The annual Animé Expo presented films, vendors' booths and merchandise all centered around the passion of many millions of people for all things Animé–Japanese animation.

This was a huge assignment for me, as 100,000 people would be attending this four-day event. As it happens, I had been hit by an intense case of vertigo the day before the expo opened, so the whole time I was at the convention center surrounded by so many people, my world was quite literally spinning all around me!

To make this project even more difficult, Gene Simmons and Paul Stanley from the rock band KISS were going to be the special guest stars who would be introducing to the Animé fans the first ever U.S. performance of Japan's #1 all girl group, Momoiro Clover Z aka MCZ. The group was going to do a live performance the first night of the expo, after Gene and Paul talked about how much they loved Japan, Japanese fans and all things related to Japanese culture.

I had to arrange for a backstage media event for Gene, Paul and MCZ, which I did, as the world spun 360-degrees around me. I was living on hardcore medication that whole week, and to this day I have no idea how I managed to pull this off. We had dozens of media members with cameras at the backstage event, during which time I spoke with Paul Stanley about his new music project, "Soul Station," and the time he and KISS performed at the Sunshine Inn back in 1973.

"I remember that gig," he told me. "I still have the poster for it."

"Me, too," I said.

When I was able to get Gene Simmons' attention, I tried to shake his hand, but he fist-bumped me instead. "Hey Gene, I worked stage crew for you guys at the Sunshine Inn in Asbury Park back in 1973," I shouted.

He drolly replied, "Don't you mean 1873?"

Gene was clearly exhausted, as he'd just gotten back into the USA from Europe that morning, and wanted solely to get some sleep.

I added, "Paul and I both still have that poster."

Gene replied, "So do I. It's in my KISS museum."

My childhood best friend, Steve, came out to L.A. for a visit. One night in my house, we watched a documentary about the '60s real-life family singing pop music group, The Cowsills. The doc was rather dark, as at the heart of this story was a father who managed the family with an iron fist and ultimately embezzled many millions of dollars from his wife and children.

In the '60s, The Cowsills were an American phenomenon and had a number of hit songs on the radio, including "Hair," "The Rain, The Park and Other Things," and "Indian Lake," as well as having sung the theme song for the hit TV series, *Love, American Style* (1969). The TV series, *The Partridge Family* (1970), had been built upon the premise of the real-life Cowsills.

After I watched the documentary with Steve, I remembered one evening back in 1967 when my parents had taken my brothers and I out to dinner at a local diner. That night, I'd heard on the restaurant's speaker system "The Rain, The Park and Other Things," and immediately got tears in my eyes. That song was such a joyous, happy, uplifting tune that it had affected me emotionally. I never forgot that experience.

<u>Cut to</u>: After Steve returned to New York, I tracked down Bob Cowsill, who was now living in the San Fernando Valley selling medical technology equipment to hospitals and doctors' offices. I told him I wanted to take him to lunch. I had an idea I thought he might spark to.

Bob and I met for lunch. I told him the first record he and his older brother, Bill, recorded was back in 1965, so the year 2015 would mark the 50th Anniversary of The Cowsills in the music industry. This lunch took place during the fall of 2014.

Bob's reply, "Oh, my God, you're right! 50 years. I never would have thought of that."

I then continued. "Bob, my best friend Steve Walter owns a very popular live music nightclub in Manhattan called the Cutting Room. I think The Cowsills should perform a special 50th Anniversary concert there next year. I'm sure Steve would book it for you and I'll handle the PR for free. Your song, 'The Rain, The Park' means a great deal to me and I'd be honored to work with you guys!"

Bob was amazed by this entire turn of events. He told me he would speak with his siblings Paul and Susan (the three of them comprising the current iteration of The Cowsills) and let me know ASAP if they could perform in New York.

A short time later, Bob confirmed the group would love to fulfill my idea. I called Steve, a date was booked, and the show was a go.

I flew into New York for this special event–one of the few times I visited there since moving out to L.A. back in 1980. The night before the concert at the Cutting Room, The Cowsills had been invited to perform during a live broadcast from the Sirius XM studios in NYC during a show hosted by radio legend, Cousin Brucie. Steve and I watched this performance through glass from the show's control room and during their performance of "The Rain, The Park," I showed Steve a tear that was trickling down my cheek.

After the Cousin Brucie show, Steve took all of us out to eat at the restaurant inside the iconic Chelsea Hotel (the site where Sid Vicious had overdosed). Steve ordered massive quantities of food-so much was presented on the table, in fact, that Susan Cowsill, who was sitting directly across from me, and I started laughing so hard we were crying.

"Steve, who are you, man? King Henry the 8th?" Susan and I had a severe case of the giggles. We simply could not stop laughing at the gluttony that appeared before us on that table.

The next night at the Cutting Room, the club was completely packed and The Cowsills dedicated their show "To Danny & Steve, thank you guys so much for getting us here. We haven't played New York City since *The Ed Sullivan Show!*"

I was on Cloud 9 during that concert and, of course, I cried during "The Rain, The Park." At the end of the show, Steve and I jumped up on stage and hugged the band. I told Susan Cowsill, "God, I just love you guys so much," and kissed her on the cheek. A friend of Steve's took photos of us all gathered onstage together.

Steve and I helped the band pack up their gear and load it onto a truck parked in front of the Cutting Room. We hugged each member of the group and watched them drive away. Steve and I were on a natural high.

"Do you realize that was the first thing we've collaborated on together since our days at the Sunshine Inn, back in the '70s?" Steve asked.

"Wow, you're right," I replied. "We've still got it."

A wonderful, memorable time for me. A simple idea I'd had, had manifested into a tiny moment in pop music history.

<u>Side note</u>: Steve's partner in the Cutting Room is *Sex and the City* (1998) co-star, Chris Noth. I met Chris during The Cowsills' rehearsal, but while shaking his hand, he never once looked at me, simply staring off into space. He was a distant, cold man and I

instantly felt his invisible shield, guarding him from all strangers, foreign and domestic.

My brother Bob was visiting me in Beverly Hills. One day while we were eating sub sandwiches outdoors in front of Jersey Mike's restaurant, Marc Summers walked past me. I hadn't seen Marc in decades, but I recognized him instantly.

"Hey Marc!" I called out. "Do you remember me?"

He studied my face. "You do look familiar, who are you again?"

I told him I met him back at Gary Collins' *Hour Magazine* (1980) show taping during my very first week ever in Los Angeles, and again when he was the warm-up comic for the TV series *What's Happening Now!!*, which I did the PR for.

"Right, yes, of course, I remember you now!" Marc replied.

In the interim years since I'd last known Marc, he had become the renowned TV host of a kids' game show called *Double Dare* (1986)–the show on Nickelodeon that introduced "green slime" to the world. Marc made a fortune from that show and following its run, morphed into a TV production mogul, producing other shows for the Food Network like *Dinner: Impossible* (2007) and *Restaurant: Impossible* (2011), both of which starred celebrity chef Robert Irvine.

Marc gave me his number, we met again, and he hired me to handle the PR for his various TV projects, including a one-man theater show. I came up with the idea that Marc hosted, or co-hosted, 25 TV series during his career and with that as a PR "hook," generated a good deal of media coverage for him, including a profile in *PEOPLE* Magazine and an appearance on *The Howard Stern radio show*.

Marc told me that his show *Restaurant: Impossible* was about to mark its 100th episode in production, and that Chef Robert Irvine was going to be doing a live "concert" for his fans, during which Marc would be serving as the MC.

I had my daughter, Anjuli, design a graphic for the top of a cake I had custom-made for Marc to present to Robert, backstage, before Irvine's concert. Marc's daughter took photos of the two men standing side-by-side that special "Happy 100th Episode" cake, which depicted Robert Irvine wearing a white chef's outfit and wielding a sledgehammer.

Marc has since retired and moved north to Santa Barbara; in fact, his next-door neighbor is Oprah Winfrey! He has remained, these past ten years, one of my very favorite people on the planet and one of my very best friends.

Marc Summers called one day to tell me he had been longtime friends with Sarah Campbell, one of Singer Glen Campbell's ex-wives, and Sarah was looking for a publicist to help her son, Dillon, with his burgeoning music career.

I met with Sarah and Dillon at a sushi restaurant and marveled at how attractive Sarah was, even in her early 70's. At that lunch, Sarah told me a number of real horror stories about how terribly Glen Campbell treated her and their son Dillon when Dillon was very young. At that time, Glen was an out-of-control alcoholic and cocaine addict–afflictions Glen admitted to in his autobiography. I was surprised and saddened to hear this, as I used to watch *The Glen Campbell Goodtime Hour* (1969) TV show religiously as a youngster.

Dillon Campbell was an emerging singer/songwriter. I got him a few radio and TV interviews in the Los Angeles area. He was a nice guy, but he was sometimes hard to locate. Several times I had to cancel media interviews I'd arranged for him, after Sarah would call me up to tell me "Dillon isn't around. I'm not sure where he is."

Episodes like that happened often, until I finally had to tell them I could no longer represent him.

Today, Sarah and Dillon live in Nashville with Dillon's wife and daughter. Sarah and I remain friends on Facebook, but I doubt I will ever see either of them again in real life.

I received a phone call from a man who was marketing "the Photo Bubble," a new product designed to help facilitate the filming of movie and TV program scenes with minimal lighting requirements. He told me his company had been hired by Old Navy for the production of a TV commercial starring Julia Louis-Dreyfus.

I attended the shoot for that commercial, which was being produced on the Sony Studios lot in Culver City. I was excited by the possibility of seeing Julia again, as it had been decades since our last encounter.

I arrived at the soundstage and saw that a huge white, yes, "bubble" had been inflated in the middle of the room. Inside the bubble was a scene that resembled a model's catwalk. In the commercial, Julia was portraying a French fashion designer who was instructing her models how to walk the catwalk, but when she learns they are wearing very affordable Old Navy clothing, Julia "loses" her French accent and becomes an American suddenly interested in purchasing some of those same Old Navy clothes for herself.

My client and I watched as Julia and a number of very attractive female models ran through their lines and shot various moments from the commercial. During a break, Julia sat on a director's chair (with her name on its back). Sitting next to her on the adjacent director's chair was her husband, Brad Hall of *Saturday Night Live*. I approached the *Seinfeld* and *Veep* star.

"Julia! My name is Dan Harary, I'm a publicist. I first met you during the very start of the Environmental Media Association and the launch of the Environmental Media Awards!"

"Oh my God, that was SUCH a long time ago," Julia replied. "I'm flattered that you remembered me from way back then."

I then turned to Brad. "Hey Brad, nice to meet you, man," and we shook hands.

"Julia, I have a very funny story to share with you. Can I tell it?"

"Sure, why not?" she said.

I was now quite excited, thinking my recounting of the "tag on the dress" story would enthrall the two of them. "When you arrived on the red carpet for the first Environmental Media Awards event, you were wearing a brand-new dress, and the dress had a huge SALES TAG sticking out of it! There were dozens of TV cameras there at the time, so I had to run up to you and rip off that tag before you did any interviews!" Brad Hall laughed, and I thought my story would make Julia chuckle at the very least.

"Oh my, really? Did I really do that? Oh, wow." Julia was completely taken aback, embarrassed and a bit humiliated. She stopped smiling, stared at the ground and went silent. I couldn't believe I'd just insulted someone I so admired.

"Oh, um, okay then, nice to see you again, Julia, take care," I replied. I turned and quickly scurried away, feeling like crap for the rest of that afternoon.

Side story: Julia had a female stand-in for lighting rehearsals who was, perhaps, the most adorable brunette I'd ever seen in my entire life. I very much wanted to flirt with her, but I didn't get a chance that morning. I was anticipating after the lunch break I would, at the very least, try to chat her up and see if I could get her phone number.

Right after lunch, I had to go to the bathroom, badly; so badly, in fact, the men's room on the soundstage was occupied and I had no choice but to use the toilet in the women's bathroom. I was dreading the idea that Julia, or any other woman on the set that day, would need this bathroom while I was in there, and it would be a rather sad day for me if one of those ladies "caught" me.

Who should be standing just outside the ladies' bathroom door when I'd finished my business and was leaving? Yep, Julia's gorgeous body double.

"Wow, did you really just go in there?" she asked me, disgusted.

"Uh, yeah. Sorry, man, kind of an emergency," I sheepishly replied.

I walked off as she entered the smelly ladies' room and I knew, of course, I'd never have any chance of even getting her name, let alone her phone number.

As I'd humiliated Julia Louis-Dreyfus, so, too, had I been humiliated by her stand-in. I guess this was divine retribution.

I secured a client who was a very prominent auctioneer of high-end furniture, antiques, artworks and memorabilia items of "the stars." I generated numerous profile articles about him and his new company. This British gentleman, Andrew Jones, had a strong celebrity clientele who either purchased his items for sale, or granted them to him for commissioned sales.

At some of Andrew's various live auction events, I met: Patricia Arquette of *Medium* (2005); renowned burlesque queen/dancer Dita Von Teese; Johnny Carson's second ex-wife, Joanna Carson; and Shera Falk, Actor Peter Falk's widow. Shera had a small sheltie collie with her at one of Andrew's auctions, and the dog discovered he was amorously interested in my trousers. The dog humped my leg furiously. Shera ran up to me and removed the doggie, apologizing.

"Shera, don't worry about it," I replied. "That's the most action I've had in months!"

I'd been getting allergy shots once a week at the office of L.A.'s most prominent allergy doctor for many, many decades. Since my doctor was such a maven in his field, he treated numerous celebrity patients.

While spending time in his waiting room, I met, during this era: Actress Mary McCormick, who I so enjoyed in Howard Stern's movie, *Private Parts* (1997). She and I talked about Howard Stern who, she told me, was one of her best friends. We also talked about a movie of hers my daughter and I both liked called, *High Heels and Low Lifes* (2001). She was lovely and I greatly enjoyed meeting her; Actor Robert Patrick, who will forever be known as the "T-1000" cyborg in the movie *Terminator 2: Judgment Day* (1991). Robert also co-starred in one of my all-time favorite TV series, *The X Files* (1993). He and I got many shots together, and we talked about life, Hollywood, and allergies; Singer Gwen Stefani was in the waiting room one day with her child in a stroller. I was sitting inches from her, but didn't want to disturb her as she seemed distressed (her kid was sick). When the nurse called her name, I stood and held the door open so she could wheel her kid's stroller into the doctor's office.

"Thank you," she said. I replied, "For you, Gwen, anything."

Another actor I met in the allergy office was Ron Livingston, an interesting fellow, best known for his work on the comedy film *Office Space* (1999) and as the man who broke up with Sarah Jessica Parker's character via post-it note on *Sex and the City*. I told Ron the time I watched *Office Space* with my brother, Bob, was one of the times we'd laughed the hardest ever in our lives. He also told me that strange women, to this day, come up to him on the street and argue with him for "breaking up with Carrie Bradshaw through a post-it note!" Great guy.

Jackass (2000) star Johnny Knoxville and I got many allergy shots in tandem. At the time, *Jackass* was a huge hit TV and film series. I asked him about getting injured and was it worth the fame? He told me he was very grateful to have made a name for himself in Hollywood, but he was realizing he had to start slowing down. He'd broken numerous bones and felt the time was coming soon for him to "become an actual adult." He also expressed his concern to me over his friend, *Jackass* co-star Steve-O, who was a serious drug addict at the time.

"I'm trying my best to keep him from overdosing," Johnny told me.

I had many additional celebrity encounters during this time frame, none of which were work-related.

Among these incidents were:

** Sally Kirkland: I was on a first date with a woman I met on Match.com, and we had tickets to see a live theater play. After I picked her up, she told me she'd invited her friend "Sally" to join us, and would I mind picking her up, too?

"No problem," I said, driving into West Hollywood. There, Actress Sally Kirkland got into my backseat. Sally is perhaps best known for her Oscar-nominated role in the movie, *Anna* (1987), and for her appearance in Oliver Stone's movie, *JFK* (1991).

At the play, I sat between Sally and my date. I could clearly see Sally was more interested in me than my date was. While I was flattered and still considered Sally attractive even at her advanced age, I managed to deflect her amorous vibes. I drove both women home that night, and never saw either one again.

** Carlos Santana: My daughter, Anjuli, was attending San Francisco State University and I often flew up to San Fran to visit her. On one such flight, as I entered the cabin of the plane, I noticed Guitarist *Extraordinaire,* Carlos Santana, sitting in First Class to my right. The second I saw him, I blurted out, "Carlos! How are you, man?"

Carlos smiled, placed his two hands together, palm against palm, and bowed his head toward me, as though he was praying. This was his expression of "thanks."

"Live long and prosper, Carlos," I replied, placing my right fist over my heart as if to say, "I love you."

** Garry Marshall: Just before boarding another flight up to San Fran to visit my daughter, I was in the airport waiting area, reading a book about the JFK assassination. I heard above me, "Is that book any good?"

The man asking me the question was legendary Producer/Director Garry Marshall, creator of *Happy Days* (1974), *Mork & Mindy* (1978), and *Laverne & Shirley* (1976).

"Yes, Garry, it's fascinating," I answered. "In fact, if you ever studied the assassination, this book will open your eyes to a number of theories you've never heard about before."

"I'll have to get it, then," he said.

I doubt he had the chance. Sadly, Garry died not long after this encounter.

** Sharon Case: I was taking beginner's guitar lessons in a group setting at the famous McCabe's guitar shop in Santa Monica. Another student in my class was the luscious blonde Actress Sharon Case, star of the TV soap operas, *Days of Our Lives* (1965) and currently, *The Young and the Restless* (1973). Sharon was so beautiful I was always distracted during that class. Instead of memorizing the fingering of guitar chords, I was busy memorizing the curves of her very alluring body.

** Selma Blair: I was buying some magazines at the large newsstand in Studio City, when Actress Selma Blair bumped into me. She apologized.

I laughed and told her, "Selma, you can bump into me anytime." She was cute and sweet, and I only wished I could think of anything further to say.

** Kim Kardashian: I was walking back home on Wilshire Boulevard from a lunch in Beverly Hills when I saw a truly voluptuous brunette woman walking directly toward me. This woman's breasts were so large, they arrived five minutes before the rest of her body did. Realizing this was Kim Kardashian, I waited until we were side-by-side.

"God, Kim (referring to her boobs), unbelievable!"

Kim replied, "Right?"

** Bruce Willis: I was waiting to be seated for a table at Junior's Deli in Westwood, when Bruce Willis walked toward me. He seemed to be in a world of his own, and purposely did not look in my direction. I was truly surprised by how tall he was. Thinking fast, and realizing he wanted nothing to do with me, I simply said, "Jersey." (Bruce is from New Jersey.)

Without even looking in my direction, he responded, "Jersey," then stormed off and hurried to his table.

** Andy Dick: My daughter and I met Andy at a Whole Foods grocery store in Beverly Hills. As he and Amber Smith had co-starred on the VH-1 series *Celebrity Rehab: Sober House* starring Dr. Drew Pinsky, I knew he'd had a crush on Amber. "Andy, I'm Dan. I was close friends with Amber Smith."

"Really? Do you have her phone number? I'd so love to get back in touch with her!"

I gave it to him and he thanked me profusely.

** Mike Rowe: Mike Rowe is the star of the hilarious Discovery Channel reality TV series, *Dirty Jobs* (2003). I met him at a Starbucks on Beverly Drive in Beverly Hills, telling him how much my son, Jordan, loved that show. He talked with me for a while about how he was trying to "evolve" his persona by starting to do other kinds of television programs. We drank our coffees side-by-side and he gave me an autograph for my son.

** Mark Rydell: I attended a tribute to Carl Reiner at the Saban Theatre in Beverly Hills. In the lobby before the show, I met Director Mark Rydell. Mark is best known for his work on the films, *On Golden Pond* (1981), *The Rose* (1979), and *Cinderella Liberty* (1973). We talked about our mutual love of Carl Reiner's *The Dick Van Dyke Show* (1961) and, of course, Sid Caesar, whose *Your Show of Shows* originally put Carl Reiner on the map.

** <u>Al Pacino</u>: I was on a date with a very attractive actress/waitress at Dan Tana's Restaurant in West Hollywood. When my date got up from our table to go to the bathroom, I realized Actor Al Pacino was sitting at the table next to mine. He watched my gal pal walk away, glanced over to me, smiled and raised his glass as if to make a toast to her beauty. I raised my glass to him, returned his smile, and felt like a million bucks.

** <u>Rhea Perlman</u>: I was shopping at Whole Foods in Beverly Hills when my cart crashed into *Cheers* (1982) star Rhea Perlman's cart. I apologized, then said, "Rhea, my name is Dan. I'm from Asbury Park, New Jersey." I then pulled out my business card to show her that it read: The Asbury PR Agency.

"Oh, very, very cool," she replied. "I'll have to show this to Danny."

She was referring, of course, to her husband Danny DeVito, who grew up just adjacent to Asbury Park–same as me. I didn't mention to Rhea that years earlier I'd insulted Danny when I met him and asked him about being a hairdresser back in the early part of his career.

** <u>John Legend</u>: I was working out at my gym, L.A. Fitness, in Beverly Hills at the corner of Wilshire Boulevard and Doheny Drive.

"Hey man, can I work in with you?" asked a very handsome African American man, standing aside a very large, Black bodyguard.

I was reclining on a bench press bench at the time. "Sure man, no problem," I replied, not realizing until an hour later that this guy was Singer/Songwriter John Legend.

** Brian May: A former secretary/friend of mine now involved in the 3D film industry invited me to a special event at Walt Disney Studios in which Queen guitar legend Brian May would be discussing his passion for photography and all things 3D. I met Brian before the event began, telling him how much I enjoyed seeing Queen live in Boston back in '77 when I was attending Boston University.

"Brian, I remember how you had rows and rows of Fender Super Reverb amplifiers behind you when you played. I never saw any other guitarist ever do that."

"Vox," he replied. "They were Vox amps and yes, I never saw anyone else do that, either."

I felt a bit foolish, but my friend did snap a photo of Brian and me together.

** Leonard Nimoy: I was in the elevator at Cedars Sinai Medical Center, returning to the lobby floor after having just gotten one of my 20,000 lifetime allergy shots, when I saw "Mr. Spock" himself–Leonard Nimoy–standing alone next to me. Leonard had just appeared in the movie, *Star Trek Into Darkness* (2013). I said, "Mr. Nimoy, it's so great to see you back on the big screen again! I really enjoyed your new movie."

Clearly touched, but also clearly quite ill (his skin had an odd color) he simply replied, "Thank you, young man. That's very nice of you to say." Leonard died not long afterward.

** George Takei: One of my favorite celebrity stories; this one is in two parts.

Part One: My mother came to L.A. for a visit. I dropped her off for a few hours along Larchmont Boulevard in Larchmont Village to go shopping, as I had a lot of work to do. I was going to retrieve her for lunch. A few hours later, I found her on Larchmont sitting outside a Starbucks, drinking coffee side-by-side with *Star Trek* Actor George

Takei. I pulled up my car along the curb, waved to George, and watched as my mom got into my car.

"I just met such a lovely man," she said. "I was telling him about how I am an actress and producer of plays back in New Jersey and he was fascinated by my stories! What a nice man!"

"Mom!" I cried. "That's Sulu! You just had coffee with 'Sulu,' a world famous, global icon!"

My mother's reply, "What's a SULU?"

<u>Part Two</u>: Years later: I was backstage at *KTLA TV* News in Hollywood in the green room with Marc Summers. I booked Marc to do an on-air interview with KTLA's entertainment reporter, Sam Rubin. As Marc and I were sitting there waiting, George Takei walked into the green room as he, too, was going to do a live interview with Sam.

I introduced myself to George and told him I had a very funny story for him.

"Sure, tell me!" he said, smiling.

"George, many years ago, I dropped my mom off for a while along Larchmont Boulevard and she ended up having a coffee with you and your dogs at a Starbucks. She had no idea who you were! When she got back into my car, I told her she'd just met Sulu, and her response, was, 'What's a Sulu?'"

At this, George started laughing so hard he was crying. "What's a SULU?! Oh my, that's the greatest thing I ever heard!" he exclaimed. He laughed so hard, Marc and I joined in. To this day, I clearly remember the joy on his face when I recounted HIS close encounter with MY MOTHER!

** <u>Ron Jeremy</u>: A journalist friend of mine invited me to a Trivia Game night at a local bar. During these evenings, random groups of strangers would end up working together as teams to answer very difficult trivia questions. I was paired up with '70s porn star Ron Jeremy and we named our team, "The Schmeckles." Alas, our team only came in second place. (Today, Ron is in jail for multiple rapes.)

** Jeff Garlin: I met *Curb Your Enthusiasm* (2000) co-star Jeff Garlin at a TV taping for another client. Since he was close friends with *Seinfeld* co-creator, Larry David, I figured I would tell him the same story I told Jason Alexander years earlier about my *Schindler's List* date/*Seinfeld* episode.

"No, no. Larry David didn't see you during your date!" Garlin declared. "No chance. No way. Larry's a crazy genius. He thought of that all by himself. You can't claim ownership of that one, Dan."

I was a bit annoyed that he so dismissed me. It confirmed that I'll never have a way to prove that I "invented" that particular circumstance.

** Tobey Maguire and Ryan Phillipe: My friend Ron and I went to the Universal Amphitheatre to see a live stand-up comedy show by British Comedian Eddie Izzard. While I was less than impressed by the show, a funny thing happened to me in the men's room afterward. I was standing in a middle urinal, peeing, when *Spider-Man* (2002) star Tobey Maguire stood at the urinal to my immediate right and Ryan Phillippe, *Cruel Intentions* (1999) star and ex-husband of Reese Witherspoon, stood at the urinal to my immediate left. Knowing just what to say, having been in this spot several times before, I stated, "Gentlemen, we simply have GOT to STOP MEETING this way!"

This joke, which had worked so nicely for me with Robert Wise, Sylvester Stallone and even Jerry Springer, fell flat. I bombed. Tobey and Ryan looked at each other like I was a freak of nature, turned and hurried away.

** Nancy Sinatra: I was having lunch with a new employee of my bank, City National Bank of Beverly Hills, outdoors at a table on Bedford Drive in Beverly Hills. He invited me to lunch to thank me for my business. I asked him if he was familiar with the history of that particular bank and he said no. I was reading a very long biography of Frank Sinatra at the time, and I told this banker friend that when Frank Sinatra, Jr., had been kidnapped, Frank, Sr., had called the manager of that same bank in the middle of the night and asked him to put together $240,000.00 to pay the ransom.

Just as I was describing the Sinatra kidnapping to this banker guy, Nancy Sinatra exited from the restaurant and walked inches from me. At that time, I had a client–a movie and TV marketing and advertising agency–that was working with Nancy on building a brand-new website for her through which Sinatra fans could purchase merchandise and memorabilia items from the Sinatra Family.

"Nancy!" I said. "My name is Dan. My client XYZ is working with you right now on your new Frank Sinatra website!" I thought, no, I ASSUMED, she was going to be delighted by this coincidence, stop to talk with me, and maybe even join me and my colleague for a coffee.

"Well, your client is really FUCKING THAT WEBSITE UP!" Nancy declared, pissed. "Everything they've done for me so far has been wrong. I'm probably going to be firing them later this week!" With that, she stormed off.

I guess the reason this story is memorable to me is this: what were the ODDS that a Sinatra would walk past me just as I was telling this new banker guy a story about THE SINATRA FAMILY? No bookie in Las Vegas would ever have taken odds on that circumstance occurring in real life.

** <u>Chris Rock/David Spade</u>: I was sitting on a bench inside a bookstore, killing time by reviewing some magazines. I was going to be meeting my friend, Ron, in a few minutes for a movie at the nearby theater within L.A.'s The Grove shopping center. When I looked up, I saw a tall African

American guy sitting about two feet from me, on the same bench, also reviewing some magazines.

"God, this guy looks A LOT like Chris Rock," I thought to myself, "but there's NO WAY it could possibly be him. This man is FAR TOO TALL."

I stared at this guy. He looked back. I said, "You really do look like—"

He instantly replied, "Yeah, I know, I know. I get that a lot. Not me." We smiled at each other and continued reading magazines.

About 15 minutes later, I met Ron inside the movie theater lobby and saw Comic Actor David Spade (who I once literally bumped into in a men's room at a comedy nightclub, many years earlier) run up to this Chris Rock lookalike guy and hug him.

Ron said, "Look, there's Chris Rock and David Spade."

To this day, I'm stunned that Chris Rock stands at 5'10" tall. I'd always assumed he was a little guy. God, that was weird.

I'm finishing out this chapter by recounting my adventures with petite Dr. Ruth Westheimer. I was hired by the producers of an annual L.A. event called, "The Sexual Health Expo" or "SHE" for short, and was tasked by these new clients to find them a keynote speaker for their 2017 gathering.

At our initial meeting, I said to my clients: "Well, it simply has GOT to be Dr. Ruth! Who else could possibly be better than her?" They laughed at me at the meeting table. "There's no way on Earth you'll be able to get her, Dan," they sneered.

"Oh, really?" I replied. "Watch me!"

I then became a man on a mission. I simply HAD to secure Dr. Ruth as the keynote speaker for the SHE Conference at any cost. I don't recall how, but I managed to track down Dr. Ruth's publicist, a guy named Pierre in New York, and got him on the phone.

Long story short, Ruth demanded a $10,000.00 speakers fee, plus First-Class roundtrip airfare to and from New York and Los Angeles, as well as top accommodations at the Beverly Hills Hotel.

Defeated, I phoned my clients and told them Ruth's demands, not thinking in a million years they would acquiesce. "You can get us DR. RUTH?" they replied. "Fuck, we'll find the money!" and they did.

For many weeks, I was in daily (multiple times a day) contact with Pierre about "Dr. Ruth wants this" and "Dr. Ruth wants that." There seemed to be no end to her demands just to get her to and from the event. On top of that, I generated numerous media interview requests for Ruth to help promote the SHE event–all by phone prior to her arrival in Los Angeles. Pierre had me constantly changing the dates, the times, and even the phone numbers that journalists were expecting to utilize to accomplish these media interviews. Everything changed over and over and over again.

Dealing with all this was exhausting.

Finally, Dr. Ruth arrived and made her way to the Beverly Hills Hotel. I met her there, along with a photographer from the *L.A. Times*. We shot her photo for an article that would be running the next day. I also got a nice photo of us together.

During my time that evening with Ruth (about an hour), she and I had time to have a calm, quiet talk and we "bonded." I told her that Steve from the Cutting Room nightclub in Manhattan was my best friend.

She replied, "I know Steve. Such a nice boy, a real mensch!"

For that year's SHE Conference, several hundred people showed up, many more than normal, given the advance publicity and promotion that Dr. Ruth would be attending in person to give a keynote talk. When Ruth arrived by limousine to the event, I scooped her upstairs on the elevator and hid her backstage in a quiet meeting room.

"Dan, Dan," Ruth said, "as soon as I'm finished talking, I need you to PROMISE ME that you will get me RIGHT BACK DOWNSTAIRS to my limo so I can return to my hotel, okay? Promise me!"

"Yes, Ruth, of course, I promise," I answered.

Eventually, a producer of the SHE event introduced Dr. Ruth to thunderous applause. I led her up the few small stairs to the stage. She was captivating, brilliant, funny, and yes, sexy, as she talked about the importance of communication within a consensual sexual relationship. She spoke for about 20 minutes, at one point sitting in a chair and reading her speech off of cue cards. (This was a bit disturbing to many in the audience, as it was readily apparent she was showing her advanced age.)

Before Dr. Ruth spoke, members of the audience submitted handwritten questions to be asked of her. When Ruth finished her speech, she said, "So now I understand many of you have some questions for me. Dan! Why don't you come up here on the stage and help me out?"

I had been standing in the wings of the stage. I was stunned to my socks! Dr. Ruth wanted ME to ask HER SEX QUESTIONS? Oh my God! Okay, sure, why not?

One of the SHE producers handed me a stack of the index cards containing the questions. I waltzed up to the microphone, introduced myself, and began reading the cards.

The questions I asked Dr. Ruth, on behalf of the audience, ranged from cock rings, anal sex and mutual masturbation, to fetishes, "golden showers," and adultery. Ruth answered each and every question thoughtfully and honestly while, of course, recognizing the humor in many of her answers.

The Dr. Ruth/Dan Harary Sex Questions Show was a big hit. We got tremendous applause at the end of our session. (I was on something of a high, myself!)

Just then Ruth approached me, whispering in my ear, "NOW, Dan! Get me out of here, NOW!"

"Sure, okay," I replied.

A second later, my clients came up to me. "Dan, we MUST get photos of ourselves with Dr. Ruth on this stage! Why is she leaving? This is part of her contract, Dan! If she doesn't pose for photos with us, we are NOT going to give her that $10,000.00 check!"

FUCK! I was completely stuck between clients who were paying good money and my promise to Dr. Ruth! I saw a look of terror in Ruth's eyes–she did NOT WANT to be walking through that huge crowd, knowing she would be besieged for photos and autographs.

As Ruth began walking off from the stage, I ran around and in front of her, and grabbed her by both shoulders. "Ruth! I know I promised to get you out of here, BUT I need you to do something for me, please! I NEED YOU to pose for some photos up here on the stage with my clients before you leave."

There was chaos and volume all around us, but Ruth and I were in a private "cone of silence," looking deeply into each other's eyes.

"Dan, if YOU need me to do something for you, yes, of course, I'll do whatever you say."

I gently nudged Ruth back onto the stage, and arranged for her to pose in photographs with all of my clients, the producers of the SHE event. Once everyone was satisfied, I personally scooped up little Dr. Ruth and, acting as a human shield, parted the Red Sea of fans before us. I hurried her into the elevator, downstairs through the lobby and back into her awaiting limousine.

"Such a mensch, Dan, such a mensch," Dr. Ruth said to me as she hugged me goodbye, entered her limo, and waved "so long" as she sped away, not a moment too soon.

For all of the hard work and constant changes that she and Pierre put me through in the weeks preceding the SHE event, I have to say, in retrospect, that bonding with Dr. Ruth Westheimer was worth every second of that trouble.

Chapter Twelve

2017 - 2019

MUSSO AND FRANK TURNS 100 / DANNY TREJO WANTS MY DAUGHTER / LUCY LIU SENDS A WINK/ ANN-MARGRET IS MY DREAM GIRL

I was on a date (from Match.com) one night in November, 2018, at the famous Musso & Frank Restaurant on Hollywood Boulevard. (I'd first been there with Actor Robert Englund back in '87.) It was a great date (or so I thought at the time), and it turned out my female companion was the ex-wife of a famous TV sitcom star. (FYI, she claimed that that star happened to owe her over $1 million in back alimony.)

I walked my date to her car when our meal was done, then walked back toward mine, which was parked in Musso's lot behind the building. Just before I unlocked my car, I glanced up and saw the enormous green Musso & Frank sign that proudly proclaimed the restaurant's prominence in Hollywood "Since 1919."

At that moment, I had an epiphany. It was November, 2018, and in just two months, this iconic venue was going to turn 100! I actually glanced around to see if any other Hollywood publicists were standing behind me!

The next Monday, I called the restaurant, but could not reach the owner. I was, however, given his name. Unable to secure his email address, I sat down and wrote him an old-fashioned letter and sent it to him, care of the restaurant's address, via snail mail. I never thought in a million years he'd read it.

Two weeks later, Mark Echeverria, the COO and a fourth-generation member of the family that owns Musso & Frank, called me! He enjoyed my letter, told me he wasn't happy with his existing PR team, and could I come in to meet with him? I set up a date and time for that meeting, then immediately reached out to my longtime friend and fellow publicist Peter, who had much more experience in handling restaurants, hotels, and resorts than I did.

Peter and I met with Mark, his lovely wife, Tina, and Andrea Scuto, the General Manager of Musso's, for lunch. It was a hit–not only did we talk about our dozens of PR ideas for the site, but Peter and I also regaled the assembled with very funny stories culled from our previous years together.

We were hired on the spot! This was mid-March, 2019.

Mark told us he was planning a number of special projects to commemorate the historic restaurant's 100th Anniversary milestone. These included: securing a Star on the Hollywood Walk of Fame for Musso's (they would become the only restaurant ever so honored); publishing a book about the history of Musso's; releasing a brand new wine label; and hosting a VIP dinner on September 27, 2019, the exact 100th anniversary date, that would include various celebrities and notables.

Between March and September, 2019, Peter and I generated countless newspaper, magazine, radio, television and online articles and stories about the history of Musso & Frank (Charlie Chaplin originally put the place "on the map" back in the venue's earliest days. He used to ride his horse to the restaurant-on the dirt road that was Hollywood Blvd. at the time-from his Chaplin Movie Studio Lot on La Brea Ave., just a short distance away. During those lunches, he would sit in the only booth inside the restaurant that had a window, to keep an eye on his horse!)

Peter and I spent countless hours at Musso's during 2019, including lunches and dinners with media members, photographers, TV crews, and various journalists from around the world.

On the 100th Anniversary date itself, September 27, 2019, I produced the ceremony we held on Hollywood Boulevard, just in front of Musso's front doors, to unveil the Star on the Walk of Fame. (We had fans and media lining the entire sidewalk.) For this event, my friend Marc Summers served as MC (as a favor to me) and Actor Danny Trejo of *Machete* (2010) served as our keynote speaker. Danny talked about how, when he first came to Hollywood, he'd spend days at Musso's trying to make connections with Hollywood agents and casting directors, to help launch him into the acting field. He'd been to "University" (prison) before then and wanted nothing more than to break into showbiz, which he felt was his means by which to steer away from a life of crime.

His talk was rather fascinating–and heartfelt.

That night, the VIP dinner at Musso's was truly wonderful. I brought my beautiful daughter, Anjuli, with me as my "plus one." Together, we spent time talking with such celebrities as: Director David Lynch of *Blue Velvet* (1986) and *Twin Peaks* (1990); Marion Ross of *Happy Days* (1974); Danny Trejo (he asked me if he could ask my daughter out on a date! I told him he was much too old!); Composer Randy Newman; Comic Actor Fred Willard – the man's skin was yellow and he clearly was ill. He died shortly thereafter); Richard Benjamin and Paul Prentiss–I told the couple I used to enjoy their '60's TV show, *He and She* (1967) and they were amazed that I remembered it; Donal Logue, co-star of the TV series, *Gotham* (2014); Jeffrey Katzenberg, co-founder of the movie studio DreamWorks SKG and a man I'd met years earlier at the *Jesus Christ Superstar Reunion* (2006) play; and Jeanne Tripplehorn, whom I told about the time I was planning my escape from Duck's PR agency and was nervously copying documents like Holly Hunter did in Jeanne's movie, *The Firm* (1993). She seemed rather intrigued by my story.

The evening was magical and everyone had a great time.

During the past few years, while dining at Musso's, I've also met: Lucy Lawless of *Xena: Warrior Princess* (1995); T.J. Miller, co-star of the sitcom, *Silicon Valley* (2014); actor Giovanni Ribisi of *Saving Private Ryan* (1998) and *Ted* (2012); and Lucy Liu, who'd gotten her own Star on the Hollywood Walk of Fame. As I happened to be at the restaurant that day, I walked past Lucy on my way to leave the building, and turned to face her for a quick second. She stared at me, I stared back. She winked at me, I winked back. She was very charismatic, and had I not been in a hurry to leave, I likely would have had a conversation with her.

Lucy's fellow *Charlie's Angels* (2000) co-stars, Drew Barrymore and Cameron Diaz, were also present that day for Lucy's special luncheon honor, but I did not get a chance to speak with them.

Handling the PR for the Musso & Frank Restaurant has been, without question, one of the highlights of my 40 years as a Hollywood publicist. The owners and staff are the nicest people in the world, the food and martinis are amazing, and the prestige factor of their 100-plus years as a true Hollywood icon has rubbed off on me in countless-and beneficial-ways.

The week of Christmas, 2019, Mark Echeverria and his wife, Tina, invited me and Peter to join them to sit at their table for a special event being hosted by the Los Angeles Press Club. The evening was to honor Director Quentin Tarantino, Actor Danny Trejo, and Movie Legend/Sex Symbol Ann-Margret.

I've been in love with Ann-Margret since I saw her movie, *C.C. and Company* (1970), in a theater in Asbury Park, back when I was 14. I believed her to be, then and now, the most extraordinarily beautiful woman God ever created on the Earth.

Ann-Margret arrived as the last person for the event and was surrounded by a phalanx of people–not sure who they were, but all five of them were clearly there to support and protect her. I gave my cellphone to Peter and asked him to take a photo of me with Ann-Margret, and he agreed. I knew it would be a difficult assignment, given that Ann was in the middle of a swarm of people.

When she approached me, I burst through her gaggle of protectors and gently grabbed her arm. "I've been waiting FIFTY YEARS to meet you!" I said into her ear. "Can I please get a photo of us together?"

"Oh, how very sweet!" she replied.

Knowing I had to move fast, I pulled her away from her gang, aimed her toward Peter and put my arm around her. Peter got the photo, and she was then scurried away very quickly.

This entire encounter lasted about 20 seconds, but it was a most enjoyable moment for me, and one of my definite favorite celebrity sightings ever!

Chapter Thirteen

2020 – 2022

BARNEY'S TURNS 100/HELLO COVID MY OLD FRIEND/CHARLIE SHEEN'S EX-WIFE CALLS/DREW CAREY LOVES TO BOWL/ALAN ARKIN SENDS A NOTE/BILLY JOEL'S DRUMMER STANDS CORRECTED/GOODBYE MIKE NESMITH/STAR TREK: 25/A MUSSO DINNER WITH A LEGENDARY BEACH BOY/THE VANITY FAIR "YOUNG HOLLYWOOD" OSCARS PARTY

At the top of 2020, Peter and I had just signed a PR contract with the owners of Barney's Beanery, another iconic, LA restaurant (based in West Hollywood) that was about to celebrate its 100th anniversary that summer. Barney's Beanery was very famous within the rock 'n roll community – it was the venue where Jim Morrison had once been kicked out after urinating on the bar, and the restaurant where Janis Joplin supposedly ate her very last meal before a heroin overdose.

The plan was for the owners to throw a huge, street fair just in front of the building on Santa Monica Blvd. that summer. Peter and

I were going to be co-producing the event, and I was even trying to negotiate a reunion between Robbie Krieger and John Densmore to perform as The Doors on the stage that was going to be erected.

Alas, in mid-March, a funny little new germ called Covid-19 announced its presence on the global stage instead. And just like that, the PR contract Peter and I had with Barney's Beanery vanished.

With the 100th anniversary of Musso & Frank in my rearview mirror, and with the Barney's contract cancelled, I found myself with a lot of free time on my hands. My other few retainer clients also became very quiet during most of 2020, so I did what probably most other Americans did during that first year of Covid: I sat on my ass, watched TV, and ate massive amounts of junk food.

My daughter Anjuli and I discovered the TV show *The Biggest Loser* (1999), and we were simply fascinated by the plights of these enormous, morbidly obese people from across the USA who had lost all hope and eaten their troubles away.

(Note: After one full year of this lethargy, I decided to get off my ass and start working out-something I'd been doing, on and off, since my sophomore year of college. From then, until today, I've been walking over five-miles every other day, and working out with weights at the gym once a week. I feel better, look better and am grateful that at my age of 66, I'm healthy enough, hopefully, to continue running my business well into the future.)

During the middle of summer, 2020 while Covid-19 was actively raging around the world, I received a phone call from nowhere from Actress Brooke Mueller, the second ex-wife of Actor Charlie Sheen. How Brooke found me I have no idea-she told me she was in need of a publicist to send out a press release to the media-IMMEDIATELY-informing the world that she and Charlie Sheen were active, capable parents to their two sons, and that her mother had no cause for trying to get legal custody of those boys away from Brooke and Charlie.

Huh?

I told Brooke I was a big fan of Charlie's *Two and a Half Men* (2003), which I really was, and that I'd be glad to help her IF I could talk with Charlie by phone FIRST to hear directly from HIS mouth exactly what HE wanted me to say.

Brooke said she'd have Charlie call me back in 10 minutes. As you have probably already guessted, I'm still waiting for that return call.

I later found out Brooke had re-entered drug rehab the SAME DAY she phoned me, and I was never able to reach her again afterwards.

Ah, Hollywood. Ya' gotta love it!

In September, 2021, CBS News contacted me. They told me they were going to be doing a story about the upcoming 50th Anniversary of the TV game show, *The Price is Right* (1972) and they wanted to interview Drew Carey at Musso & Frank Restaurant for that piece. Apparently, Musso's is where Bob Barker and Drew Carey met back in 2007, when Bob "passed the baton" to Drew, to host that show upon Bob's retirement.

I made the arrangements and met Drew Carey that morning at Musso's. Very nice guy, incredibly infectious laugh. The CBS News interviewer, Lee Cowan, asked Drew about how he got into standup comedy, his struggles with poverty and depression, and how his appearance on *The Tonight Show* in 1991 turned his entire life around. Drew talked about how he felt "unworthy of everything" since he came from Cleveland.

"Folks from Cleveland back then always seemed to be saying 'I'm sorry' just because they existed," Drew explained.

After the interview, I told Drew, "When they were little, I used to take my kids bowling behind the Jerry's Deli in Studio City, and we used to see you there."

Drew replied, "Yeah, I went there all the time! I love bowling. It's a great stress reliever. The best bowling alleys around are in Las Vegas, believe it or not."

Drew seemed truly unaffected by his fame and was more than happy to pose for a photo with me. I didn't get a chance to tell him how much my daughter and I loved his show, *Whose Line Is It Anyway?* (1998). We used to laugh hysterically at that show, quite often ending up rolling on the floor, crying tears of joy.

Before COVID 19 arrived and changed everyone's plans around the world, Mark Echeverria and I had been planning a special event for Musso's 102nd Anniversary on Sept. 27, 2021. The restaurant was going to open to the public its brand-new, private dining rooms–a project seven years in the making. The idea was to have some celebrities cut a large, red ribbon in front of the new rooms, and have local TV camera crews cover the event.

I reached out to the co-stars of the TV series, *The Kominsky Method* (2018)–Michael Douglas and Alan Arkin–to see if they might be available to join us for the 9/27/21 ceremony. That series shot many of its funniest scenes at a red leather booth inside Musso's.

I was told by Michael Douglas' PR people that he would be out of town.

Alan Arkin actually replied to me via personal email: "Hi Dan, Alan Arkin here. Thank you so much for the invitation. I've been going to Mussolini's on and off for perhaps 40 years and have touted it to countless numbers of people, too. It's one of the few places left in Hollywood that has any texture and sense of history. Unfortunately, as much as I'd like to, I won't be able to attend the event. We live just north of San Diego, and it's a three-hour drive for us. I'm at an age where it's too hard for me to do all that in a day. In addition, because of Covid, we're not doing a lot of socializing, so much as it saddens us, we will have to say no to your invite, but I send all of my best wishes to all those who will be there celebrating. Musso & Frank is a wonderful institution, and very deserving of its reputation. Best, Alan Arkin."

Ultimately, Mark Echeverria, his wife, Tina, and their entire family and I held a private, ribbon-cutting ceremony to open those new private dining rooms on November 1, 2021. We did not have any media attend the event, but I did send out a press release and accompanying PR photos, which ran in various local media outlets including the *Los Angeles Times*.

During late fall, 2021, I had a series of celebrity meet and greets which took place pretty much all in a row. These were:

- ** Liberty DeVito: I met famed, longtime Billy Joel Drummer, Liberty DeVito, while visiting my childhood friend, Steve Walter, at his Cutting Room nightclub in Manhattan in October. Liberty was a "regular" at the Cutting Room, and he and I discussed his autobiography, which he'd recently written and released. I even told him that a few locations in L.A. that he wrote about were incorrect, to which he responded, "Well, I'll add them to the list. Billy Joel told me I had several things wrong in the book, also!"
- ** Micky Dolenz (again): My longtime friend Toby and his wife, Lynda, invited me to see The Monkees Present the Mike &

Micky Show at Hollywood's Greek Theater. I'd seen Micky with The Monkees numerous times over the years, and I'd also seen The Mike & Micky Show a few years previous. So I was hesitant to attend, but did end up going and I'm glad I did. The show was on November 14, 2021. Mike Nesmith, dressed in white, looked like a ghost and was clearly unhealthy during the show. He didn't play the guitar–I don't think he could even have held one in his arms–and didn't "sing" his songs either. Rather, he "spoke" the lyrics to his famous tunes instead.

Mike also, during the show, would simply walk off the stage in the middle of a song for no apparent reason, then return many minutes later. It was disturbing and a bit shocking to see him appearing in such a sorry state.

As Toby's son, Nathan, worked at the Greek Theater, I was able to get backstage after the concert. I made my way up to Micky Dolenz and asked him if he remembered me from the '80s. Given my full beard and moustache, along with my Covid mask, he didn't, alas, but when I spoke with him about Steve's nightclub, the Cutting Room, he responded, "Oh, yeah, I love that place. I'm so glad Steve was able to get that club open again after Covid. It's really a great space." Micky and Steve have been longtime friends.

Mike Nesmith died on December 10, 2021, less than one month after the show I attended. It was his last concert ever. As I'd also seen the <u>very first time</u> he'd re-joined the other three *Monkees*–at the Greek Theater in summer 1986 (a show that made me cry!)–I was very grateful that I had the honor to see his <u>final performance</u> as well.

The Monkees were my childhood heroes and it was fitting that I got to pay my respects to Michael Nesmith, a rock star I truly loved since 1966.

** <u>*"Star Trek: First Contact"* Stars</u>: On behalf of my longtime client, Todd Masters, the multi-Emmy Award winning

Special FX Makeup Artist, I produced an event in Hollywood to commemorate the 25th anniversary of the release of the hit film, *Star Trek: First Contact* (1996). Todd had supplied the special makeup FX to that film. He collaborated with its Director, Jonathan Frakes, the Visual Effects Society, and myself to present this "behind-the-scenes" look at the making of this terrific movie.

That evening, in addition to meeting Jonathan Frakes, I also met the wonderful Actress Alfre Woodard and, for the second time, Actor LeVar Burton. The evening was a huge success, with many hundreds of Hollywood industry-types attending, in spite of the ongoing Covid era.

** <u>Beach Boy Brian Wilson</u>: At the start of February, 2022, I was contacted by *Rolling Stone* Magazine Editor Jason Fine and a filmmaker named Brent Wilson, to see if I could help them get a dinner reservation inside one of the new, VIP private dining rooms at Musso & Frank's in Hollywood for February 8th. Working with legendary Beach Boy founder Brian Wilson, they'd produced a documentary film entitled *Long Promised Road* (2021). The reason for their requested dinner was that-since they were expecting an Oscar nomination which would have been announced that morning for "Best Song" for the tune "Right Where I Belong," written by Brian and Rock Star/Songwriter Jim James, which appeared within the documentary-it would be a celebration. Unfortunately, the song did not get the nod for a 2022 "Best Song" Oscar that morning.

I managed to get the guys (seven total) a special reservation inside one of Musso's VIP dining rooms for February 8. When I arrived at the site to ensure all was going well, Jason and Brent invited me to stay and join the gang for dinner! I was utterly surprised and truly not expecting that honor at all.

For three hours, I was one of seven other men dining with a living legend-the original Beach Boy himself, Brian Wilson. We each took turns asking Brian questions about his life, his career, his songwriting and producing, some of his live concerts, etc.

Brian, nearly 80 at the time, was in a wheelchair and his mental focus would stray. He'd often appear to be staring off into space, but when asked a direct question face-to-face, he would rise to the occasion and deliver short, emphatic and very to-the-point answers.

I asked him, "Hey Brian, what was the very best rock concert you ever saw that wasn't the Beach Boys?" His reply? "San Diego." (Giving me a sense of his thought-process.)

Funny side note: I sat directly across from Jim James, a major rock star with the band My Morning Jacket. I had no idea who he was, and wasn't particularly impressed by his "fame stature," but I can say he was a truly great guy and super fun to talk to.

Rolling Stone Editor Jason Fine, who's had an especially close relationship with Brian since 1998, essentially served as the "Brian Whisperer" during the meal and was able to elicit some of the more colorful and lengthened responses from Brian. In fact, in the movie *Long Promised Road*, Jason and Brian, alone, appear together on screen, driving in a car, while visiting various sites of interest within Los Angeles that are meaningful to Brian and The Beach Boys.

In the doc, Jason is able to navigate Brian's heartfelt emotional answers to dozens of questions about his decades as an icon.

Brian Wilson is a true musical genius and a living legend, and I was honored to have had the opportunity to spend a few hours in private with him and his friends.

In early spring 2022, I was contacted by a woman in charge of Special Events for *Vanity Fair Magazine*, asking IF I thought Musso & Frank might be interested in hosting a Pre-Oscars Party for "Young Hollywood" stars? Seizing this unique opportunity, I called Mark Echeverria at Musso's and explained the request to him. His initial response? "Dan, can we trust these young kids not to destroy the place?" I told him: "*Vanity Fair Magazine* events are very prestigious, and I think it would be great for us to develop this new relationship. Plus, the 'Al Pacinos' of the world already know and love Musso's – I think it's time that we reached out to the 'next generation' of Hollywood performers, to inform them about the history and stature of Musso's within the industry." Thankfully, Mark agreed with me. Andrea Scuto, Musso's General Manager and I, then responded back to the *Vanity Fair* people that the event was a "GO!"

The entire party was organized within just about three weeks, which is a remarkably quick time frame. I was looking forward to "working the red carpet" for this event, to try to meet some additional celebrities to include into this book. When I had a Zoom meeting with Rebecca, one of the event people from *Vanity Fair*, I asked her if there were any "stand-out big names" of performers she was expecting to attend.

"Dan, I don't recognize ANY of the names on our RSVP list," she replied.

The night of the big event came – I arrived early and observed the decorator's crew "transforming" Musso & Frank restaurant into a tropical themed paradise, with palm trees replacing the tables and chairs and with a specially designed "Rum Room" in the back, sponsored by Bicardi. The normally "red" red carpet was "gold" for this party – in honor of Bicardi's Gold Rum liquor!

7PM sharp came, and the "Young Hollywood" stars began to arrive like clockwork. I was standing on the "gold carpet" next to the paparazzi photographers, hoping to meet and chat up at least a few famous people so I could include them into this–my final section of this book.

During the course of the next two hours, over 200 "celebrities" walked the gold carpet and were photographed by the rabid photographers shooting pictures for the wire services and for various social media networks and channels. As I stood watching these young kids – ages ranging from 21 to 34, all attractive, shiny people - and especially pretty girls – I was struck by a lightning bolt:

I didn't know who ANY of these "famous young celebrities" were! Not a one!

After all the big Hollywood events I've worked, and all of the red carpets I've been on, helping media get the interviews and photos that they wanted from top, world-class stars, this *Vanity Fair* "Young Hollywood" event was the first of its kind – ever – in my career. These so-called celebrities were either: minor cast members of TV shows no one's ever heard of, or budding singers and musicians with no or little discernable talent, or gorgeous female – and quite a few male - models hoping to "make it" in showbiz, or actors/actresses who had very small roles in movies that only their parents and closest friends probably saw.

I did chat with several of these young people after they left the media station on the gold carpet, but I'm a bit embarrassed to say I didn't know their names or "who they were!" They were all friendly and sweet and charming, but only three of these young kids were of note to me, solely for the sake of this book:

** Jack Alcott was the co-star of the Showtime TV series *Dexter: New Blood* (2021,) which I loved. I've been a fan of Michael C. Hall ever since *Six Feet Under* (2001,) so I recognized Jack by saying, "Hey, aren't you the kid from the new *Dexter*?" He and I, along with his publicist, had a nice talk about that series and about how talented Michael C. Hall is. Jack was a great kid, very sincere and charming. I wish him a lot of luck in the future.

** Isabella Ward played the role of "Tere" in Steven Spielberg's *West Side Story* (2021) remake. She was a beaming light of smiles and I thought she was adorable. I told her my story about how – when I met Spielberg – he and I discussed his mother's blintzes. "Oh, my God, I love that story so much!" she said. I Google'd her after the party and discovered she is a very accomplished dancer who, as "Tere," was one of the Sharks in that 2021 movie.

** Cameron Monaghan is a tall, red-headed kid who I recognized on the gold carpet immediately. "You're the kid that played 'The Joker' in the TV show *Gotham* (2014) right?" I asked. "That's me," he replied. I told him I thought he was one of the best "Jokers" ever, and he seemed to appreciate the compliment. As to what he's up to now? "I'm doing a lot of voice-over and character work for a variety of *Star Wars* (1977) games and video projects," he told me. "Hey, do you have a business card?" I handed him my card and he said he'd call me soon "to discuss some possible projects we might be able to work on together."

Another very nice young man. I don't expect to ever hear from him, though.

After those celebrities walked the gold carpet, they entered into the virtually unrecognizable Musso & Frank interior. I stood back a bit with Andrea Scuto, along with Aleesio and Jose, the two top Maitre'Ds, as we simply observed the jam-packed restaurant from a slight distance. "I would venture to say that never, in the 103-year history of this place, have so many young kids been here at the same time," I noted. "That's for sure," responded Jose. "We've never seen anything like this – this is a real 'Young Hollywood' party!"

Realizing it was simply too crowded for me to even get a drink from the bar, I decided to call it a night, and split at 9pm. As I was walking back to my car, I realized that the term "celebrity" in the age of Tik-Tok and Instagram is loosely applied to today's performers. If anyone and everyone in 2022 can be a "star," doesn't that just water down the power and allure of that word? Who are the Hollywood stars of today? Of course, we still have Pacino and DeNiro and Streep and Hanks, but when that generation is gone, what then? Can you name any truly big "new stars" that have emerged on the scene during the past few years?

I paid my $12 for parking and began the 45-minute drive back home. Just as I arrived in my driveway and turned off my ignition, another big thought hit me:

I met Richie Havens at The Sunshine Inn on March 24, 1972.

This Vanity Fair/Musso & Frank party was on March 22, 2022.

I've been meeting and working with celebrities for EXACTLY 50 years ALMOST TO THE DAY!

I also came to realize that, clearly, the "glory days" of my working as a Hollywood Publicist with world-famous performers has run its course. Other than Paul McCartney and Barack Obama, I can't think of any top celebrities anywhere in the world I'd even want to meet or talk to, in my old age.

I've had a good, 50-year run! I'm grateful for all that I'm accomplished in the worlds of Hollywood, media and the entertainment industry.

Now it's time for me to take a good, long nap. And when I wake up, I need to start writing more books about my lifetime of interesting, amusing, and off-the-wall, "this could only happen to Dan Harary" adventures.

AFTERWORD

As I was winding down the writing of this book, my fuzzy brain suddenly sprang back to life and I recalled a number of very quick "celebrity close encounters" that I'd experienced and relegated to the back of my memory banks. These include:

- ** Bumping into Tim Allen of *Home Improvement* (1991) and Christopher Lloyd of *Back to the Future* (1985) at two separate Hollywood movie theaters;
- ** Meeting Jane Lynch of *Glee* (2009) at a TV industry event in Century City;
- ** Bumping into Jay Mohr of *Jerry Maguire* (1996) at The Improv comedy club;
- ** Pushing shopping carts side-by-side with Diane Lane of *Under the Tuscan Sun* (2003) at my local Bed, Bath & Beyond store;
- ** Eating at the next table to Billy Baldwin of *Backdraft* (1991) and Chynna Phillips (Wilson Phillips) at my favorite Westside L.A. breakfast restaurant, John O'Groats;
- ** Standing in line just behind Gary Cole of *Veep* (2012) at my local pharmacy;
- ** Eating sandwiches side-by-side with Barry Livingston, who played "Ernie Douglas" on *My Three Sons* (1960);
- ** Sighting Jodie Foster (*Taxi Driver* -1974), Jessica Alba of *Sin City* (2005), and Jason Bateman of *Ozark* (2017) at my local Whole Foods supermarket in Beverly Hills;
- ** Eating frozen yogurt at the Century City Mall, standing just feet from Director Oliver Stone of *Platoon* (1986) and Marcia Cross, the attractive redhead from *Desperate Housewives* (2004);

** Holding open the front door of the restaurant Carlitos Gardel on Melrose Ave., as Javier Bardem and Penelope Cruz entered, having just been delivered by a long, white limo;

** And handling the PR for a short, African American film called Passage (2021). At the Hollywood premiere of that film, I met actress Marla Gibbs (*The Jeffersons*/1975) and U.S. Congresswoman Karen Bass, who, as of the writing of these words, is running to become the next Mayor of Los Angeles.

As fate would have it, quite recently my daughter and I bumped into Jay Leno and his wife, Mavis, three weeks in a row at a Vons supermarket in West Hollywood! Jay remembered me from my time, decades earlier, as his publicist. He seemingly remains unaffected by his subsequent fame and truly remains "a nice guy." Why I still never thought to take a photo of he and I together remains a baffling mystery to me!

These days, when I talk with my family and friends back East, they'll often ask me, "So, what new celebrities have you met?" It is kind of funny that I seem to have had a magnetic "pull" toward famous people these past 50 years, some of that a result of my profession, but much of it simply random chance.

As anyone who lives in Southern California knows all too well, bumping into celebrities around town during the course of everyday normal life is something that can simply just occur on its own. Yet, for some reason, I've always been able to spot a celebrity "a mile away," and have often impressed those I'm with by my "celebrity sensor" detective abilities.

I'd have to say in retrospect that of the countless celebrities I've met, my favorites have been Micky Dolenz, Alice Cooper, Hugh Hefner, Steven Spielberg, Mel Brooks, Sam Kinison, Julia Louis-Dreyfus, Dee Wallace, Rene Russo, Kevin Costner, Dr. Ruth, Beach Boy Brian Wilson and, last but certainly NOT least, Ann-Margret!

As of the writing of this book, I still handle the public relations for the famous Musso & Frank Restaurant. More likely than not, I'll still be "close encountering" more celebrities in the coming years ahead.

But, as I noted above, it seems to me that in this modern era, the words "famous" and "celebrity" and "star" no longer have quite the same cachet they referred to, for so many Hollywood years.

PHOTO CREDITS

A big THANK YOU to all of the various photographers, publicists, managers, filmmakers, personal assistants, and friends who granted me their permission to use the photos presented within FLIRTING WITH FAME. These photos helped me forever capture and document many of the special moments in my life when I was interacting with the celebrities recounted on these pages.

Photo Credits/Photos Courtesy:

Amber Smith (Dan with Amber Smith)
Bob Cowsill (Dan with The Cowsills Singing Group)
Brian Leng & Anne-Marie Johnson (Dan and cast of TV show, *What's Happening Now!!*)
Caryn Richman (Dan with Caryn Richman; Dan with Alan "The Skipper" Hale, Jr.)
Christina Papadopoulos (Permission to use photo of Dan with Drew Carey)
Dan Harary/Author's Collection (Dan with Sylvester Stallone; Dan with Tom Hanks; Richie Havens Poster; Bruce Springsteen Poster; Joan Rivers' Autograph; Jay Leno's Autograph)
David Salidor (Permission to use photo of Dan with Micky Dolenz)
Gene Arias (Dan with Jerry Seinfeld)
Glenn Schwartz/Former Publicist for Milton Berle (Dan with Milton Berle)
Heather Burgett (Dan with Victoria Principal and Brooke Shields; Dan with Ray Harryhausen)
Jason Fine (Dan with Beach Boy Brian Wilson, Jim James, Jason Fine & Brent Wilson)

Jerry Macaluso (Dan with Jenna Jameson)

Joshua Lingenfelter, Chef Irvine Productions (Dan with Chef Robert Irvine)

June Lockhart and Dee Wallace (Dan with Dee Wallace, Jon Provost, June Lockhart, Bob Weatherwax and Lassie on set of *The New Lassie*, Universal Studios, 1991)

Lee Roth (Dan with Steven Spielberg)

Lynn Barstow/McGhee Entertainment & Heather Burgett (Dan with Paul Stanley and MCZ Group)

Mark Sennet (Dan with Michael Landon)

Michael Garfinkel (Dan with Bob Barker; Dan with Kirk Douglas)

Michael Ochs/Getty Images (Dan with Michael Jackson)

Mitch Zamarin (Dan with Jack Black)

Office of Dr. Ruth Westheimer/Pierre Lehu (Dan with Dr. Ruth)

Office of Mel Brooks (Dan with Mel Brooks and Joan Harary)

Office of Robert Englund Management/Thirdhill Entertainment (Photo of Dan with Robert Englund)

Patrick Piper (Dan with Sid Caesar)

Peter Berk (Dan with Ann-Margret)

Robert Short (Dan with Oscar Winner Bob Short)

Sam Maxwell (Dan with Playmate Lynda Weismeier; Dan with Playmate Kym Malin)

Shannon Bena (Dan with Brian May)

Steve Walter (Dan with Kirsten Dunst)

The Hugh M. Hefner Foundation (Image of Dan and Hugh Hefner, Courtesy of the Hugh M. Hefner Foundation and its Board of Directors)

Tim Long (Dan with Bob Hope and Steve Allen; Dan with Steve Allen; Dan with Bob Denver; Dan with Alice Cooper; Dan with Vice President Al Gore; Dan and Lois Laurel)

Tiana Reneau/Authenticm.com (Dan and Cheri Oteri)

Veronica Puleo (Dan with Jason Alexander)

Zane Levitt (Dan with Karen Black)

Celebrity Encounters Index

Listings Alphabetically by Category, First Name, and Page Number

Actors

Cameron Monaghan, 252
Christopher Stone, 80
Dean Butler, 59
Divine, 73
Donal Logue, 239
Doug Jones, 210
Jack Alcott, 251
Jack Warden, 72
Lance Henricksen, 210
Lorenzo Lamas, 109
Mark Moses, 202
Paul Bartel, 73
Roddy McDowell, 81
Tim Matheson, 68

Actresses

Angie Dickinson, 45
Bijou Phillips, 158
Brooke Mueller, 243-244
Brooke Shields, 28, 29, 129
Carol Kane, 32
Caryn Richman, 59, 148
Claudia Black, 133
Cynthia Preston, 210-211
Elena Wohl, 68
Esther Williams, 96
Fran Drescher, 26
Gigi Rice, 97
Isabella Ward, 252
Jayne Meadows, 96
Jeanne Tripplehorn, 239
Jill Clayburgh, 27
JoBeth Williams, 47
Juliet Prowse, 70
June Lockhart, 81
Katherine Helmond, 45
Lainie Kazan, 131
Lily Collins, 83
Linda Hamilton, 135
Mary McCormack, 224
Mika Boorem, 134
Molly Cheek, 97
Nancy Allen, 210
Patricia Kalember, 151
Rae Dawn Chong, 73
Roma Downey, 136
Ruta Lee, 72
Selma Blair, 226
Shannon Wilcox, 68
Sharon Case, 226
Summer Glau, 133
Theresa Russell, 136

Astronauts

Buzz Aldrin, 94, 205
Eugene Cernan, 94

Comedians/Comediennes

Andy Dick, 227
Arsenio Hall, 58
Artie Lange, 69
Bill Maher, 51
Billy Crystal, 212, 214
Charles Fleischer, 210
Cheech Marin, 111-112
Cheri Oteri, 134-135
Chris Rock, 232-233
Don Rickles, 208
Eugene Levy, 123
Fred Willard, 239
Garry Shandling, 50-51
George Lopez, 202-203
Jack Carter, 96, 212
Jay Leno, 65-66, 255
Jay Mohr, 254
Jerry Lewis, 108
Jerry Seinfeld, 40-41, 104
Joan Rivers, 20
Louis Nye, 96
Martin Short, 123
Milton Berle, 70-71, 103
Paul Lynde, 37
Richard Lewis, 212-213
Robert Wuhl, 26
Sam Kinison, 105
Shecky Greene, 96, 212
Shelley Berman, 96
Sid Caesar, 50, 64-65
Sinbad, 91
Steve Allen, 94-96
Stuttering John Melendez, 69
Tommy Chong, 73
Whoopi Goldberg, 83

Directors

Anthony Bongiovi, 211
Bryan Singer, 136
Carl Reiner, 212
Clint Eastwood, 57
David Lynch, 239
Garry Marshall, 226
James Gunn, 210
Jodie Foster, 254
John Cassavetes, 27
John Derek, 33
John Landis, 112
Mark Rydell, 227-228
Mel Brooks, 137-138, 212-214
Oliver Stone, 254
Paul Mazursky, 137
Peter Bogdanovich, 27
Quentin Tarantino, 240
Robert Wise, 43
Ron Howard, 103
Ted Lange, 81
Tim Burton, 77
Tony Dow, 81
Steven Spielberg, 196-200
Woody Allen, 22-24

Entertainment Industry Producers/Executives/Notables:

Abby Singer, 38-39
Allan Carr, 50
Bill Allen, 94
Bob Banner, 37
Christie Hefner, 49-50
David Geffen, 205
Gary Dell'Abate, 69, 75
George Schlatter, 205

Gil Junger, 97
Helen & Jerry Kushnick, 66-67
Jean Firstenberg, 42
Jeffrey Katzenberg, 136, 239
Jim Henson, 57
John Kricfalusi, 143
Johnny Grant ("The Mayor of Hollywood"), 82
Mark Burnett, 136
Marvin Levy, 27, 198
Matt Weiner, 212
Norman Lear, 212-213
Phil Rosenthal, 212-213
Ron Meyer, 197
Sherry Lansing, 205
Stanley Jaffe, 27
Ted Turner, 91

Ghostbusters

Bill Murray, 36
Dan Aykroyd, 91
Ernie Hudson, 58
Harold Ramis, 58

Miscellaneous Notables

Dan Cain, *Sexcetera* Anchorman, 49
Dillon Campbell (Glen Campbell's son), 220-221
Dr. Patrick Soon-Shiong (One of L.A.'s richest men), 205
Joanna Carson (Johnny Carson's ex-wife), 223
Kevin Peter Hall (*Harry & the Hendersons*), 98
Leah Adler (Steven Spielberg's mother), 199
Lois Laurel (Stan Laurel's daughter), 109-110
Noah Blake (Robert Blake's son), 97
Patti Davis Reagan (President Reagan's daughter), 149
Ron Reagan, Jr. (President Reagan's son), 103-104
Sam Rubin, KTLA Entertainment Reporter, 230
Sarah Campbell (Glen Campbell's ex-wife), 220-221
Shera Falk (Peter Falk's widow), 223
Theresa Flynt (Larry Flynt's daughter), 141
Yoko Ono, 208-209

Movie Stars

Al Pacino, 228
Alan Arkin, 245-246
Amy Smart, 138-139
Ann-Margret, 240-241
Arnold Schwarzenegger, 123-124
Barbra Streisand, 47, 61
Billy Baldwin, 254
Billy Bob Thornton, 206
Billy Dee Williams, 50
Bo Derek, 33
Bob (and Dolores) Hope, 96
Brendan Fraser, 201
Bruce Davison, 97-98
Bruce Willis, 227
Burt Reynolds, 103
Cameron Diaz, 240
Charlton Heston, 101-102
Chevy Chase, 91
Christian Slater, 73
Christopher Lloyd, 254
Connie Stevens, 212
Danny Trejo, 239-240
Dee Wallace, 80-81
Debra Winger, 42
Diane Lane, 254

Dick Van Dyke, 36
Drew Barrymore, 99, 240
Dudley Moore, 36
Dustin Hoffman, 43
Elliott Gould, 50
Eric Roberts, 72
Esther Williams, 96
Giovani Ribisi, 240
Gregory Peck, 72
Harrison Ford, 45
Harvey Keitel, 147
Hillary Swank, 146
Kirk Douglas, 125-126
Jack Black, 135-136
Jack Lemmon, 21
Jacqueline Bisset, 36
Jamie Lee Curtis, 91
James Woods, 131
Jane Fonda, 91
Jason Statham, 148-149
Javier Bardem, 255
Jessica Alba, 254
John Lithgow, 50
Jon Voight, 213
Jonah Hill, 200
Karen Black, 73-74
Keanu Reeves, 149
Kevin Costner, 85, 88-89
Kirk Douglas, 125-126
Kirsten Dunst, 145
Lesley Ann Warren, 126-127
Lily Tomlin, 205
Lou Diamond Phillips, 148
Lucy Liu, 240
Mark Wahlberg, 100-101
Meryl Streep, 86-87
Michael Caine, 51-52
Michael Chiklis, 138
Michele Pfeiffer, 57
Nicholas Cage, 72
Paula Prentiss, 239
Penelope Cruz, 255
Raquel Welch, 203
Rene Russo, 151-152
Richard Benjamin, 239
Robert Englund, 68-69, 104, 210
Robert Redford, 91
Robert Patrick, 224
Richard Dreyfus, 57
Ryan Phillippe, 231
Sally Field, 59-60
Sally Kirkland, 225
Sammy Davis, Jr., 71
Sean Astin, 135, 144
Shelley Winters, 126
Shirley MacLaine, 91
Sidney Poitier, 36
Sean Connery, 45
Scarlett Johansson, 134
Sylvester Stallone, 87-88
Tobey Maguire, 231
Tom Hanks, 89, 110
Tony Roberts, 23
Wynona Ryder, 76
Zsa Zsa Gabor, 50, 73-74

Multi-Media Notables

Dr. Ruth Westheimer, 233-236
Henry Diltz, 99
Ike Pappas, 107-108
Matt Groening, 129
Jim Henson, 57
Muhammed Ali, 47
Ray Harryhausen, 131
Richard Simmons, 102-103

Playboy Magazine Playmates

Crystal Smith, 49

Dona Speir, 53
Dorothy Stratten, 27
Kym Malin, 54-55
Lynda Weismeyer, 53-54
Shannon Tweed, 52

Politicians

Mayor Tom Bradley, 58
Vice President Al Gore, 93
Congresswoman Karen Bass, 255

Pop Music Stars

Alanis Morissette, 208
Amy Grant, 75
Anita Baker, 75
Barry Manilow, 201
Belinda Carlisle, 72
Bobby McFerrin, 75
Buddy Rich, 111
Carnie Wilson, 72
Charlotte Caffey, 139
Charo, 148
Christopher Cross, 130
Chynna Phillips, 254
Danny Elfman, 75
Davy Jones, 72
Donna Summer, 74
Gwen Stefani, 224
John Legend, 228
Kenny Rogers, 32
Lady Gaga, 2
Linda Ronstadt, 75
Madonna, 60
MCZ/Japanese Girl Singing Group, 215
Michael Jackson, 89
Michelle Phillips, 72
Micky Dolenz, 4, 61-62, 146-147, 246-247
Mike Melvoin, 136

Mike Nesmith, 43-44
Nancy Sinatra, 23, 232
Notorious B.I.G. (aka Biggie Smalls), 128
Olivia Newton-John, 75
Pat Boone, 70
Randy Newman, 239
The Cowsills (Bob, Paul, Susan), 216-218
The Monkees, 4, 247
Tracy Chapman, 75
Weird Al Yankovic, 51, 75
will i. am, 205

Porn Stars

Houston, 142
Kylie Ireland, 142
Marilyn Chambers, 38
Nikita Denise, 142
Jasmin St. Clair, 142
Jenna Jameson, 140-142
Julie Meadows, 142
Ron Jeremy, 230-231

Publishing Industry Notables

Hugh Hefner, 49
Matty Simmons, 67-68
Stan Lee, 131-132

Radio Industry Stars

Cousin Brucie, 217
Howard Stern, 19-20, 69
Larry King, 64
Tim Conway, Jr., 135

Rock Music Stars

Alice Cooper, 61-62
America: Dewey Bunnell and Gerry Beckley, 130

Andy Summers, 143-144
Annie Haslam, 19
Bonnie Raitt, 99
Brian May, 229
Beach Boy Brian Wilson, 248-249
Beach Boy Carl Wilson, 32
Bruce Springsteen, 3, 9, 10-16
Bruce Springsteen Band: Danny Federici, Garry Tallent, Vinnie Lopez, 10-11, 14
Carlos Santana, 225-226
Carmine Appice, 150-151
Christine McVie, 9
Clarence Clemons, 11, 13, 16-17
David Crosby, 98-99
Eddie Van Halen, 72
Gene Simmons, 9, 215-216
Grace Slick, 99
Graham Nash, 98-99, 125
Greg Lake, 5
Jackson Browne, 99
Jim James, 248-249
John Entwistle, 84
John Fogarty, 57
Jon Camp, 19
Liberty DeVito, 246
Max Weinberg, 112-113
Mick Fleetwood, 9, 209
Neil Giraldo, 135
Paul McCartney, 20-21
Paul Stanley, 215-216
Pete Townsend, 83-84
Phil Collins, 83-84
Ray Manzarek, 72
Richie Havens, 1, 6-7
Roger Daltrey, 83
Ron Bushy, 5
Stephen Stills, 105
Steve Van Zandt, 25
Sting, 91-92
Wendy Melvoin, 136

Special FX Makeup Artists

Barney Burman, 203
Rick Baker, 210
Robert Short, 75-77
Todd Masters, 209

Stage Performers

Ben Vereen, 135
Katrina Lenk, 139
Franz Harary, 61, 90, 148
Ted Neeley, 135
Yvonne Elliman, 135

Star Trek Cast Members

Alfre Woodard, 248
George Takei, 229-230
Jonathan Frakes, 248
Leonard Nimoy, 229
LeVar Burton, 130, 248
Nichelle Nichols, 130
Majel Rodenberry, 130
William Shatner, 105-106

Super Models

Amber Smith, 177-192
Cindy Crawford, 100
Cristina Ferrare, 103
Dita Van Teese, 223
Kiera Chaplin, 144
Kim Alexis, 109
Pamela Anderson, 121
Tawny Kitaen, 112

TV Stars

Adam Corolla, 103, 144
Alan Hale, Jr., 60
Andy Griffith, 103
Anthony Anderson, 150
Audrey Meadows, 72
Barry Livingston, 254
Battlestar Galactica Cast: Edward James Olmos, Mary McDonnell, Katee Sackhoff, Trisha Helfer, 132-133
Bea Arthur, 96
Bob Barker, 125, 127
Bob Denver, 60
Brad Hall, 221-222
Charlene Tilton, 59
Charlie Sheen, 243-244
Chef Robert Irvine, 219-220
Chris Noth, 218
Cobie Smulders, 212
Cotter Smith, 90
Dan Lauria, 138-139
Danny DeVito, 52
Dan Rather, 205
Danny Masterson, 150
David Spade, 232-233
Dennis Weaver, 68
Diane Sawyer, 91
Dinah Shore, 45
Dixie Carter, 113-114
Drew Carey, 244-245
Ed Sullivan, Preface
Empty Nest Cast: Richard Mulligan, Dinah Manoff, Kristy McNichol, Park Overall, 96-97
Fran Drescher, 26
Gary Cole, 254
Geraldo Rivera, 103
Graham Kerr, 104
Harry and the Hendersons Cast: Bruce Davison, Molly Cheek, Gigi Rice, Noah Blake, Kevin Peter Hall, 97-98
Harvey Korman, 74
Heather Locklear, 52
Henry Winkler, 146
Jaclyn Smith, 59
Jane Lynch, 254
Jane Seymour, 59
Janice Pennington, 127
Jason Alexander, 214-215
Jason Bateman, 254
Jayne Meadows, 96
Jean Smart, 114
Jeff Garlin, 231
Jeffrey Tambor, 146
Jennifer Love Hewitt, 145-146
Jeremy Piven, 150
Jerry Springer, 113
Jimmy Kimmel, 144
Joan Collins, 50
John Henning, 21
John Ritter, 27
Johnny Knoxville, 224-225
Jon Provost, 80
Julia Louis-Dreyfus, 90, 92-93, 203-204, 221-222
Kaley Cuoco, 137
Kate Jackson, 47
Kelsey Grammar, 103
Kim Kardashian, 226
Kirstie Alley, 125
Laraine Newman, 138
Larry David, 204
Larry Hagman, 34
Lassie, 80, 82
Lucy Lawless, 240

Lydia Cornell, 125
Marc Summers, 57-58, 219-220, 230, 239
Marcia Cross, 254
Marion Ross, 239
Marla Gibbs, 255
Mary Tyler Moore, 108
Mel Harris, 90
Michael Landon, 88
Michelle Lee, 212
Mike Farrell, 74
Mike Rowe, 227
Monty Hall, 74
Neil Patrick Harris, 212
Olsen Twins: Mary-Kate & Ashley, 111
Pat Sajak, 148
Patricia Arquette, 223
Patrick Duffy, 34
Paul Lynde, 37
Rhea Perlman, 228
Robert Vaughn, 51
Roma Downey, 136
Ron Livingston, 224
Ruth Buzzi, 72
Ryan Stiles, 147-148
Ted Danson, 91
Tempest Bledsoe, 57
Tim Allen, 254
T.J. Miller, 240
Valerie Harper, 74
Victoria Principal, 35, 129
Wayne Brady, 202
What's Happening Now Cast: Ernie Thomas, Heywood Nelson, Shirley Hemphill, Anne-Marie Johnson, Reina King, Fred Berry, 57
Yeardley Smith, 129

Writers

Larry Grobel, 50
Neil Simon, 50
Neil Strauss, 184-185
Ray Bradbury, 36

www.ingramcontent.com/pod-product-compliance
Lightning Source LLC
Chambersburg PA
CBHW071242230426
43668CB00011B/1550